# AN HISTORICAL
# INTRODUCTION
# TO
# AMERICAN
# EDUCATION

CROWELL SERIES IN AMERICAN EDUCATION

*James C. Stone*

ADVISORY EDITOR FOR EDUCATION

# AN HISTORICAL INTRODUCTION TO AMERICAN EDUCATION

Gerald Lee Gutek

*Associate Professor of Education, Loyola University, Chicago*

THOMAS Y. CROWELL COMPANY     NEW YORK

ESTABLISHED 1834

*To My Wife, Patricia*

370.973
Q98h
76385
Nov. 1971

L.C. Card 68-13381

ISBN  0-690-39437-3

Manufactured in the United States of America

First Printing, January, 1970
Second Printing, January, 1971

# Preface

The condition of American education is frequently discussed and often debated by both the professional educator and the interested layman. Too many times, these discussions have been carried on without the benefit of historical perspective. Written with the point of view that many current educational issues are rooted in the past, *An Historical Introduction to American Education* is intended for both the prospective teacher and for the interested layman. While not written as a definitive history of all phases of the American educational system, the significant developments are treated.

*An Historical Introduction to American Education* evolved from a series of lectures that I presented to students enrolled in the American Education course at Loyola University of Chicago; these students read and discussed much of the material included in the book. Subsequent revisions of the material bear the mark of their criticism, suggestions, and difficulties in dealing with the history of American education. I am much indebted to my students who in many ways helped me to restate and reorganize my thoughts on the history of the American school. Since the book grew out of classroom discussion, I feel that it is suited for readers who desire an overview of the American educational experience in historical perspective.

While the work is suited for use in classes in professional education, American educational history is viewed as a part of the broad sweep of the American past. As such, American education has been related to the economic, religious, social, and political currents that influenced its development. Throughout the book, the cultural and humanistic impulses affecting the American school have been stressed.

The organizational pattern of the book treats the Colonial and Revolutionary origins of American education; traces the development of the common school, secondary school, and college; discusses the evolution of teacher education as an area of special interest to prospective teachers; and deals with John Dewey and the progressive movement. The problem of racial integration is discussed as an area of crucial concern which faces the educational profession. Selected documents illustrating the subject treated in each chapter have been included so that the student of the history of education, as any student of history, can become familiar with some of the primary sources upon which history is based.

In the preparation of this book, I am much indebted to many people. I am grateful to Professor Archibald W. Anderson, late Professor of the History of Education of the University of Illinois, who first interested me in the history of education. Appreciation is extended to Miss Susan Breen, Miss Belinda Lam, and Mr. John Breault, who assisted in the preparation of materials in the early stages of the work. Special acknowledgment is due to Mrs. Beatrice Van Cleave and Miss Esperanza Abrajano, who typed the final draft of the manuscript. Most of all, I am appreciative of my wife, Patricia, who through her sustained interest encouraged me to write the book. To all these individuals, I am grateful. Final responsibility, however, is mine because what has been said is what I wanted to say.

G. L. G.

# Contents

# 1

# The Role of
# the History of American
# Education in Teacher Education

## THE AUTHOR'S POINT OF VIEW

At the outset of any book, it is helpful for the reader to be aware of the point of view of the author. In historical writing, the facts, or the data, are only the raw materials of the narrative or exposition. The data may be judged as valid or invalid, genuine or false, relevant or irrelevant on the basis of historical method; but its selection and interpretation always reflect the historian's beliefs and values.

The author believes that the history of education is valuable in its own right as a subject for study. As the history of the human race, or the history of a particular civilization or a particular nation, provides insight and perspective for each individual as a participant and recipient of a culture, the history of education also offers insight and perspective for the teacher. As the study of his nation's history contributes to the loyalty and appreciation of a citizen for his homeland, so a knowledge of educational history builds professional loyalty and commitment among teachers and educators.

In recent times, Americans have become increasingly aware of education as a powerful instrument of civilization. More than a few observers have termed education one of the most vital factors in a race between civilization and catastrophe. Contemporary American schools and teachers have thus shouldered enormous challenges. In the light of this increased awareness numerous critics have raised questions regarding the quality and quantity of American education. Since it offers a practical perspective

1

on a subject of national interest and concern, the history of education is worthy of study by both the professional educator and the American public.

Throughout the history of education, various philosophers and theorists have offered conflicting definitions of education. In fact, it is the task of the educational professional and the public to re-examine and re-assess the meaning of education. To aid him in this continuing process, the reader is invited to view education as the means of cultural transmission and cultural reconstruction; as a process of change; as an instrument of survival; and as a personal right and obligation belonging to every man simply because he is a member of society. The reader may then test the adequacy of these various perspectives in the light of the historical development of American education.

## EDUCATION IN THE CULTURAL MATRIX

Education is the process by which the immature members of society are introduced into full participation in their culture. Although many social agencies, such as the home, church, state, and mass media, aid informally in this process, advanced cultural groups such as our present form of civilization have established an agency specifically designed to facilitate the process of cultural transmission. This specialized agency is the school. As a carefully constructed environment, staffed by specialists in education, the school transmits the cultural heritage from generation to generation. In this way, the school exercises a preserving or conserving function, by drawing on the culture's tools, skills, and knowledge and passing them along to the immature.

In its role as a specialized cultural agency, the school cannot exist isolated from the culture it serves, but is intimately related to that particular society and cultural heritage. Because it is a vital agency in the structure of the society, it is also subject to pressure from a number of forces: social, economic, political, religious, and moral. American education, for example, draws its substance from the cultural heritage which is particularly American.[1]

In addition to the preservation or conservation of a society's cultural heritage, the school also exercises the function of social improvement or reconstruction. The heritage the school is designed to transmit is vast and complex, and within it there are elements both worthy and unworthy of

[1] For a further elaboration of the view that education occurs in a civilizational context, the reader is referred to George S. Counts, *Education and American Civilization* (New York: Bureau of Publications, Teachers College, Columbia University, 1952).

transmission. To the school falls the immense problem of selecting some parts of the heritage for transmission and rejecting others. To the extent that it is selective, the school also serves a moral purpose. Those charged with introducing the immature to full participation in their culture must make their selection according to some criteria generally agreed upon within that culture. American educators at all levels have usually chosen these cultural elements according to a democratic social philosophy.

Although the American school has been committed to the education of a democratic citizenry since the days of Horace Mann and Henry Barnard, it has never been a simple task to define the criteria that underlie a democratic education. In contrast to the rigid formulas and prescriptive definitions of totalitarian systems, democracy is purposefully open; that is, it is sustained by freedom of inquiry and experimentation. Since its ultimate authority rests in "government by the people," each generation of Americans must redefine the democratic criteria and democratic education in light of the exigencies of its own time. Thus, the American teacher has the twofold responsibility of introducing each generation to its democratic heritage, and providing it with the knowledge and skills needed to continue to reformulate and sustain the democratic ethic in the face of contemporary challenges, both domestic and foreign.

In the continuing task of defining the democratic criterion of "government by the people," each generation of Americans must reconfirm its heritage. Though not located in any one specific document, nor fully expressed at any one time, the democratic criterion has evolved as part of that heritage. Such documents as the Declaration of Independence and the United States Constitution demonstrate its political origins, and the philosophical and legislative efforts of such men as Washington, Jefferson, Jackson, Lincoln, Wilson, and Roosevelt have contributed to its legacy. In the rough "one man, one vote" egalitarianism of the frontier can be found the origins of social democracy. These origins have been described by Emerson, Thoreau, Whitman, Sandburg, and many others. Although the sources of the American democratic ideal are diverse, together they provide the basis for a democratic education. While such diversity makes precise definition difficult, it facilitates pluralistic freedom. Although they may disagree on specific social, political, religious, and economic programs, the vast majority of Americans share a general commitment to the democratic ethic and process—the idea of political and legal equality for all citizens. Subscribing to the principles of freedom of speech, press, assembly, and worship, they believe that their elected representatives can best achieve the common good through the democratic methods of discussion, debate, deliberation, and decision. Because they believe that an informed citizenry is necessary for the functioning of both the ethic and the method, they have made education the right of every American child. Equality of educational opportunity is not only a political necessity; it is also essential for intellectual, social, political, and economic opportunity.

Despite the theoretical commitment of most Americans to the democratic ethic, they have not always applied it practically. There have been and continue to be occasions when racial, religious, social, and economic discrimination have deprived Americans of their guaranteed rights. Some people have disregarded the democratic methodology and resorted to violence. Not all American children have enjoyed equal educational opportunity, either. In this area too, discrepancies exist between theory and practice, but Americans have become increasingly aware of these discrepancies and are attempting to put democratic theory into action. As public education strives to fulfill the promise of equal educational opportunity for all children, it fulfills its commitment to the democratic ethic.

As part of its task of selection, the school tries to balance the students' environment by choosing elements of the culture most likely to produce integrated individuals within an integrated society. An integrated society is not necessarily a monolith characterized by a common level of conformity, but is rather a harmonious blend of divergent elements in a unified social fabric. For example, the United States has been termed a nation of immigrants of various ethnic and religious persuasions. Although they share a common commitment to the democratic process, American citizens enjoy a wide range of political, social, and religious beliefs. A democratic society may include many forms of pluralism and at the same time conform to basic ethical and methodological precepts that serve as an integrative value system. The school communicates these values in a graduated environment by selecting cultural elements, skills, and knowledge according to the maturity level of the learner.[2]

### Education as Past, Present, and Future

In the foregoing discussion, the conservative and reconstructive functions of the school as a social agency have been suggested. It is also clear, however, that, as a social enterprise, education does not occur in a vacuum. It is a dynamic and on-going experience which has its roots in the past, but which also actively affects the present situation and influences the future as each new generation is educated. If the course of education in America were plotted on a continuum of past, present, and future, the function of educational history could be more clearly indicated. First, the

[2] For a philosophic discussion of the specialized function of the school see John Dewey, *Democracy and Education* (New York: The Macmillan Company, 1916).

problems of education today have grown out of the past and are intimately connected with it. In order to understand contemporary issues, the student of professional education must be aware of how they developed. Instead of anchoring himself securely in the safety of finished events, he should use the past as a means of interpreting the present and as an instrument for shaping the future. Second, a total program of teacher education must concern itself with current problems. It is necessary for the education student to examine contemporary philosophies, social views, theories, methods, curricula, organization, psychology, and administration, since these are the working tools of the educational practitioner and theorist. Third, the educational experience is a means of controlling the course of future events. Educators must think in terms of the future in order to prepare society to cope with whatever events and issues may develop to affect it. Both the educational leader and the student must take all three of these elements into consideration. The history of American education presented here is intended only as an introductory foray into the first area in the continuum. It is designed to prepare the student for a more mature examination of the other two areas of the continuum and to serve as his point of departure for more intensive study of American education.

The viewpoint taken in this work is opposed to what might be called the "four walls philosophy" of the school. Some educators have continued to view education as a process that goes on inside a school, apart from the social order of which it is an intimate part. The "four walls philosophy" is narrowly confined to the mechanics of education—buildings, books, desks, blackboards, audio-visual aids—to the point that it neglects the substance of education as it is supplied and sustained by the culture. This is not to say that the materials and technologies connected with the educational enterprise are unimportant; they are indeed, but only as instruments and tools which will advance the purposes of education, not as ends in themselves.

The history of American education is a valuable tool in assessing this culture for its influence on the course of education, and education for its influence on the course of the culture. In *Experience and Education* John Dewey discusses the close relationship between the issues and problems of contemporary life and the past:

> . . . the achievements of the past provide the only means at command
> [sic] for understanding the present. Just as the individual has to draw in
> memory upon his own past to understand the conditions in which he in-
> dividually finds himself, so the issues and problems of present social life
> are in such intimate and direct connection with the past that students
> cannot be prepared to understand either these problems or the best way

of dealing with them without delving into their roots in the past. In other words, the sound principle that the objectives of learning are in the future and its immediate materials are in present experience can be carried into effect only in the degree that present experience is stretched, as it were, backward. It can expand into the future only as it is also enlarged to take in the past.[3]

Dewey warns against taking a myopic view of the present that would ignore the context of past experience. If present problems are to be solved through action based on intelligent reflection, then the reconstruction of experience requires a survey of conditions already existing. These conditions are products of the past. According to Dewey:

> The institutions and customs that exist in the present and that gave rise to present social ills and dislocations did not arise overnight. They have a long history behind them. Attempts to deal with them simply on the basis of what is obvious in the present is bound to result in adoption of superficial measures which in the end will only render existing problems more acute and more difficult to solve.[4]

## Education as Change

The American historical experience has been characterized by profound changes which have transformed the original simple, rural, agrarian social order into a highly complex, urban, and industrialized technological civilization. The ramifications of this transformation have affected all facets of American life—religious, economic, social, political. In fact, it has been a continuing process, one that is still producing great changes in our life. As part of the fluid social order the schools, too, have been profoundly affected. In the same way that a static and stratified society is alien to the American tradition, the idea of a rigid, closed school system and curriculum is also alien to the American educational experience. Mechanical invention and scientific discoveries of the twentieth century have not only produced technological change but have also had a social impact. For example, the invention and mass production of the automobile has facilitated travel, reduced geographical isolation, and contributed to a more mobile society. The discovery and harnessing of atomic energy not only poses scientific and technological problems, but raises crucial ethical issues on which may hinge man's very survival on this planet. To meet these new challenges, American teachers must be aware of the full impli-

[3] John Dewey, *Experience and Education* (New York: The Macmillan Company, 1958), p. 93. Originally published in 1938. Copyright by Kappa Delta Pi, an honor society in education. Reprinted by permission of Kappa Delta Pi.
[4] *Ibid.*, p. 94.

cations of the inter-relationship of technological and social change, and of the impact of change upon educational patterns. As members of a mobile society, teachers must be willing to experiment, to seek more effective methods of education. To adequately introduce the immature generation to participation in society means that the educational profession must not be content to educate for the current condition of society; it must also be concerned with how that society will be and should be in the future. In practical terms, this means that the education of teachers, too, is never finished, never completed, but is a continually active process.

In the past, some educators have been concerned only with the difficulties of transmitting a cultural heritage as if that heritage had been fully developed. While this is one function of a teacher, it is only half of his task. Too often, teachers have introduced young people to a way of life that has already become obsolete because the curriculum of the schools has lagged behind people's real needs.

The changes wrought by technology are constantly confronting the teacher and the educational profession. Racial and social integration, survival in a nuclear age, massive poverty, functional illiteracy, and worthy use of leisure time are only a few of the complex problems they must deal with in the crucial decades ahead.

## EDUCATION AS A PERSONAL FUNCTION

Thus far we have been concerned with the social aspects of education and its specialized agency, the school. However, at a time when society's emphasis is on the mass, it is important to remember that the business of education is always with the individual: the specific child, man or woman being educated. Although it is a socializing process, education remains fundamentally a unique, individualized, and personal matter. When education is considered as a process of induction into society, it is clear that individualization and socialization need to be properly balanced.

As the immature member of the group or society masters the cultural tools of reading and writing, he attains the freedom to participate and make decisions within the social framework. As he acquires more sophisticated skills and knowledge he continually increases both his framework of decision-making and the freedom to exercise it. As a participant in the group process, his freedom is thereby increased. Thus the process of participation is one of a reciprocal relationship between an individual and society.

However, it denies individual personality to insist upon the same kind and degree of socialization from everyone. Each man is different, a unique individual. Education should be a personal instrument by which he fulfills his own possibilities. At the same time it should aid him to estimate and achieve self-determination and self-realization.

In order that teachers may better evaluate the development of their profession, it is necessary to examine the American educational experience in terms of its strengths and weaknesses over time. Further, since most problems of any kind tend to be rooted in past experience, it is necessary for us to study its history as a part of the process of solving the problems now facing American schools. The following survey of the history of education in America is intended to provide a better understanding of our educational system today by presenting its history, development, structure, and problems.

## PLAN OF THE WORK

In this study of the history of education in America I have deliberately focused attention on its origins and institutional development, the rise of educational methodology, and pressing problem areas. The book first describes American education during the colonial and revolutionary periods, and then traces the evolution of the common school, the high school, and the college, and the growth of teacher education. Education as a process or methodology is discussed in relation to the European reformers Rousseau, Pestalozzi, Froebel, and Herbart. John Dewey's experimentalism and the progressive movement are treated as a unique American contribution to education. From among the myriad conflicts facing American education today, the problem of racial integration has been selected for historical treatment.

Following the descriptive analysis in each chapter, source readings have been appended so that the reader may examine the significant primary material for himself. It is hoped that these documents may offer greater insight into the particular historical development being discussed. At the conclusion of each chapter, further selected references are listed as sources for reading and study.

## References

COUNTS, GEORGE S. *Education and American Civilization.* New York: Bureau of Publications, Teachers College, Columbia University, 1952.

DEWEY, JOHN. *Democracy and Education.* New York: The Macmillan Company, 1916.

DEWEY, JOHN. *Experience and Education.* New York: The Macmillan Company, 1938.

# 2

# The Colonial
# Educational Experience

## INTRODUCTION

The history of American education begins with the efforts of the English colonials to recreate in the New World the school system they had known before. When a school is established, it is a clear indication that the group sponsoring the school means to perpetuate itself by providing its children in a systematized way with the knowledge and values it deems necessary for survival. The colonists' schools thus reflected their desire to stay and conquer the wilderness.

The patterns of settlement in North America varied according to geographical, climatic, and topographical conditions. Along with these diverse patterns, variations also followed in the life style of the different colonial regions. New England in its Puritan conformity, the Middle Atlantic colonies in their pluralism, and the South in its plantations, all reflected the tendency to develop unique characteristics, as the common English experience was altered by the American environment. The variations in educational processes and institutions which began to mark these regions of settlement likewise reflected the imprint of the new environment.

Colonial education was influenced greatly by the cultural heritage that the colonists brought with them from Europe. To understand their ideas about education, it is necessary to examine some of the precedents that existed in Europe. The Renaissance humanism of the fourteenth and fifteenth centuries stressed the classical forms and tradition and the Greek and Latin languages as marks of the educated man. Linked with this classical humanism was a strong concern with religion, which was part of the heritage of the Protestant Reformation and Catholic Counter-Reformation. The religious element emphasized doctrinal education. Another factor in European culture at that time was the accelerated pace of commercial exchange, which considerably increased the value of a man who could read, write, and calculate.

Both the intellectual inheritance and the commercial revolution made their impact upon colonial education. The Latin Grammar school continued the emphasis on classical education, while the vernacular schools reflected the demands of doctrinal conformity and basic literacy. As the commercial classes grew in numbers and in importance, they demanded a more utilitarian education. Although all of the English colonies in North America shared the tradition of European intellectual and commercial life, certain differences unique to each region developed early in the New England colonies, the Middle colonies, and the Southern colonies.

## THE NEW ENGLAND COLONIES

The New England colonies were settled primarily by the Puritans, who based their lives and their beliefs upon the theological doctrines of the Swiss religious reformer, John Calvin. Their educational orientation was also influenced heavily by his writings, for several aspects of Calvinism were especially relevant to education. First, the doctrine of predestination held that only a certain religiously observant elite was destined for salvation, while the unenlightened masses were doomed to hell-fire and damnation. Second, a certain correlation was indicated between the man of property and the good man. The elect were the industrious, and could therefore be known by their external prosperity. This philosophy helped to establish the Protestant ethic as an integral part of American life, which considered hard work and the acquisition of property as positive values in and of themselves. Third, a spirit of religious conformity developed which led to the punishment for dissent from orthodox doctrine as both a theological and political infraction. It can be seen that the Puritans based their government, particularly that of the Massachusetts Commonwealth, upon a theocratic concept of the state. Education was regarded as an instrument by which the believer might become literate in sacred Scripture, Calvinist doctrine, and the general laws of the Commonwealth. Furthermore, education was a means of achieving social and religious stability both individually and communally. The Puritan Fathers believed that they had a social blueprint, designed in Heaven, that needed no reconstruction.

New England colonial education emphasized the conservative aspect of its role by transmitting a heritage which allowed little room for change.

Education of that period also took pains to convey the particular world-view of Calvinist theology. Since a literate clergy and a literate laity were important to Calvinism, reading and writing were emphasized.

Another important feature of New England colonial education was the close relationship of church, state, and school. When the first schools were established they were considered adjuncts of the church-state. This was in sharp contrast to the later view that the church, school and state should function separately.

## Puritan View of the Child

New England colonial education was permeated by a notion of child psychology which maintained that the infant was conceived in sin and born to corruption.[1] According to this theory, a child was a savage creature who needed constant upbraiding and discipline to curb his evil inclinations and desires. The New England boy or girl was not regarded as a child, interested in play and games, but was treated as a miniature adult and made to conform to adult behavior and regulations. Consequently, discipline in both home and school was extremely harsh, with corporal punishment a frequent feature of the child's educational experience. In admonishing parents as to the proper nurture of their children, the New England clergyman Jonathan Edwards warned:

> Let me now, therefore, once more, before I finally cease to speak to this congregation, repeat and earnestly press the counsel which I have often urged on heads of families here, while I was their pastor, to great painfulness in teaching, warning and directing their children; bringing them up in the nurture and admonition of the Lord; beginning early, where there is yet opportunity, and maintaining a constant diligence in labors of this kind; remembering that, as you would not have all your instructions and counsels ineffectual, there must be government as well as instructions, which must be maintained with an even hand and steady resolution, as a guard to the religion and morals of the family and the support of its good order. Take heed that it not be with any of you as with Eli of old, who reproved his children but restrained them not; and that, by this means, you don't bring the like curse on your families as he did on his.
>
> And let children obey their parents, and yield to their instructions, and submit to their orders, as they would inherit a blessing and not a curse. For we have reason to think, from many things in the word of God, that nothing has a greater tendency to bring a curse on persons in this

[1] Stanford Fleming, *Children and Puritanism: The Place of Children in the Life and Thought of the New England Churches, 1620–1847* (New Haven: Yale University Press, 1933). Fleming's book is an excellent treatment of the life of the New England child in relation to the Puritan theology.

world, and on all their temporal concerns, than undutiful, unsubmissive, disorderly behavior in children towards their parents.[2]

## Puritan Stress on Education

The New England Puritans, like their European Calvinistic counterparts, greatly valued literacy. They believed it an easy matter for Satan to corrupt the ignorant. In order to ensure a literate people, the Massachusetts General Court in 1642 required the parents and guardians of children to attend to their dependents' ability to read and to understand the principles of religion and the laws of the Commonwealth. Although the Law of 1642 provided for education, it did not order compulsory school attendance and maintenance. It is interesting to note that the Massachusetts Law of 1642 closely paralleled the English Poor Law of 1601, which required the apprenticeship of pauper children. This English Law broadened the definition of "poor parents" from those actually receiving charity to those who were deemed unable to support their children. The Poor Law of 1601 contained two major provisions: that taxes be levied on all property owners within a given parish for the support of paupers; and that all poor and dependent children be bound out as apprentices in order to learn a useful trade. Motivated by the Poor Law, the New England Calvinists feared that a class of ignorant citizens would not only be prone to the devil's wiles, but might also become a dependent class draining the state's prosperity.

In 1647, the General Court of Massachusetts enacted the famous "Old Deluder Satan Law," which required every town of fifty or more families to appoint a teacher of reading and writing. Towns of one hundred or more families were to employ a Latin teacher as well, to prepare students for entry to the colonial college. Enacted in 1647, the "Old Deluder Satan Law" read:

> It being one Chiefe project of ye ould deluder, Satan, to keepe men from the knowledge of ye Scriptures, as in former times by keeping ym in an unknowne tongue, so in these lattr times by perswading from ye use of tongues, yt so at least ye true sence & meaning of ye originall might be clouded by false glosses of saint seeming deceivers, yt learning may not be buried in ye grave of our fathrs in ye church and commonwealth, the Lord assisting our endeavors,—
>
> It is therefore ordred, yt evry towneship in this jurisdiction, aftr ye Lord hath increased ym number to 50 housholdrs, shall then forthwth appoint one wthin their towne to teach all such children as shall resort to

[2] H. Norman Gardiner, ed., *Selected Sermons of Jonathan Edwards* (New York: The Macmillan Company, 1904), p. 148.

him to write & reade, whose wages shall be paid eithr by ye parents or mastrs of such children, or by ye inhabitants in genrall, by way of supply, as ye major part of those yt ordr ye prudentials of ye towne shall appoint; provided, those yt send their children be not oppressed by paying much more yn they can have ym taught for in othr townes; & it is furthr ordered, yt where any towne shall increase to ye numbr of 100 families or householdrs, they shall set up a grammar schoole, ye mr thereof being able to instruct youth so farr as they shall be fited for ye university, provided, yt if any towne neglect ye performance hereof above one yeare, yt every such towne shall pay 5£ to ye next schoole till they shall performe this order.[3]

Although it is easy to exaggerate the importance of these early school laws, they did establish certain significant points: 1) the state could require education; 2) the state could require towns to maintain teachers; 3) civil authorities could supervise and control schools; 4) public funds could be used to support education. It is an oversimplification to suggest that these laws anticipated the publicly supported and state-supervised schools that were set up later. However, the passage of this legislature does serve to indicate the importance which the Puritans of Massachusetts attached to literacy.

## Elementary Education: The New England Town School

The New England town school was devoted to the teaching of reading, writing, and religion, which were taught by a master. The primary subject was reading, and it was taught according to the ABC method. The student first learned the letters of the alphabet, then syllables, words, and finally sentences. His first text was the Hornbook, a sheet of parchment covered by a transparent material, which contained the alphabet, vowels, and syllables, the doctrine of the Trinity and the Lord's Prayer.

One of the most popular of the colonial school books was the famous *New England Primer*. It appeared in 1690 and ran through numerous editions, and was often referred to as the "Little Bible of New England." This slim volume contained twenty-four rhymes to aid the child in learning the alphabet. Each letter was illustrated with a little woodcut or drawing. The first of these rhymes was the well-known "In Adam's Fall, We Sinned All." This little phrase illustrates the close relationship between reading and religion that was the hallmark of New England elementary education. The *New England Primer* also contained vowels, syllables, "An Alphabet of Lessons for Youth," "The Dutiful Child's Promises," the Lord's Prayer,

[3] Nathaniel Shurtleff, ed., *Records of the Governor and Company of the Massachusetts Bay in New England* (Boston: n.p., 1853), II, 203.

the Creed, the Ten Commandments, "The Duty of Children Towards Their Parents," "Names and Order of the Books of the Old and New Testaments," "The Shorter Catechism Agreed Upon by the Reverend Assembly of Divines at Westminster," and a woodcut of Mr. John Rogers burning at the stake in Smithfield as the first Protestant martyr of Queen Mary's reign.[4]

The student was expected to master the contents of this slim list of printed materials by memorizing them. Writing was learned by copying the printed page or by transcribing the lessons dictated by the teacher. The classroom was ungraded with all students housed in the same classroom irrespective of their age. The teacher, who might be anyone from a ministerial student to an indentured servant, controlled the students by means of the harsh discipline prescribed by religious doctrine.

### Secondary Education: Latin Grammar School

The Latin Grammar school was attended by the sons of the New England social, political, and religious elite. Children destined for this elite kind of secondary education did not enter the Latin school directly from the town school, but first learned to read and write the vernacular from lessons with a private teacher or tutor. As its name indicates, the Latin Grammar school was one of the schools where Latin and Greek were taught as the languages of the educated class—those persons destined to become the religious and political rulers of New England. Students attending the school were destined for the ministry of the Puritan Church or positions of political leadership in the colonies.

This institution formed a direct link between the new American educational environment and its European antecedents. The emphasis on the classics, Latin, and Greek was a direct carryover from the classical humanistic tradition of the Renaissance; the religious influence stemmed from the Protestant Reformation. Students entered the Latin Grammar school at the age of eight and studied there for another eight years. Instructional materials were drawn from the Latin classics: Cicero, Terence, Caesar, Livy, Virgil, and Horace. The advanced students read the Greek authors Isocrates, Hesiod, and Homer as well. No attention was given to subjects that might be considered immediately utilitarian, such as mathematics, science, history, or modern languages.

[4] Paul Leicester Ford, ed., *The New England Primer* (New York: Dodd, Mead, and Co., 1899).

## Higher Education: The New England College

The New England Puritans were greatly concerned with having an educated ministry whose members read the Scriptures and doctrines. To provide for the higher education of ministers of the Church, Harvard College was established in 1636. The Harvard curriculum embodied the old medieval curriculum of the liberal arts, Trivium and Quadrivium. Comprised of three major disciplines, the Trivium dealt with grammar, rhetoric, and logic. The four subjects of the Quadrivium were arithmetic, geometry, music, and astronomy. In addition, Hebrew, Greek, and ancient history were offered because they were useful in Scriptural reading.

## The New England Educational Experience

Several features marked the New England educational experience, as typified by the Commonwealth of Massachusetts: first, education was considered an instrument of both literacy and religious indoctrination; second, it was an essentially conservative means of transmitting a particular cultural heritage; third, it was localized in order to serve the needs of a rural village society. Although the direct influence of the New England town school on later American education is often exaggerated, this unit of educational organization and administration did contribute considerably to the concept of local control. When the common school was established in the nineteenth century, the states delegated substantial powers to local school districts. Although this made education responsive to the citizens in the district, it also produced significant quantitative and qualitative variations from district to district.

## COLONIAL SOUTH: A CULTURAL MATRIX

Because the climate favored the growing of staple subtropical crops such as tobacco, rice, sugar, indigo, and later cotton, the large plantation came to dominate the southern landscape. The society that grew up around the plantation was an agricultural one, supported by a growing number of Negro slaves. Little communication existed between plantations, so the sense of community characteristic of the New England town was absent.

The large plantation also promoted rigid, immobile social class distinctions. Although strong economic rivalries existed between the landowning plantation gentry and the lower socio-economic group, the "poor whites" who had been pushed to the infertile back country, a kind of coalition developed between these two groups. In contrast to New England, where community values were religiously based, the southern colonies developed a value structure that rested upon a set of social, economic, and moral relationships centering around the Negro slave system and based on the concept of white supremacy.[5] The economic hostility between the plantation owners and the back-country poor whites was submerged by their mutual interest in the slave system and by the desire of both groups to control the Negro population.

## Southern White Gentlemen's Code

The plantation owners represented a leisure class of people in an agricultural structure who wanted to establish a chivalrous code of life based upon the Cavalier myth.[6] Although historically there is little truth to the notion that the southern gentry were originally displaced aristocrats, the southern plantation owners believed the myth to be a factual account of their ancestry. The education of southern gentlemen contained two major emphases: an ethical code based upon a conception of chivalry; and practical instruction in the management of the basic agricultural unit, the plantation. The merging of a concept of chivalry and a method of plantation management was not necessarily dictated by either logic or economics, but resulted instead from a rather romanticized view of history.

Like leisure classes in other times, southern gentlemen developed an interest and ability in oratory. It is interesting to note that oratorical ability has often had both aristocratic and democratic connotations. Excellence in speech has long been rated highly by leisure classes. Since the days of Athenian democracy, oratorical prowess has also characterized democratic societies. Southern writers have frequently referred to the slave-holding South as a latter-day Athens, since Athenian life at the time of Pericles was similarly supported by a large slave population that enabled the free citizens to follow cultural pursuits. The unusual blending of aristocratic and democratic elements in the South produced a generation of orator-statesmen that included Washington, Jefferson, Madison, and

[5] In this description of the American South the author has condensed almost 150 years of southern history. Although the large plantation did not emerge immediately, the pattern already existed by the close of the seventeenth century. The southern white code evolved as an expression of racially conditioned mores and folkways in the period between the Revolution and the Civil War.

[6] Some plantation owners considered themselves to be the descendants of the Cavaliers, the English aristocrats who supported the Stuart cause against Cromwell's "Roundheads." According to the "Cavalier myth," these displaced aristocrats emigrated to the American South, where they re-established the old aristocratic way of life in the form of plantation society. Historically, the "Cavalier myth" is more legend than fact.

Monroe, all of whom were instrumental in the early republic's political experience. As an educational exemplar, the orator has served as a model for the well-rounded, liberally educated man who is a persuasive public speaker.

The population patterns which resulted from the plantation economy also made formal education difficult. A small population was scattered over a large land area. Because of the long distances between plantations and the lack of well-defined community life, a good deal of the formal education of the socio-economic elite was provided by tutors.

Because of the problems of establishing a formal structure for transmitting the social code, southern educational patterns also embraced much that was informal. The plantation itself served as an informal school where young men and women could learn "proper manners" by directly imitating their parents. The young man learned the skills of plantation management from his father. The daughter of the elite family was reared to occupy the exalted social position of mistress of the plantation. As the future wife of a plantation owner, she was trained to carry out the domestic duties of managing the household and the servants. Like her brother she often had the benefits of private tutoring, and learned the social graces from her mother. Children of wealthy families often completed their education by going to European or colonial colleges.

## Poor White Education

Although the poor white, who was usually confined to small farms on infertile land, often occupied an economic position inferior to that of the Negro slave, he learned to feel superior because he was white. Thus a set of mores and folkways based upon the economic and social conditions of a slave society evolved that reinforced the doctrine of white supremacy. Economically restricted by the plantation system, the poor white was doomed to eke out his subsistence as best he could, and only fear of the Negro checked his hostility to the plantation owner. In the southern backwoods, education was concerned with the arts of survival rather than the intricacies of a classical tradition. Education for the poor white boy was entirely informal; he learned through the direct experience of farming and hunting with his father. The girl learned simple domestic tasks from her mother. While such informal lessons served the immediate needs of survival in an inhospitable environment, they produced a large class of illiterate people, a condition that tended to inhibit the progress of the South in later years.

## *Negro Education*

The education of the Negro slave was functionally related to the needs of a plantation-based economy. In being uprooted from his native Africa, the Negro was torn from his own culture and thrust into an environment not merely inhospitable but completely alien. As a slave, the Negro was undergoing induction into a society vastly different from that of his homeland. He was forced to adapt from the life of a hunter-herdsman-farmer to that of a plantation laborer. As in the case of the poor white, the Negro slave's education was direct and informal as he learned the vocational skills of his economic level. Although the field hands only learned the simple agricultural skills, some of the slaves received more specializing training as mechanics, blacksmiths, or domestic servants. Fearful of slave insurrections, the southern plantation owner made no attempt to provide formal education. Literacy in the sense of reading and writing was not available to most of the slaves, although there were a few exceptions.

## *Formal Education*

Thus far formal education in the South has not been considered, for the simple reason that, except for the tutoring provided for the upper-class children of plantation society, it was not readily available. Since the southern social order lacked opportunities for community life, it did not develop a well-defined system of formal education. However, certain types of formal education eventually did evolve in some areas of the South.

Influenced by the English Poor Law of 1601, which had required training for the dependent poor, the colonies of Virginia and North Carolina made it compulsory for orphans and pauper children to be apprenticed. Orphans were indentured to masters of specific trades to learn a particular skill. The master, in addition to teaching his trade, was also required to provide instruction in reading and writing.

Another development of more formal education in the South was the establishment of various private denominational schools. These denominational or charity schools were supported by private endowments or gifts. The Anglican missionary society, the Society for the Propagation of the Gospel in Foreign Parts, maintained elementary schools which provided religious instruction, reading, writing, and rudimentary arithmetic. But these attempts to establish formal education were sporadic and never reached the level of organization achieved by the Puritans in New England.

As was the case in England, and the other North American colonies, higher education in the South was restricted to the sons of the upper class.

Some members of this elite were sent to England for further education. In 1693 William and Mary College was established in Virginia to educate the ministry of the Anglican Church. Originally, it had three departments of instruction: a grammar school, a School of Philosophy, and a Theology School. In 1779 the college was reorganized, and the scope of the curriculum was broadened to include natural philosophy, mathematics, law, medicine, moral philosophy, fine arts, and modern languages.

For most of the population in the South, therefore, colonial education was informal rather than formal. Because of population distribution and the economic system, such formal education as did exist was highly aristocratic and confined to the elite group of white plantation owners. Educational progress in the South lagged behind that of New England because of the lack of a sense of community goals comparable to the religious orientation in New England.

## THE MIDDLE ATLANTIC COLONIES: PLURALISM

Located between New England and the southern colonies, the Middle Atlantic colonies included New York, New Jersey, Pennsylvania, and Delaware. While New England was characterized by patterns of religious and racial homogeneity and the South by patterns of economic homogeneity, the Middle Atlantic colonies comprised an extremely pluralistic society. Religious pluralism was evidenced by such diverse sects as Dutch Reformed, Anglican, Lutheran, Quaker, Presbyterian, Roman Catholic, and Jewish. The presence of the English, Dutch, Swedes, French, Danes, Jews, Irish, Scottish, and Germans resulted in widely varying racial and linguistic patterns as well. Various economic endeavors included farming, manufacturing, commerce, and related activities.

Because of the diverse traditions, languages, and religions, there was no common fund of shared experience upon which to build a required or extensive educational enterprise. Various linguistic and religious groups attempted to perpetuate themselves through isolation, which each one thought would preserve the elements particular to its culture. Conflicting motives and goals also retarded the growth of institutional patterns of formal education. We have earlier defined education as the process of introducing the immature to their culture; but the middle colonies' experience was complicated by the existence of multiple cultural patterns.

### Educational Patterns in New York

Until 1664, New Amsterdam was a Dutch colonial possession. The most powerful religious agency there was the Dutch Reformed Church, a

Calvinistic sect which, like its New England counterpart, believed in an educated ministry and laity. While the Dutch West India Company supported education, the Church exercised control over it. Under Church auspices elementary or reading and writing schools were maintained. After the English seized the colony these schools persisted, as the small Dutch community struggled to preserve its cultural identity against the English influx.

The English established a number of charity schools, supported by the Anglican Church and protected by the colonial governor, where instruction was given in reading, writing, arithmetic, catechism, and religion. The primary emphasis was on the elementary level of education, although a statute was passed to provide for the teaching of Latin and Greek.

Whenever formal institutions fail to respond to economic conditions, informal substitutes come into existence. Despite the difficulty of maintaining a set of organized educational institutions, therefore, a number of private schools developed, and the government's neglect of education encouraged their growth. More and more members of the rising commercial class attended these schools, for special skills were offered that were needed for trading, such as navigation, accounting, and modern languages. The "private venture school" was an educational response to the demand for practical skills and knowledge.

### Educational Patterns in Pennsylvania

Pennsylvania followed a pattern similar to New York's; the English Quakers who first established a colony there were soon joined by Scots-Irish Presbyterians and German Pietists. Each group had its own notion of culture and of how to transmit it. Quaker elementary schools stressed religion, reading, writing, and arithmetic. The Quakers rejected the harsh forms of corporal punishment prevalent during that period and gave greater attention to the individual nature of each child. Although the English founded charity schools, the German colonists rejected them as part of an English plot to undermine Germanic culture. Among the German teachers was Christopher Dock, who wrote the first book about education in the New World. As in New York, the absence of strong governmental concern with education caused private venture schools and private tutors to fill the educational gap.

## CONCLUSION

Although certain features were unique to each colonial region, the colonies also shared this early stage of the American educational experience in many ways. Because church and school were intimately connected, the religious influence was strong in all areas where the school served as a formal instructional agency, and much of the educational content was religious. This element persisted into the eighteenth and even into the nineteenth centuries. Also, the society served by the school was predominantly rural and agrarian.

The American colonial educational experience, then, basically consisted of the reconstruction of imported English institutions in light of the New World environment. It also included the failure of some elements of the imported educational tradition to meet environmental challenges. For example, the New England town school was an attempt to offer literacy to the people of the settlement within the immediate societal framework. The Latin Grammar school with its emphasis on Latin and Greek represented a failure of secondary education to adjust to the demands of this new world. However, in a non-utilitarian sense the Latin Grammar school did provide a sense of continuity with the tradition of the Western world.

When the American colonists rose in rebellion against England, they were beginning to come to grips with the realities of this new environment. The struggles of the revolutionary generation of Americans, discussed in the following chapter, indicate the attempts by American intellectual leadership to fashion and direct an educational experience appropriate to the unique environment they had discovered.

# References

BAILYN, BERNARD. *Education in the Forming of American Society.* Chapel Hill: University of North Carolina Press, 1960.

BENEDICT, AGNES E. *Progress to Freedom: The Story of American Education.* New York: G. P. Putnam's Sons, 1942.

CUBBERLEY, ELLWOOD P. *Public Education in the United States: A Study and Interpretation of American Educational History.* Boston: Houghton—Mifflin Co., 1934.

DEXTER, EDWIN G. *A History of Education in the United States.* New York: The Macmillan Company, 1904.

FLEMING, STANFORD. *Children and Puritanism: The Place of Children in the Life and Thought of the New England Churches, 1620–1847.* New Haven: Yale University Press, 1933.

FORD, PAUL L., ed. *The New England Primer.* New York: Dodd, Mead and Co., 1899.

GARDINER, H. NORMAN, ed. *Selected Sermons of Jonathan Edwards.* New York: The Macmillan Company, 1904.

JOHNSON, CLIFTON. *Old-Time Schools and School Books.* New York: The Macmillan Company, 1904.

KILPATRICK, WILLIAM II. *The Dutch Schools of New Netherland and Colonial New York.* Washington: Government Printing Office, 1912.

KNIGHT, EDGAR W. *A Documentary History of Education in the South Before 1860.* Chapel Hill: University of North Carolina Press, 1949.

# SELECTIONS

*The life style of the New England colonist was permeated by the theology of John Calvin. Various ministers of the Gospel in the New World elabo-rated this theology and recast it in the New England form of Puritanism. Among the most famous of these divines was Jonathan Edwards. Although his writings are complex and deal with a variety of themes ranging from metaphysics to aesthetic experience, Edwards never strayed far from the Puritan intellectual and religious framework. It is important to interpret the New England educational experience in the light of this frame of ref-erence. The selections which follow are taken from Edwards' sermon, "Sinners in the Hands of an Angry God."*

## Jonathan Edwards' Sinners in the Hands of an Angry God

The God that holds you over the pit of hell, much as one holds a spider or some loathsome insect over the fire, abhors you, and is dreadfully provoked; his wrath towards you burns like fire; he looks upon you as worthy of nothing else, but to be cast into the fire; he is of purer eyes than to bear to have you in his sight; you are ten thousand times so abominable in his eyes, as the most hateful and venomous serpent is in ours. You have offended him infinitely more than ever a stubborn rebel did his prince: and yet it is nothing but his hand that holds you from falling into the fire every moment. 'Tis ascribed to nothing else, that you did not go to hell the last night; that you were suffered to awake again in this world after you closed your eyes to sleep; and there is no other reason to be given why you have not dropped into hell since you arose in the morning, but that God's hand has held you up. There is no other reason to be given why you han't gone to hell since you have sat here in the house of God, provoking his pure eyes by your sinful wicked manner of attending his solemn worship. Yea, there is nothing else that is to be given as a reason why you don't this very moment drop down into hell.

SOURCE: H. Norman Gardiner, ed., *Selected Sermons of Jonathan Edwards* (New York: The Macmillan Company, 1904), pp. 88–89, 96–97.

23

O sinner! consider the fearful danger you are in. 'Tis a great furnace of wrath, a wide and bottomless pit, full of the fire of wrath, that you are held over in the hand of that God whose wrath is provoked and incensed as much against you as against many of the damned in hell. You hang by a slender thread, with the flames of divine wrath flashing about it, and ready every moment to singe it and burn it asunder; and you have no interest in any Mediator, and nothing to lay hold of to save yourself, nothing to keep off the flames of wrath, nothing of your own, nothing that you ever have done, nothing that you can do, to induce God to spare you one moment.

.   .   .   .   .

And you that are young men and young women, will you neglect this precious season that you now enjoy, when so many others of your age are renouncing all youthful vanities and flocking to Christ? You especially have now an extraordinary opportunity; but if you neglect it, it will soon be with you as it is with those persons that spent away all the precious days of youth in sin and are now come to such a dreadful pass in blindness and hardness.

And you children that are unconverted, don't you know that you are going down to hell to bear the dreadful wrath of that God that is now angry with you every day and every night? Will you be content to be the children of the devil, when so many other children in the land are converted and are become the holy and happy children of the King of kings?

And let every one that is yet out of Christ and hanging over the pit of hell, whether they be old men and women or middleaged or young people or little children, now hearken to the loud calls of God's word and providence. This acceptable year of the Lord that is a day of such great favor to some will doubtless be a day of as remarkable vengeance to others. Men's hearts harden and their guilt increases apace at such a day as this, if they neglect their souls. And never was there so great danger of such persons being given up to hardness of heart and blindness of mind. God seems now to be hastily gathering in his elect in all parts of the land; and probably the bigger part of adult persons that ever shall be saved will be brought in now in a little time, and that it will be as it was on that great outpouring of the Spirit upon the Jews in the Apostles' days, the election will obtain and the rest will be blinded. If this, should be the case with you, you will eternally curse this day, and will curse the day that ever you was born to see such a season of the pouring out of God's Spirit, and will wish that you had died and gone to hell before you had seen it. Now undoubtedly it is as it was in the days of John the Baptist, the axe is in an extraordinary manner laid at the root of the trees, that every tree that bringeth not forth good fruit may be hewn down and cast into the fire.

Therefore let every one that is out of Christ now awake and fly from the wrath to come. The wrath of Almighty God is now undoubtedly hanging over great part of this congregation. Let every one fly out of Sodom. *"Haste and escape for your lives, look not behind you, escape to the mountain, lest ye be consumed."*

The New England Primer, *which first appeared in 1690, was one of the most popular and widely used textbooks in the colonial elementary school. Known as the "Little Bible of New England," it combined the basic rudiments of literacy and religious education. The selections reprinted here are the rhymes by which the New England school child mastered the letters of the alphabet, followed by "The Dutiful Child's Promises."*

# The New England Primer

A    In Adam's Fall
     We Sinned All.

B    Thy Life to Mend
     This Book Attend.

C    The Cat doth play
     And after slay.

D    A Dog will bite
     A Thief at night.

E    An Eagle's flight
     Is out of sight.

F    The Idle Fool
     Is whipt at School.

G    As runs the Glass
     Man's life doth pass.

H    My Book and Heart
     Shall never part.

J    Job feels the Rod
     Yet blesses God.

K    Our King the good
     No man of blood.

L    The Lion bold
     The Lamb doth hold.

M    The Moon gives light
     In time of night.

N    Nightingales sing
     In Time of Spring.

O    The Royal Oak
     It was the Tree
     That sav'd His
     Royal Majestie.

P    Peter denies
     His Lord and cries.

Q    Queen Esther comes
     In Royal State
     to Save the Jews
     From dismal Fate.

R    Racol doth mourn,
     for her first born.

S    Samuel anoints
     Whom God appoints.

T    Time cuts down all
     Both great and small.

U    Uriah's beauteous Wife
     Made David seek his Life.

W    Whales in the Sea
     God's Voice obey.

X    Xerxes the great did die,
     And so must you and I.

Source: Paul L. Ford, ed., *The New England Primer* (New York: Dodd, Mead, and Co., 1897). The rhymes and alphabet have been edited and the woodcuts omitted by the author of this book.

| Y | Youth forward slips<br>Death soonest nips. | Z | Zacheus he<br>Did climb the Tree<br>His Lord to see. |

# The Dutiful Child's Promises

I Will fear GOD, and honour the KING
I will honour my Father & Mother
I will Obey my Superiours
I will Submit to my Elders
I will Love my Friends
I will hate no Man
I will forgive my Enemies, and pray to God for them
I will as much as in me lies keep all God's Holy Commandments

# 3

# Educational
# Patterns and Ideas
# During a Revolutionary Period

## INTRODUCTION: EARLY FEDERAL PERIOD

The American Revolutionary period produced a whole generation of statesmen, who first sundered the ties that bound them politically to the old order and then strove to guide the new nation through the uncharted regions of a republican covenant. The Declaration of Independence and the Constitution gave form and direction to the new political order. The leaders of this revolutionary generation realized that a republic of self-governing citizens would function effectively only if such a government rested on a firm foundation in the education of its citizens. If there was a system of education proper to monarchy, then there was one appropriate to free men. Benjamin Franklin and Thomas Jefferson were foremost among those who sought to assess the condition of education and plan the reforms needed to assure the continuing existence of the United States as a sovereign and independent nation.

After the American Revolution brought the colonial period to an abrupt end, the diverse colonial settlements became blended together in the emerging national consciousness of the early republican period. The United States was an experiment in political forms being cast in a new environment, as new social and political institutions were constructed by the republican government. While the colonial forms of education persisted into the republican era, there was much theorizing over the institutional organization and curricular content that education should adopt as a means of introducing people to a new government and cultural experience. A major part of this theorizing centered about the problem of how to replace the old loyalties with a set of values and commitments based on the new concept of self-government.

Under the Articles of Confederation, one of the infant Congress' major problems was that of administering the Northwest Territory. To encourage the settlement of this area, the first Northwest Ordinance was adopted in 1785. This Ordinance called for the territory to be surveyed and divided into townships of six square miles each, which were then subdivided into thirty-six sections. The income derived from the sixteenth section was to be set aside for school funds. Although much of this income was dissipated, the precedent for the establishment of school funds was set. The Ordinance of 1787 encouraged education as "necessary to good government and the happiness of mankind." Although the Ordinances of 1785 and 1787 predated state ratification of the federal Constitution, they contained elements that would have continuing significance for education. The federal government had expressed a concern for the support of educational institutions that anticipated the programs of assistance adopted in the late nineteenth and twentieth centuries.

Although land was reserved for the purpose of school support, the federal Congress avoided making specific injunctions as to how the funds derived from this land should be administered. This lack of specific directive resulted from widespread fear of centralizing educational powers in a federal authority. Throughout the eighteenth and nineteenth centuries education remained localized and decentralized.

The United States Constitution, which was ratified in 1789, did not mention education. Under the "reserved powers clause" of the Tenth Amendment in the Bill of Rights, the responsibilities and prerogatives of education remained vested in each of the individual states of the Union. Following the New England tradition of controlling education through the township, most of the states delegated substantial educational powers to local school districts. Although education remained a state function, local school districts and school boards thus gained the initiative in matters of educational support and control. The great qualitative and quantitative variations that have developed since then in American public schools reflect local districts' ability to support education.

The absence of provision for education in the Constitution has been used as an argument to block federal involvement by the opponents of federal aid to education. Although the system of local control has persisted, many Americans have become increasingly aware of the importance of education to the nation as a whole. The large-scale federal programs of assistance enacted in the twentieth century are evidence of this.

## FIRST EFFORTS TOWARD MASS EDUCATION

Since the early federal government was reluctant to become involved in financing education, the states finally began to exert themselves in this area. The first state to take action was Massachusetts, which passed compulsory support laws based upon its earlier experience with the town schools. In the new states to the west, New England was considered the model of educational support and control. Because of its unique problems and attitudes, the South continued to lag. The Middle Atlantic states experimented with various kinds of private education such as the monitorial school, the Sunday school, and the traditional privately endowed school.

Individual experiments with systems of mass education are interesting chapters in the history of American educational methodology. The monitorial method of education, which was based upon the work of the Anglican clergyman, Andrew Bell, and the Quaker teacher, Joseph Lancaster, attracted widespread attention in the period of 1780–1820, and was particularly popular in large cities such as New York and Philadelphia. It called for a master teacher to instruct a number of older students, who would in turn teach classes of younger students. The most appealing feature of this system was its low cost, since the services of only one skilled teacher were needed. At first, the monitorial method was thought to be an effective means of teaching reading, writing, spelling, and arithmetic on a mass scale. By the late 1820's, however, the enthusiasm it had aroused waned as critics argued that mechanical memorization was no substitute for genuine education.

The Sunday school movement in the United States was also an attempt to provide large numbers of children with a basic education. It held classes one day a week, Sunday, when the factories and mills were closed and the child laborers were free from their toil. Instruction was given in reading, writing, and religion. Although it was apparent that one day of instruction a week was inadequate to produce a literate population, some of the churches recognized the value of the Sunday school as an instrument of religious education. The Sunday school has remained a popular institution in many Protestant denominations.

It is difficult to assess the value of such private experiments with mass education. Institutions like the monitorial system and the Sunday school blocked the movement for the publicly supported common school for some time in the Middle Atlantic region. On the other hand, the educational experiments created a wider interest in education and led many individuals to recognize the need for public education.

## Plans for a National System of Education

Meanwhile, numerous plans for a national system of education were suggested. While many of the proposals formulated during the early republican era were never actually carried out, the educational theories of such men as Benjamin Rush, Robert Coram, Samuel Knox, and Samuel Smith did contribute to the nineteenth-century development of the common school. Allen O. Hansen, in *Liberalism and American Education in the Eighteenth Century*, 1926, has analyzed these plans for a national system of education.[1]

The concepts of "nationalism" and "science" were constant themes in the writings of the American intellectuals of the late eighteenth and early nineteenth centuries. Writers such as Benjamin Rush recognized that a residue of old loyalty to England on the part of many people might delay the development of a sense of identification with the United States. A feeling of nationalism might also be impeded by regional loyalties that were allowed to take precedence over national commitment. The cultivation of a sense of American identity meant the building of a common commitment and loyalty to the United States as an independent and sovereign nation.

The concept of a "scientific attitude" was based upon the intellectual ferment of the eighteenth century Enlightenment, which was rooted in the basic conviction that man could discover the laws of the universe through the instrument of science. A "scientific attitude" called for open-minded objectivity and willingness to experiment. Old loyalties and commitments had to be examined and if necessary altered or abolished in the light of scientific discovery. The gentlemen of the revolutionary age believed that "science" applied to social and political relationships as well as to natural and physical reality. If men were willing to experiment and to look forward to the future rather than to rely on the past, then a better and more progressive society would result. Closely allied to the "scientific attitude" was the notion of "progress." If men were guided by scientific principles instead of ignorance, then improvement of both men and society would inevitably follow.

The American intellectuals of the revolutionary era blended the concepts of "nationalism" and "science" into an ideal which they believed

[1] Allen O. Hansen, *Liberalism and American Education in the Eighteenth Century* (New York: The Macmillan Company, 1926).

appropriate for adoption as a guiding principle in the United States. As the Revolution had swept away the old political order, so a revolutionary system of education could likewise remove anti-science prejudices from the American mind. Benjamin Rush, urging a unique brand of education that would reinforce the principle of patriotism, suggested that the federal government should set up an educational structure that would remain flexible enough to absorb constant modifications. Such a national system, Rush said, should be directed toward the building of an attitude distinctively American and scientific.

Robert Coram, in 1791, called attention to the economic basis of educational support. There was a great deal of variation in the ability of local areas to support their schools. As a result, because they were poorly endowed, the rural schools were inferior to the more prosperous urban schools. Stressing the intimate relationship between educational opportunity and social, political, and economic equality, Coram strongly advocated a uniformly supported system of national education. Samuel Knox proposed an educational plan that would combine instruction in classical humanities and American nationalism. Another theorist, Samuel Smith, saw education as providing a means of social control. Smith believed that the United States had a mission to serve as the model of democracy for the rest of the world. These, however, were only various points of emphasis in the plans presented to the American Philosophical Society; actually, there were two major areas of agreement among this group: one, that a national system of education should be used to establish and promote a distinctive American culture; and two, that an educational commitment to the scientific attitude would promote progress.

As is indicated by the work of Rush, Coram, Smith, and Knox, old-world customs and attitudes clearly failed to provide an adequate foundation for the loyalties and creative intelligence necessary for the proper administration of the new government. Realizing that a system of education was called for that could serve the unique needs of the American people, such philosopher-statesmen as Benjamin Franklin and Thomas Jefferson each formulated plans for the development of such a system. The plans proposed by Franklin and Jefferson deserve close scrutiny by the student of the American educational experience. These plans reveal the intimate relationship which both men felt existed between education and the social and political order. Although Franklin's plan was actually proposed before the Revolution occurred, it was a revolutionary plan in that it recognized the unique conditions of the American environment in the light of changing social and economic patterns. Jefferson's plan was introduced during the years of the Revolution, and it demonstrated clearly the emphasis placed on educating the new kind of citizen—men capable of self-government.

## BENJAMIN FRANKLIN'S EDUCATIONAL PLAN

Benjamin Franklin's life has come to be considered archetypical of the opportunities available to the new class of tradesmen in North America. Born into a large but poor family, Franklin's youth was spent in diligent labor and industry. His formal education consisted of only one year at the Boston Grammar School and a few private lessons in writing and arithmetic. When he became an apprentice in the printing trade, Franklin's further education was provided by his own continuing efforts to acquaint himself with the classics and the literature of his day. One of his lifelong principles was that there should be no separation between theory and practice in either life or education, and his numerous educational projects always reflected this.

In Philadelphia, Franklin inaugurated such groups as the Library Subscription Society and the Junto. The Subscription Society was successful in founding the first subscription library in North America. In the meetings of the Junto, a discussion group, Franklin and other young men debated the current intellectual controversies of the day.

In 1743 he organized the American Philosophical Society. His *Poor Richard's Almanack* was an instrument of informal education for countless Americans. The homely admonitions of *Poor Richard* epitomized the practical and utilitarian values of frugality, diligence, and thrift that characterized the rising American middle class. Franklin's distrust of the merely ornamental and solely intellectual aspects of education impelled him to establish an English Grammar school in Philadelphia. Franklin's many political contributions to this country, as Minister to France from 1776 to 1785 and as delegate to the Constitutional Convention, are well known to every student.

In its theoretical outline, Benjamin Franklin's educational plan combined two basic elements of study, the humanistic and the utilitarian; the relative merits of these twin functions of education still vex administrators today. In person and in his attitudes Franklin represented the growing middle class of businessmen and professionals who were becoming impatient with the inherited traditions and institutions that favored the landed aristocracy of the old order. The new class wanted an educational system that would serve practical and utilitarian ends. At the same time, Franklin realized that if American education were to reflect the American dream of progress and opportunity for all, it needed to help provide a feeling of nationalism that would break down the colonial provincialism that had hitherto divided Americans. Franklin also emphasized the need for Americans to develop a scientific outlook to aid in the national experiment.

In 1749, Franklin proposed a curriculum for the education of Pennsylvania youth [2] that, in effect, constituted a program of studies for an English Grammar school as opposed to the old Latin Grammar school. Instead of the narrow classical studies of the Latin Grammar school, his plan called for a broad and practical curriculum that would emphasize both ethical and professional elements. Attitudinal preferences, or values, were stressed equally with skills and knowledge.

The proposed curriculum encompassed many subjects and resembled the modern comprehensive high school. English grammar, classics, composition, rhetoric, and public speaking were a part of language studies; but the important distinction was that classes were to be conducted in English, the vernacular of trade and daily life, rather than in Latin. Utilitarian crafts were also included: carpentry, shipbuilding, engraving, printing, painting, cabinetmaking, carving, and gardening. Although Franklin referred to these areas as elementary art works, they were actually vocational skills.

Mathematics was to be offered as a practical subject rather than as strictly theoretical study. Mathematical studies included arithmetic, geometry, astronomy, and accounting. History was to supply students with exemplars or models based upon the lives of famous historical figures. Greek, Roman, English, and colonial history were offered, with emphasis on the moral lessons they supplied.

Although English was the language spoken, and the first one taught, students could elect a second language according to anticipated vocational needs. Latin and Greek might be studied by prospective ministers; Latin, Greek, and French by doctors; French, German, and Spanish by merchants. Other subjects included in the curriculum were natural science, agriculture, technology, physical education, and character education.

Although Franklin's plan was never actually put into practice in Pennsylvania, it contained certain flaws even in its theoretical form. Its en-

[2] A detailed discussion of Franklin's proposals can be found in the following: John H. Best, ed., *Benjamin Franklin on Education* (New York: Bureau of Publications, Teachers College, Columbia University, 1962); Robert Ulich, *History of Educational Thought* (New York: American Book Company, 1945); and Merle Curti, *The Social Ideas of American Educators* (New York: Littlefield, Adams Co., 1960), which contains sections on both Franklin and Jefferson.

riched curriculum, responsive as it was to the needs of the rising commercial class, was a vast improvement over the narrow course of studies of the Latin Grammar school. But it remained primarily an impressive program of subjects that were not arranged into a clearly logical or graduated curriculum. Also, because to him education was completely a private affair, Franklin failed to develop a scheme for its public application.

## THOMAS JEFFERSON'S PLAN OF EDUCATION

Unlike Franklin, Thomas Jefferson enjoyed both social and formal educational opportunities. Born of a prosperous plantation family, in Virginia's Albemarle County in 1743, Jefferson attended the local English vernacular and Latin Grammar schools. His formal education was completed with his graduation from William and Mary College. He was honored as a distinguished man of letters by election to the American Academy of Arts and Sciences, and served as president of the American Philosophical Society from 1797 to 1815. As a leading statesman during the formative republican period, Jefferson held the positions of member of the Virginia legislature, delegate to the Continental Congress, Governor of Virginia, Minister to France, Secretary of State, Vice President and President.

While Thomas Jefferson is usually remembered as the author of the Declaration of Independence and as the third President of the United States, he was an educational theorist as well as a statesman. He often said that his epitaph should refer to only three of his accomplishments: writing both the Declaration of Independence and the Virginia Bill of Rights, and founding the University of Virginia.

In 1779 Jefferson introduced into the Virginia legislature a "Bill for the More General Diffusion of Knowledge." [3] Implicit in his proposal were three assumptions: first, that republican government and democratic decision-making required an educated and literate citizenry; second, that education should be a political rather than a religious function; third, that educational control should be vested in state governments. It was significant that the proposals of both Jefferson and Franklin implied a shift in emphasis from the religiously oriented education of the colonial period to the more secular approach that characterized the later development of American public education.

[3] Jefferson's educational ideas are analyzed in Gordon C. Lee, "Learning and Liberty: The Jeffersonian Tradition in Education," *Crusade Against Ignorance: Thomas Jefferson on Education* (New York: Bureau of Publications, Teachers College, Columbia University, 1962).

## School Units in Jefferson's Plan

According to Jefferson's plan, the counties of Virginia were to be subdivided into wards and each ward was to support an elementary school. The school was to provide instruction in reading, writing, arithmetic, and the history of Greece, Rome, England, and America. The teacher was to be supported by the school district. All white children in the district were to attend the ward school for three years of publicly financed elementary education. After three years, the parents could maintain the enrollment of their children in the school by paying tuition. The significance of Jefferson's plan was that each white child in the state was provided with an elementary education, even though it was a limited one.

Jefferson also recommended the establishment of twenty grammar (secondary) schools in the state of Virginia.[4] The supervisor of each district would select the most able student in every elementary school who was unable to pay the tuition for the grammar school. These scholarship students were to continue in the grammar school for two to three years, where they would study Latin, Greek, English, geography and higher mathematics. The most promising student from among this group would then receive an additional six years of education and the rest of the class be dismissed. The highest ranking twenty students, selected annually, would continue as far as the grammar school education extended. At the end of this period, half would be dismissed to become teachers in the elementary schools and the remaining ten would go on to higher studies at William and Mary College.

The significance of Jefferson's proposal, which was never enacted, lies in its educational content and perspective. Jefferson wanted education to exercise a sifting function, by selecting the most able citizens through the schools and preparing them for leadership roles in the new society. His proposal contained both democratic and aristocratic elements: first, it was democratic in that it provided for the education of all (white) children at least on a rudimentary level; second, it recommended a publicly supported and publicly controlled education system; third, it was aristocratic in that it tended to produce an intellectual elite; fourth, although it was an

[4] During the colonial and Revolutionary periods, a "grammar school" referred to a school which provided secondary education. This was in contrast to the "elementary" or "vernacular" school which provided the basic tools of reading, writing, and arithmetic. During the nineteenth century, however, the "common school" was so frequently referred to as a "grammar school" that a grammar school education was usually understood as an elementary education. However, for Jefferson, a "grammar school" provided a secondary education that was college preparatory in nature.

improvement over existing conditions, the educational advantage would remain in the hands of the economically wealthy, in that all of this group could stay in school as long as they wished providing they could pay for their education.

While the educational plans of Jefferson, Franklin, and other theorists of the Revolutionary period were imperfect in many respects, they indicated an awareness of the problems of a new social order wrought by political revolution. Although most of the theories were not enacted, they did reflect the concern among intellectuals and others to provide an educated citizenry who could effectively carry out the functions of a republican government. As has been noted, they also represented a shift from a religious emphasis in education to one that focused upon its social and political obligations in a republican society.

## CONCLUSION

The proposals of Franklin, Jefferson, Rush, and others indicated that the leaders of the American Revolution recognized the importance of education as a means of preparing citizens for the responsibilities of democratic self-government. These leaders also knew that the individual man's knowledge and understanding were directly related to the harmony and prosperity of the state. As the frontier moved westward, as population increased, and as greater political stability was achieved, the ideas of the Revolutionary generation were tempered and molded by the realities of the American environment and experience. Franklin's ideas for a more practical curriculum and the use of English as the language in which to teach it typified the utilitarian temperament of the nation. Jefferson's proposal for the diffusion of knowledge to the general populace contributed to the democratic concept of the common school that was articulated by Horace Mann in the nineteenth century.

During the nineteenth century, both the elementary curriculum of the public common school and the secondary curriculum of the private academy came to reflect the practical goals of American life. As it became available to more and more individuals, education contributed to the continuation and elaboration of the American experiment in republican government. As it served to equalize and harmonize the conflicting interests of various ethnic and religious groups, it was an instrument of social integration. The practical aspects of education became apparent in the provisions for training in the various professions and vocations. As denominational control over education gradually diminished, the American school began to instill a non-sectarian, commonly accepted system of values.

# References

ARROWOOD, CHARLES F. *Thomas Jefferson and Education in a Republic.* New York: McGraw-Hill Book Company, 1930.

BEST, JOHN H., ed. *Benjamin Franklin on Education.* New York: Bureau of Publications, Teachers College, Columbia University, 1962.

CURTI, MERLE. *The Social Ideas of American Educators.* New York: Littlefield, Adams Co., 1959.

HANSEN, ALLEN O. *Liberalism and American Education in the Eighteenth Century.* New York: The Macmillan Company, 1926.

HONEYWELL, ROY J. *The Educational Work of Thomas Jefferson.* Cambridge: Harvard University Press, 1931.

LABAREE, LEONARD W., ed. *The Papers of Benjamin Franklin.* New Haven: Yale University Press, 1961.

LEE, GORDON C., ed. *Crusade Against Ignorance: Thomas Jefferson on Education.* New York: Bureau of Publications, Teachers College, Columbia University, 1962.

ULICH, ROBERT. *History of Educational Thought.* New York: American Book Company, 1945.

WOODY, THOMAS. *Educational Views of Benjamin Franklin.* New York: McGraw-Hill Book Company, 1931.

# SELECTIONS

*Foremost among Benjamin Franklin's convictions about the development of American education was his belief that it was necessary for English to be the language of instruction. Stressing utility, he felt that concentration on Latin and Greek as the languages of learning ill prepared Americans to harness a wilderness environment. Too much time was wasted in the study of dead languages. Second, he believed, like Noah Webster, that the evolution of an American form of English as a common language would serve to provide a greater sense of community in the New World. Third, Franklin felt that English as a common language would facilitate the assimilation of foreign language groups. He believed this to be a matter of special concern for Pennsylvania with its large concentration of German-speaking residents. The selection which follows was first attached as an appendix, written by Franklin, to a sermon preached by the Reverend Richard Peters on January 7, 1751. In it Franklin presented his proposed plan of instruction for an English Grammar school.*

## Franklin's Idea of an English School

It is expected that every Scholar to be admitted into this School, be at least able to pronounce and divide the Syllables in Reading, and to write a legible Hand. None to be receiv'd that are under ( ) Years of Age.

### FIRST OR LOWEST CLASS

Let the first Class learn the *English Grammar* Rules, and at the same time let particular Care be taken to improve them in *Orthography*. Perhaps the latter is best done by *Pairing* the Scholars, two of those nearest equal in their Spelling to be put together; let these strive for Victory, each propounding Ten Words every Day to the other to be spelt. He that spells truly most of the other's Words, is Victor for that Day; he that is Victor most Days in a Month, to obtain a Prize, a pretty neat Book of some Kind useful in their future Studies. This Method fixes

Source: Leonard Labaree et al., eds., *The Papers of Benjamin Franklin* (New Haven: Yale University Press, 1961), IV, 102–8. Reprinted by permission of Yale University Press.

the Attention of Children extreamly to the Orthography of Words, and makes them good Spellers very early. 'Tis a Shame for a Man to be so ignorant of this little Art, in his own Language, as to be perpetually confounding Words of like Sound and different Significations; the Consciousness of which Defect, makes some Men, otherwise of good Learning and Understanding, averse to Writing even a common Letter.

Let the Pieces read by the Scholars in this Class be short, such as Croxall's Fables, and little Stories. In giving the Lesson, let it be read to them; let the Meaning of the difficult words in it be explained to them, and let them con it over by themselves before they are called to read to the Master, or Usher; who is to take particular Care that they do not read too fast, and that they duly observe the Stops and Pauses. A Vocabulary of the most usual difficult Words might be formed for their Use, with Explanations; and they might daily get a few of those Words and Explanations by Heart, which would a little exercise their Memories; or at least they might write a Number of them in a small Book for the Purpose, which would help to fix the Meaning of those Words in their Minds, and at the same Time furnish every one with a little dictionary for his future Use.

## THE SECOND CLASS TO BE TAUGHT

Reading with Attention, and with proper Modulations of the Voice according to the Sentiments and Subject.

Some short Pieces, not exceeding the Length of a *Spectator*, to be given this Class as Lessons (and some of the easier *Spectators* would be very suitable for the Purpose). These lessons might be given over Night as Tasks, the Scholars to study them against the Morning. Let it then be required of them to give an Account first of the Parts of Speech, and Construction of one or two Sentences; this will oblige them to recur frequently to their Grammar, and fix its principal Rules in their Memory. Next of the *Intention* of Writer, or the *Scope* of the Piece; the Meaning of each Sentence, and of every uncommon Word. This would early acquaint them with the Meaning and Force of Words, and give them that most necessary Habit, of Reading with Attention.

The Master then to read the Piece with the proper Modulations of Voice, due Emphasis, and suitable Action, where Action is required; and put the Youth on imitating his Manner.

Where the Author has us'd an Expression not the best, let it be pointed out; and let his Beauties be particularly remarked to the Youth.

Let the Lessons for Reading be varied, that the Youth may be made acquainted with good Stiles of all Kinds in Prose and Verse, and the proper Manner of reading each Kind. Sometimes a well-told Story, a Piece of a Sermon, a General's Speech to his Soldiers, a Speech in a Tragedy, some Part of a Comedy, an Ode, a Satyr, a Letter, Blank Verse, Hudibrastick, Heroic, & c. But let such lessons for Reading be chosen, as contain some useful Instruction, whereby the Understandings or Morals of the Youth, may at the same Time be improv'd.

It is requir'd that they should first study and understand the Lessons, before they are put upon reading them properly, to which End each Boy should have an

English Dictionary to help him over Difficulties. When our Boys read English to us, we are apt to imagine *they* understand what *they* read because *we* do, and because 'tis their Mother Tongue. But they often read as Parrots speak, knowing little or nothing of the Meaning. And it is impossible a Reader should give the due Modulation to his Voice, and pronounce properly, unless his Understanding goes before his Tongue, and makes him Master of the Sentiment. Accustoming Boys to read aloud what they do not first understand, is the Cause of those even set Tones so common among Readers, which when they have once got a Habit of using, they find so difficult to correct: By which Means, among Fifty Readers we scarcely find a good One. For want of good Reading, Pieces publish'd with a View to influence the Minds of Men for their own or the publick Benefit, lose Half their Force. Were there but one good Reader in a Neighbourhood, a publick Orator might be heard throughout a Nation with the same Advantages, and have the same Effect on his Audience, as if they stood within the Reach of his Voice.

## THE THIRD CLASS TO BE TAUGHT

Speaking properly and gracefully, which is near of Kin to good Reading, and naturally follows it in the Studies of Youth. Let the Scholars of this Class begin with learning the Elements of Rhetoric from some short System, so as to be able to give an Account of the most usual Tropes and Figures. Let all their bad Habits of Speaking, all Offences against good Grammar, all corrupt or foreign Accents, and all improper Phrases, be pointed out to them. Short Speechs from the Roman or other History, or from our *Parliamentary Debates,* might be got by heart, and deliver'd with the proper Action, &c. Speeches and Scenes in our best Tragedies and Comedies (avoiding every Thing that could injure the Morals of Youth) might likewise be got by Rote, and the Boys exercis'd in delivering or acting them; great Care being taken to form their Manner after the truest Models.

For their farther improvement, and a little to vary their Studies let them now begin to read *History,* after having got by Heart a short Table of the principal Epochas in Chronology. They may begin with Rollin's *Antient and Roman Histories,* and proceed at proper Hours as they go thro' the subsequent Classes, with the Best Histories of our own Nation and Colonies. Let Emulation be excited among the Boys by giving, Weekly, little Prizes, or other small Encouragements to those who are able to give the best Account of what they have read, as to Times, Places, Names of Persons, &c. This will make them read with Attention, and imprint the History well in their Memories. In remarking on the History, the Master will have fine Opportunities of instilling Instruction of various Kinds, and improving the Morals as well as the Understandings of Youth.

The Natural and Mechanic History contain'd in *Spectacle de la Nature,* might also be begun in this Class, and continued thro' the subsequent Classes by other Books of the same Kind: For next to the Knowledge of *Duty,* this Kind of Knowledge is certainly the most useful, as well as the most entertaining. The Merchant may thereby be enabled better to understand many Commodities in Trade; the Handicraftsman to improve his Business by new Instruments, Mixtures and Materials; and frequently Hints are given of new Manufactures, or new

Methods of improving Land, that may be set on foot greatly to the Advantage of a Country.

## THE FOURTH CLASS TO BE TAUGHT

*Composition.* Writing one's own Language well is the next necessary Accomplishment after good Speaking. 'Tis the Writing-Master's Business to take Care that the Boys make fair Characters, and place them straight and even in the Lines: But to *form their Stile,* and even to take Care that the Stops and Capitals are properly disposed, is the Part of the English Master. The Boys should be put on Writing Letters to each other on any common Occurrences, and on various Subjects, imaginary Business, &c. containing little Stories, Accounts of their late Reading, what Parts of Authors please them, and why. Letters of Congratulation, of Compliment, of Request, of Thanks, of Recommendation, of Admonition, of Consolation, of Expostulation, Excuse, &c. In these they should be taught to express themselves clearly, concisely, and naturally, without affected Words, or high-flown Phrases. All their Letters to pass through the Master's Hand, who is to point out the Faults, advise the Corrections, and commend what he finds right. Some of the best Letters published in our own Language, as Sir William Temple's, those of Pope, and his Friends, and some others, might be set before the Youth as Models, their Beauties pointed out and explained by the Master, the Letters themselves transcrib'd by the Scholar.

Dr. Johnson's *Ethices Elementa,* or first Principles of Morality, may now be read by the Scholars, and explain'd by the Master, to lay a solid Foundation of Virtue and Piety in their Minds. And as this Class continues the Reading of History, let them now at proper Hours receive some farther Instructions in Chronology, and in that Part of Geography (from the Mathematical Master) which is necessary to understand the Maps and Globes. They should also be acquainted with the modern Names of the Places they find mention'd in antient Writers. The Exercises of good Reading and Proper Speaking still continued at suitable Times.

## FIFTH CLASS

To improve the Youth in *Composition,* they may now, besides continuing to write Letters, begin to write little Essays in Prose; and sometimes in Verse, not to make them Poets, but for this Reason, that nothing acquaints a Lad so speedily with Variety of Expression, as the Necessity of finding such Words and Phrases as will suit with the Measure, Sound and Rhime of Verse, and at the same Time well express the Sentiment. These Essays should all pass under the Master's Eye, who will point out their Faults, and put the Writer on correcting them. Where the Judgment is not ripe enough for forming new Essays, let the Sentiments of a *Spectator* be given, and requir'd to be cloath'd in a Scholar's own Words; or the Circumstances of some good story, the Scholar to find Expression. Let them be put sometimes on abridging a Paragraph of a diffuse Author, sometimes on dilating or amplifying what is wrote more closely. And now let Dr. Johnson's *Noetica,* or first Principles of human Knowledge, containing a Logic, or Art of Reasoning, &c. be read by the Youth, and the Difficulties that may occur to them be explained by the Master. The Reading of History, and the Exercises of good Reading and just Speaking still continued.

## SIXTH CLASS

In this Class, besides continuing the Studies of the preceding, in History, Rhetoric, Logic, Moral and Natural Philosophy, the best English Authors may be read and explain'd; as Tillotson, Milton, Locke, Addison, Pope, Swift, the higher Papers in the *Spectator* and *Guardian,* the best Translations of Homer, Virgil and Horace, of *Telemachus, Travels of Cyrus,* &c.

Once a Year, let there be publick Exercises in the Hall, the Trustees and Citizens present. Then let fine gilt Books be given as Prizes to such Boys as distinguish themselves, and excel the others in any Branch of Learning; making three Degrees of Comparison; giving the best Prize to him that performs best; a less valuable One to him that comes up next to the best; and another to the third. Commendations, Encouragement and Advice to the rest; keeping up their Hopes that by Industry they may excel another Time. The Names of those that obtain the Prizes to be yearly printed in a List.

The Hours of each Day are to be divided and dispos'd in such a Manner, as that some Classes may be with the Writing-Master, improving their Hands, others with the Mathematical Master, learning Arithmetick, Accompts, Geography, Use of the Globes, Drawing, Mechanicks, &c. while the rest are in the English School, under the English Master's Care.

Thus instructed, Youth will come out of this School fitted for learning any Business, Calling or Profession, except such wherein Languages are required; and tho' unaquainted with any antient or foreign Tongue, they will be Masters of their own, which is of more immediate and general Use; and withal will have attain'd many other valuable Accomplishments; the Time usually spent in acquiring those Languages, often without Success, being here employ'd in laying such a Foundation of Knowledge and Ability, as, properly improv'd, may qualify them to pass thro' and execute the several Offices of civil Life, with Advantage and Reputation to themselves and Country.

*B.F.*

---

*Thomas Jefferson's educational theory reflected the shift in attitude in the United States from a religious viewpoint to a secular one. Jefferson felt that the newly established republic required a body of educated citizens if it was to endure. The selection which follows, "A Bill for the More General Diffusion of Knowledge," was proposed by Jefferson to the legislature of Virginia for the purpose of making education accessible to a larger segment of the population. The significant feature of the proposal was its at-*

tempt to provide basic literacy for the white population by guaranteeing three years of education for all white children in the state. Equally important was Jefferson's attempt to prepare an educated leadership by means of a system of state-supported scholarships.

# A Bill for the More General Diffusion of Knowledge

Whereas it appeareth that however certain forms of government are better calculated than others to protect individuals in the free exercise of their natural rights, and are at the same time themselves better guarded against degeneracy, yet experience hath shewn, that even under the best forms, those entrusted with power have, in time, and by slow operations, perverted it into tyranny; and it is believed that the most effectual means of preventing this would be, to illuminate, as far as practicable, the minds of the people at large, and more especially to give them knowledge of those facts, which history exhibiteth, that, possessed thereby of the experience of other ages and countries, they may be enabled to know ambition under all its shapes, and prompt to exert their natural powers to defeat its purposes; And whereas it is generally true that that people will be happiest whose laws are best, and are best administered, and that laws will be wisely formed, and honestly administered, in proportion as those who form and administer them are wise and honest; whence it becomes expedient for promoting the publick happiness that those persons, whom nature hath endowed with genius and virtue, should be rendered by liberal education worthy to receive, and able to guard the sacred deposit of the rights and liberties of their fellow citizens, and that they should be called to that charge without regard to wealth, birth or other accidental condition or circumstance; but the indigence of the greater number disabling them from so educating, at their own expence, those of their children whom nature hath fitly formed and disposed to become useful instruments for the public, it is better that such should be sought for and educated at the common expence of all, than that the happiness of all should be confided to the weak or wicked:

Be it therefore enacted by the General Assembly, that in every county within this commonwealth, there shall be chosen annually, by the electors qualified to vote for Delegates, three of the most honest and able men of their county, to be called the Aldermen of the county; and that the election of the said Aldermen shall be held at the same time and place, before the same persons, and notified and conducted in the same manner as by law is directed for the annual election of Delegates for the county.

SOURCE: Julian P. Boyd, ed., *The Papers of Thomas Jefferson* (Princeton, N.J.: Princeton University Press, 1950), II, 526–33. Copyright 1950, by Princeton University Press. Reprinted by permission of the publishers.

The person before whom such election is holden shall certify to the court of the said county the names of the Aldermen chosen, in order that the same may be entered of record, and shall give notice of their election to the said Aldermen within a fortnight after such election.

The said Aldermen on the first Monday in October, if it be fair, and if not, then on the next fair day, excluding Sunday, shall meet at the court-house of their county, and proceed to divide their said county into hundreds, bounding the same by water courses, mountains, or limits, to be run and marked, if they think necessary, by the county surveyor, and at the county expence, regulating the size of the said hundreds, according to the best of their discretion, so as that they may contain a convenient number of children to make up a school, and be of such convenient size that all the children within each hundred may daily attend the school to be established therein, distinguishing each hundred by a particular name; which division, with the names of the several hundreds, shall be returned to the court of the county and be entered of record, and shall remain unaltered until the increase or decrease of inhabitants shall render an alteration necessary, in the opinion of any succeeding Aldermen, and also in the opinion of the court of the county.

The electors aforesaid residing within every hundred shall meet on the third Monday in October after the first election of Aldermen, at such place, within their hundred, as the said Aldermen shall direct, notice thereof being previously given to them by such person residing within the hundred as the said Aldermen shall require who is hereby enjoined to obey such requisition, on pain of being punished by amercement and imprisonment. The electors being so assembled shall choose the most convenient place within their hundred for building a school-house. If two or more places, having a greater number of votes than any others, shall yet be equal between themselves, the Aldermen, or such of them as are not of the same hundred, on information thereof, shall decide between them. The said Aldermen shall forthwith proceed to have a school-house built at the said place, and shall see that the same be kept in repair, and, when necessary, that it be rebuilt; but whenever they shall think necessary, that it be rebuilt, they shall give notice as before directed, to the electors of the hundred to meet at the said school-house, on such day as they shall appoint, to determine by vote, in the manner before directed, whether it shall be rebuilt at the same, or what other place in the hundred.

At every of these schools shall be taught reading, writing, and common arithmetick, and the books which shall be used therein for instructing the children to read shall be such as will at the same time make them acquainted with Graecian, Roman, English, and American history. At these schools all the free children, male and female, resident within the respective hundred, shall be intitled to receive tuition gratis, for the term of three years, and as much longer, at their private expence, as their parents, guardians or friends, shall think proper.

Over every ten of these schools (or such other number nearest thereto, as the number of hundreds in the county will admit, without fractional divisions) an overseer shall be appointed annually by the Aldermen at their first meeting, eminent for his learning, integrity, and fidelity to the commonwealth, whose business and duty it shall be, from time to time, to appoint a teacher to each school, who shall give assurance of fidelity to the commonwealth, and to remove him as he shall see cause; to visit every school once in every half year at the least; to examine the schollars; see that any general plan of reading and instruction recommended by the visiters of William and Mary College shall be observed; and to superintend the conduct of the teacher in every thing relative to his school.

Every teacher shall receive a salary of         by the year, which, with the expences of building and repairing the school-houses, shall be provided in such manner as other county expences are by law directed to be provided and shall also have his diet, lodging, and washing found him, to be levied in like manner, save only that such levy shall be on the inhabitants of each hundred for the board of their own teacher only.

And in order that grammar schools may be rendered convenient to the youth in every part of the commonwealth, Be it farther enacted, that on the first Monday in November, after the first appointment of overseers for the hundred schools, if fair, and if not, then on the next fair day, excluding Sunday, after the hour of one in the afternoon, the said overseers appointed for the schools in the counties of Princess Ann, Norfolk, Nansemond and Isle-of-Wight, shall meet at Nansemond court-house; those for the counties of Southampton, Sussex, Surry and Prince George, shall meet at Sussex court-house; those for the counties of Brunswick, Mecklenburg and Lunenburg, shall meet at Lunenburg court-house; those for the counties of Dinwiddie, Amelia and Chesterfield, shall meet at Chesterfield court-house; those for the counties of Powhatan, Cumberland, Goochland, Henrico and Hanover, shall meet at Henrico court-house; those for the counties of Prince Edward, Charlotte and Halifax, shall meet at Charlotte court-house; those for the counties of Henry, Pittsylvania and Bedford, shall meet at Pittsylvania court-house; those for the counties of Buckingham, Amherst, Albemarle and Fluvanna, shall meet at Albemarle court-house; those for the counties of Botetourt, Rockbridge, Montgomery, Washington and Kentucky, shall meet at Botetourt court-house; those for the counties of Augusta, Rockingham and Greenbrier, shall meet at Augusta court-house; those for the counties of Accomack and Northampton, shall meet at Accomack court-house; those for the counties of Elizabeth City, Warwick, York, Gloucester, James City, Charles City and New-Kent, shall meet at James City court-house; those for the counties of Middlesex, Essex, King and Queen, King William and Caroline, shall meet at King and Queen court-house; those for the counties of Lancaster, Northumberland, Richmond and Westmoreland, shall meet at Richmond court-house; those for the counties of King George, Stafford, Spotsylvania, Prince William and Fairfax, shall meet at Spotsylvania court-house; those for the counties of Loudoun and Fauquier, shall meet at Loudoun court-house; those for the counties of Culpeper, Orange and Louisa, shall meet at Orange court-house; those for the counties of Shenandoah and Frederick, shall meet at Frederick court-house; those for the counties of Hampshire and Berkeley, shall meet at Berkeley court-house; and those for the counties of Yohogania, Monongalia and Ohio, shall meet at Monongalia court-house; and shall fix on such place in some one of the counties in their district as shall be most proper for situating a grammar school-house, endeavouring that the situation be as central as may be to the inhabitants of the said counties, that it be furnished with good water, convenient to plentiful supplies of provision and fuel and more than all things that it be healthy. And if a majority of the overseers present should not concur in their choice of any one place proposed, the method of determining shall be as follows: If two places only were proposed, and the votes be divided, they shall decide between them by fair and equal lot; if more than two places were proposed, the question shall be put on those two which on the first division had the greater number of votes; or if no two places had a greater number of votes than the others, as where the votes shall have been equal between one or both of them and some other or others, then it shall be decided by fair and equal lot (unless it can be agreed by a majority of votes) which of the places having equal numbers shall be thrown out of the competition, so that the question shall be put on the remaining two, and if on this ultimate question the votes shall be equally divided, it shall then be decided finally by lot.

The said overseers having determined the place at which the grammar school for their district shall be built, shall forthwith (unless they can otherwise agree with the proprietors of the circumjacent lands as to location and price) make application to the clerk of the county in which the said house is to be situated, who shall thereupon issue a writ, in the nature of a writ of ad quod damnum, directed to the sheriff of the said county commanding him to summon and impannel twelve fit persons to meet at the place, so destined for the grammar school-house, on a certain day, to be named in the said writ, not less than five, nor more than ten, days from the date thereof; and also to give notice of the same to the proprietors and tenants of the lands to be viewed, if they be to be found within the county, and if not, then to their agents therein if any they have. Which freeholders shall be charged by the said sheriff impartially, and to the best of their skill and judgment to view the lands round about the said place, and to locate and circumscribe, by certain metes and bounds, one hundred acres thereof, having regard therein principally to the benefit and convenience of the said school, but respecting in some measure also the convenience of the said proprietors, and to value and appraise the same in so many several and distinct parcels as shall be owned or held by several and distinct owners or tenants, and according to their respective interests and estates therein. And after such location and appraisement so made, the said sheriff shall forthwith return the same under the hands and seals of the said jurors, together with the writ, to the clerk's office of the said county and the right and property of the said proprietors and tenants in the said lands so circumscribed shall be immediately devested and be transferred to the commonwealth for the use of the said grammar school, in full and absolute dominion, any want of consent or disability to consent in the said owners or tenants notwithstanding. But it shall not be lawful for the said overseers so to situate the said grammar school-house, nor to the said jurors so to locate the said lands, as to include the mansion-house of the proprietor of the lands, nor the offices, curtilage, or garden, thereunto immediately belonging.

The said overseers shall forthwith proceed to have a house of brick or stone, for the said grammar school, with necessary offices, built on the said lands, which grammar school-house shall contain a room for the school, a hall to dine in, four rooms for a master and usher, and ten or twelve lodging rooms for the scholars.

To each of the said grammar schools shall be allowed out of the public treasury, the sum of            pounds, out of which shall be paid by the Treasurer, on warrant from the Auditors, to the proprietors or tenants of the lands located, the value of their several interests as fixed by the jury, and the balance thereof shall be delivered to the said overseers to defray the expence of the said buildings.

In these grammar schools shall be taught the Latin and Greek languages, English grammar, geography and the higher part of numerical arithmetick, to wit, vulgar and decimal fractions, and the extraction of the square and cube roots.

A visiter from each county constituting the district shall be appointed, by the overseers, for the county, in the month of October annually, either from their own body or from their county at large, which visiters or the greater part of them, meeting together at the said grammar school on the first Monday in November, if fair, and if not, then on the next fair day, excluding Sunday, shall have power to choose their own Rector, who shall call and preside at future meetings, to employ from time to time a master, and if necessary, an usher, for the said school, to remove them at their will, and to settle the price of tuition to be paid by the scholars. They shall also visit the school twice in every year at the least, either together or separately at their discretion, examine the scholars, and see that any general plan of instruction recommended by the visiters of William and Mary College shall be observed. The said masters and ushers, before they enter on the execution of their office, shall give assurance of fidelity to the commonwealth.

A steward shall be employed, and removed at will by the master, on such wages as the visiters shall direct; which steward shall see to the procuring provisions, fuel, servants for cooking, waiting, house cleaning, washing, mending, and gardening on the most reasonable terms; the expence of which, together with the steward's wages, shall be divided equally among all the scholars boarding either on the public or private expence. And the part of those who are on private expence, and also the price of their tuitions due to the master or usher, shall be paid quarterly by the respective scholars, their parents, or guardians, and shall be recoverable, if withheld, together with costs, on motion in any Court of Record, ten days notice thereof being previously given to the party, and a jury impannelled to try the issue joined, or enquire of the damages. The said steward shall also, under the direction of the visiters, see that the houses be kept in repair, and necessary enclosures be made and repaired, the accounts for which, shall, from time to time, be submitted to the Auditors, and on their warrant paid by the Treasurer.

Every overseer of the hundred schools shall, in the month of September annually, after the most diligent and impartial examination and enquiry, appoint from among the boys who shall have been two years at the least at some one of the schools under his superintendance, and whose parents are too poor to give them farther education, some one of the best and most promising genius and disposition, to proceed to the grammar school of his district; which appointment shall be made in the court-house of the county, on the court day for that month if fair, and if not, then on the next fair day, excluding Sunday, in the presence of the Aldermen, or two of them at the least, assembled on the bench for that purpose, the said overseer being previously sworn by them to make such appointment, without favor or affection, according to the best of his skill and judgment, and being interrogated by the said Aldermen, either on their own motion, or on suggestions from the parents, guardians, friends, or teachers of the children, competitors for such appointment; which teachers shall attend for the information of the Aldermen. On which interregatories the said Aldermen, if they be not satisfied with the appointment proposed, shall have the right to negative it; whereupon the said visiter may proceed to make a new appointment, and the said Aldermen again to interrogate and negative, and so toties quoties until an appointment be approved.

Every boy so appointed shall be authorised to proceed to the grammar school of his district, there to be educated and boarded during such time as is hereafter limited; and his quota of the expenses of the house together with a compensation to the master or usher for his tuition, at the rate of twenty dollars by the year, shall be paid by the Treasurer quarterly on warrant from the Auditors.

A visitation shall be held, for the purpose of probation, annually at the said grammar school on the last Monday in September, if fair, and if not, then on the next fair day, excluding Sunday, at which one third of the boys sent thither by appointment of the said overseers, and who shall have been there one year only, shall be discontinued as public foundationers, being those who, on the most diligent examination and enquiry, shall be thought to be of the least promising genius and disposition; and of those who shall have been there two years, all shall be discontinued, save one only the best in genius and disposition, who shall be at liberty to continue there four years longer on the public foundation, and shall thence forward be deemed a senior.

The visiters for the districts which, or any part of which, be southward and westward of James river, as known by that name, or by the names of Fluvanna and Jackson's river, in every other year, to wit, at the probation meetings held in the years, distinguished in the Christian computation by odd numbers, and the visiters for all the other districts at their said meetings to be held in those years, distinguished by even numbers, after diligent examination and enquiry as before directed, shall chuse one among the said seniors, of the best learning and most hopeful genius and disposition, who shall be authorised by them to proceed to William and Mary College, there to be educated, boarded, and clothed, three years; the expence of which annually shall be paid by the Treasurer on warrant from the Auditors.

# 4

# Evolution of the Common School

## INTRODUCTION: CURRENTS OF SOCIAL REFORM

The common school represents one of the most important American contributions to the history of education. It was an equally significant factor in the cultural, social, and intellectual development of the United States as a nation. In the common schools of this country, citizens of the new republic received their first lessons in democracy.

Although the common schools have been defined in various ways, they were usually elementary, and devoted to the cultivation of literacy and citizenship in all the people. Offering a program combining the skills of reading, writing, and arithmetic, these predecessors of the contemporary public school educated generations of Americans to carry out the duties and privileges of life in a republic. In this way, the common schools helped to weld a democracy that encompassed many people of various religious, ethnic, and social backgrounds.

During the nineteenth century, the westward migration of the homesteaders extended the new country's frontiers across the North American continent, and common schools were established in many of the new settlements. At the same time the population was increased by successive waves of European immigrants landing on the eastern shore and either settling in the cities or joining the journey to the Pacific. For the immigrants and their children, the common school was an instrument of Americanization which facilitated the learning of a new language and a new way of life.

The dynamic energy created by both the Atlantic immigration and the westward migration contributed to the emergence of the national character. As an instrument of cultural transmission, the common school played a large role in the development of that character.

49

While the early republican theorists had supplied many of the ideas for the experiment in national unity, it was the later generations of educational leaders and statesmen who established the common school as the agent for both cultural unification and transmission of the society. As the modulations from colony to fledgling republic to industrial nation took place, much of the European tradition was radically altered, and in the march to the Pacific Ocean a number of the inherited practices of European society were obliterated. Two of these trends were especially noteworthy: first, the sectarian religious motivation which had previously dominated educational enterprise was replaced by civil, patriotic, and utilitarian concerns; second, the earlier rigid, closed class structure was swept away by the more democratic fellowship of the frontier.

The course of nationhood was not only perilous, as evidenced by the Civil War; it also involved patient and often extensive transformation. In the early nineteenth century, the United States experienced a period when every area of life was subjected to critical examination by a generation that believed man could improve his life by reforming his society. In the new zeal for reform, a welter of proposals swept the nation. Temperance, abolition of slavery, women's rights, utopian socialism, penal improvement, and popular education were all advocated. While many of the reforms proved transitory, the agitation for public education through common schooling remained to become one of the greatest achievements of American society.

Toward the beginning of the century, however, social and educational reformers were still uncertain as to the most efficient means of establishing public education. While almost all of them agreed on the desirability of a literate citizenry, they disagreed as to how it should be achieved. Experiments with various methods of educating many people quickly were made and then rejected. The concept of the Sunday school, imported from England, involved teaching basic literacy and morality to working-class children who attended school on the one day of the week the factories were idle. The Sunday school was usually a charity venture, privately financed by well-intentioned philanthropists. The monitorial approach to mass education was also attempted. Based upon the educational experiments of the Englishmen Lancaster and Bell, this system was designed to bring about basic literacy by means of a master teacher training a number of student teachers called monitors, who in turn trained other students who served as monitors. Although the monitorial system enjoyed a flare-up of popularity because it cost so little, it too proved an inadequate method of achieving widespread education. While these and other private experiments failed to achieve the desired level of popular education, they aided the common school movement by creating greater demand for a system of universal public education.

## ARGUMENTS FOR UNIVERSAL EDUCATION

An important factor in the movement for universal education was the motivation of the reformers. Many of them were concerned with the people's need for political enlightenment. Democratic processes and procedures required an electorate capable of choosing its officials, and an officialdom capable of governing, and for both an educated, literate citizenry was a necessity.

Equally important in the demand for universal education was the increasing force of nationalism. Common schools could establish common values and loyalties and weld groups with diverse ethnic and religious backgrounds together into a common American identity. In addition to these civic demands, the rising middle and working classes wanted a more utilitarian education which would prepare skilled businessmen and workers. Although the motives of the middle-class businessmen and factory workers may have operated at cross purposes, the means they sought merged in an ill-defined demand for widespread elementary education.

A fourth motive, and one of crucial importance in the struggle for public education, was that Americans viewed education as a means of social improvement and economic advancement. To many Americans, education was something intrinsically good, in and of itself. Americans believed that with equality of educational opportunity established through a public school system, definite social progress could be achieved. Although this view of education is naive, it remains a popular American belief. More realistically, education can serve as an instrument to various ends. If social progress is to result as an educational end, the means to achieve it must be deliberately made a part of the educational process.

While there were many who favored some system of public education, more conservative elements opposed the idea with a variety of arguments. Tax-conscious property owners claimed that it violated the natural sanctity of property rights to tax one man in order to educate another's child. Other opponents saw public education as a movement designed to establish the domination of one political party over another. For example, the political party in power at the time of the school system's establishment might attempt to control the appointment of school teachers and administrators through patronage. Further, the dominant party might seek to inculcate its particular political dogma into the curriculum in order to indoctrinate the young.

Since the common schools were to be publicly supported and open to all children, others regarded the campaign for common schools as a socialist conspiracy that was determined to obliterate class distinctions by herding all the children in the nation into one group of institutions. Some religious sects alleged that public schools would be godless, and would dismiss religious values in favor of secular ones. Certain foreign language groups feared that a common school system would obliterate their distinctive languages, customs, and mores.

## PROPONENTS OF THE COMMON SCHOOL

The social reformers who viewed mass education as a means of realizing the American dream defined the common school as an institution that would provide its students with basic cultural and literary skills. But it was to be more than just another vernacular school in the European sense; it was to be the means of transforming the nation into a cultural sociopolitical entity. Common did not mean lowly or base-born, but expressed the idea of a cultural community in which ideas, experiences, beliefs, aspirations, and values would eventually become uniquely American.

With this view of the common school in mind, prominent defenders mounted podiums in countless meeting halls to plead their cause. Political figures such as Horace Mann, Henry Barnard, James G. Carter, and Thaddeus Stevens argued tirelessly for the enactment of common school legislation. The American Lyceum movement organized by Josiah Holbrook in 1826 took up the appeal to popularize the common school. Educational publications such as William Russell's *American Journal of Education*, Henry Barnard's *Connecticut Common School Journal*, and Horace Mann's *Common School Journal* carried editorials calling for the enactment of common school laws by various state legislatures.

Although the European vernacular school differed greatly from the system proposed for the United States, the centralized elementary educational system in Prussia appealed to many Americans. Not many of them admired the militarism of the Prussian example, but they did appreciate its efficiency and organization. Many of the reforms of Pestalozzi and Fellenberg were included as a part of Prussian teacher education. Further, the system boasted such innovations as a uniformly prescribed curriculum, standard teacher certification requirements, and general taxation for school support. Calvin Stowe, emulating the report of Victor Cousin to the French government concerning Prussian schools, made a similar one to the Ohio legislature. He concluded by pointing out that if a monarchy could supply universal education for its subjects, a republic such as the United States could do no less for its citizens.

While the movement for compulsory, publicly supported and controlled education varied from state to state and region to region in intensity and effectiveness, some general observations can be made. As early as 1827 the state of Massachusetts made the total support of schools by taxation compulsory. Other states in New England and the Midwest followed that model. The movement to widespread, publicly supported education followed more gradually in the Middle Atlantic states and did not really develop in the South until the Reconstruction period after the Civil War.

A general outline of the process of establishing compulsory common school education can be described in four major phases. First, the state enacted permissive legislation by recognizing school districts as legal units which could each serve as a taxing body, providing that the majority of the people within the district were so agreed. The important point was that, by means of permissive legislation, the school district was recognized as a unit with administrative and taxing powers. In the second phase the state, though it did not require the formation of such districts, encouraged them by providing grants of monies from the general school fund to those districts which agreed to support public schools. The state monies came from permanent school funds derived from the sale of public land, state taxes or lotteries, and allotments from federal revenues. The third phase constituted compulsory but still not completely free public education. While the state now required the formation of school districts, the tax support was often inadequate to provide elementary education for all the children living in the school district. As a result, the districts were obliged to use the rate bill, a charge levied upon parents on the basis of the number of children attending the district school. The tuition payments supplied by the rate bill supplemented funds derived from public sources. The last step was the establishment of compulsory and completely tax-supported public education as increased sources of revenue became available for school support. The growth of industry in the eastern states provided an increased tax base in revenue derived from industrial properties. As more people moved into the western states, the establishment of a stable community life facilitated the collection of revenue for those schools. Occasionally, the surplus income of the federal government derived from the tariff would be distributed among the states and used for the common school fund. As more money became available for school financing, the rate bill was gradually discontinued, and elementary education was opened to children from all social and economic classes.

## Horace Mann

One of the leaders in promoting acceptance of the common school was the educational statesman Horace Mann. He was born in 1796 in Franklin, Massachusetts, and raised as a Calvinist, although he later became a Unitarian. He received his bachelor's degree at Brown University, read law, and was admitted to practice in 1823. In 1827 he was elected to the Massachusetts legislature, where he supported educational reform. In 1838 he was appointed Secretary of the Massachusetts Board of Education. Through his *Annual Reports* and work as editor of the *Common School Journal* he contributed a great deal to the cause of public education in Massachusetts and throughout the nation. After retiring as Secretary of the Board in 1849, he served in Congress, and later became President of Antioch College. He died in 1859 an honored American statesman and educator.

To begin to understand Mann's significance, one must first examine his theoretical posture. He was essentially an eclectic, whose speeches and writings indicate no clearly defined philosophical structure.[1] However, five broad currents of thought permeated his educational theorizing: remnants of Calvinism; American transcendentalism; the republican-democratic ethic; industrial capitalism; and phrenology.[2]

Horace Mann rejected the stern Calvinist predestinarianism of his youth for the gentle, more liberal Unitarianism that attracted other New England intellectuals, such as Ralph Waldo Emerson and Theodore Parker, during the first half of the nineteenth century. Unwilling to accept doctrines based on the innate corruptibility of human nature, he believed that organized education could liberate human intelligence and thus effect both individual and social reformation. Although liberal in his theology, Mann recommended the teaching of a "common Christianity" in the public schools. Still remaining a Calvinist in some ways, he continued to believe in the stewardship theory of wealth. He expected wealthy men to act as economic guardians, using their resources for the public welfare.

A New England intellectual himself, Mann did not escape the transcendentalist idealism of Emerson and the whole philosophical school at Concord. Emersonian idealism provided a means of intellectual escape from the harsh realities of an embryonic industrialism. Transcendentalists believed that the human mind could achieve communion with the Abso-

[1] Frank C. Foster, "Horace Mann as Philosopher," *Educational Theory*, X (January, 1960), 9–25.
[2] Merle Curti, *The Social Ideas of American Educators* (New York: Littlefield, Adams, and Co., 1959), pp. 101–38.

lute, the Universal Mind or Oversoul, through intuitive self-evaluation and detachment from materialism. Transcendentalist education sought not only to teach purely factual lessons but also to endow education with a deeper and more complex significance. Because knowledge was such a powerful tool for doing good and avoiding evil, Mann wanted the common schools to be instrumental in creating a far-seeing intelligence and a purer morality.

Devoted to the democratic ethic, he saw public, common schooling as an instrument of the American republic. An intimate relationship existed between liberty, self-government and universal education; political and social liberties could be secure only if men were educated enough to make intelligent decisions. The common school was to serve as a school of democracy, a center of civic education, and a training-ground for responsible public service.

In speaking of the relationship of common education to republican institutions, Mann warned:

> The truth has been so often asserted, that there is no security for a republic but in morality and intelligence, that a repetition of it seems hardly in good taste. But all permanent blessings being founded on permanent truths, a continued observance of the truth is the condition of a continued enjoyment of the blessing. I know we are often admonished that, without intelligence and virtue, as a chart and compass, to direct us in our untried political voyage, we shall perish in the first storm; but I venture to add that, without these qualities, we shall not wait for a storm, —we cannot weather a calm. If the sea is as smooth as glass we shall flounder, for we are in a stone boat. Unless these qualities pervade the general head and the general heart, not only will republican institutions vanish from amongst us, but the words prosperity and happiness will become obsolete. And all this may be affirmed, not from historical examples merely, but from the very constitution of our nature. We are created and brought into life with a set of innate, organic dispositions or propensities, which a free government rouses and invigorates, and which, if not bridled and tamed by our actually seeing the eternal laws of justice, as plainly as we can see the sun in the heavens,—and by our actually feeling the sovereign sentiment of duty, as plainly as we feel the earth beneath our feet, —will hurry us forward into regions populous with every form of evil.[3]

The span of Mann's life coincided with the beginnings of the American system of mass industrial production, and he was well aware that economic and political power was gravitating from the agriculturalist to the

[3] Horace Mann, *Lectures and Annual Reports on Education* (Cambridge, Mass.: Published for the Editor by the Cornhill Press of Boston, 1867), p. 151.

industrialist. If the common school concept was to succeed in practical terms, it had to have the support of the growing middle class of business-men, professionals, and entrepreneurs. Business and industrial property would constitute much of the taxation base needed to finance a common school system.

In framing his appeal for a tax-supported system of common schools, Mann developed a theory of humane and responsible capitalism which greatly resembled the stewardship concept contained in the Protestant ethic. In the course of each generation, certain intelligent and efficient in-dividuals worked so diligently that they accumulated wealth beyond that needed for their own sustenance. As responsible men, these stewards had a moral and a civic responsibility to direct their surplus wealth into in-vestments which would pay social dividends. Mann was thus using the profit motive to argue his theory when he pointed out that investment in public education would contribute to the growth of social intelligence, and enable men to exploit natural resources with greater efficiency. Wealth would be increased, and every class would benefit. Although Mann saw abuses in the ruthless capitalism of the nineteenth century, he believed in working with the system rather than against it. In urging the propertied class to support common-school education, he said:

> Does any possessor of wealth, or leisure, or learning, ask, "What interest have I in education of the multitude?" I reply, you have at least this in-terest, that, unless their minds are enlightened by knowledge and con-trolled by virtuous principle, there is not, between their appetites and all you hold dear upon earth, so much the defense of a spider's web. Without a sense of the inviolability of property, your deeds are but waste-paper. Without a sense of the sacredness of person and life, you are only a watch-dog whose baying is to be silenced, that your house may be more securely entered and plundered. Even a guilty few can destroy the peace of the virtuous many. One incendiary can burn faster than a thousand industri-ous workmen can build;—and this is true of social rights as of material edifices.[4]

Mann was clearly pointing out to the men of wealth and position that it was in their own self-interest to provide for common school education. Property rights would be best maintained in a social context in which the masses were educated to respect property and encouraged to acquire their own. For example, the various introductory reading texts, such as the McGuffey series, stressed the values of hard work, industriousness, and frugality. Respect for both private and public property ranked high in the values stressed by the common-school teachers of the nineteenth century.

[4] *Ibid.*, pp. 197–98.

The common-school movement in America coincided with the rise of European socialism and anarchism. Mann and others believed that common civic education would serve as a deterrent to the successful importation of anarchism and its spread among the immigrants and native American workingmen.

Mann also accepted an intellectual fad of his day—phrenology. The phrenologists believed that the mind was composed of faculties governing human attitudes and conduct and that character could therefore be modified as the appropriate faculties were either exercised or allowed to atrophy through disuse. Education could therefore build the good society by improving the character of individual children in mechanical ways. This doctrine has been discarded by contemporary educators.

It is clear from Mann's theoretical posture that he never developed a clearly defined philosophy of education. Some parts of his theoretical framework were inconsistent with other elements. His great faith in the power of schooling as an instrument of social progress was naive. Although formal education can contribute to social and individual progress, the school is only one of several social institutions. The effectiveness of a program of formal instruction depends upon the educational commitment made by the total society. Mann's trust in phrenology was unfounded in reality. However, his belief in the improvability of man, in educational opportunity, and in the democratic ethic were sources of inspiration for the widespread acceptance of the common school concept in American education.

Mann's life was devoted to the development of the common school. According to his concept, education was to be state-supported and publicly controlled. He felt that the dual aristocratic system of education was alien to the American concept of equalitarian democracy; the common school would be free and open equally to all. Educational opportunity would be the legacy of every American child regardless of his social, religious, and economic background.

The common school would also avoid the stigma attached to state education that had developed with the paupers' and apprentices' schooling provided for by the English Poor Laws. It would be of such excellent quality that all parents would want to send their children to the public elementary school, and eventually it would be superior to private schools. It would also serve as a unifying force, assimilating immigrants, foreign language groups, and other diverse elements in American society into one nation. Through children's association with each other, social class conflicts would be resolved.

As the school represented the interests of the entire community, its expenditures were to be publicly obtained and controlled. As the school board was non-sectarian, its elected officials were to be responsive to the community as a whole rather than to any particular religious, economic, or social class.

## AN EDUCATED TEACHING PROFESSION

As common schools were established, as a result of Mann's struggle for public education, it became necessary to prepare enough competent teachers to staff these institutions. In his surveys of Massachusetts' district schools, Mann found evidence of a very poor level of teaching performed by unqualified and inadequately prepared teachers. To remedy this unfortunate situation, he set up teacher institutes, established normal schools, and worked for the improvement of teacher's salaries. Teacher's institutes were periodic in-service meetings in which teachers met to discuss their mutual problems and to hear lectures on educational topics. The normal schools were teacher training institutions which specifically prepared prospective teachers in common-school subjects, pedagogy, and instructional methodology. The increase in teachers' salaries was designed to attract more competent individuals to teaching.

To popularize his efforts to improve teaching Mann also applied himself to educational publication. In his *Annual Reports* and *Common School Journal* he attracted public attention to the need for improving the quality and quantity of public school education.

In discussing the education of teachers, Mann asked:

> In order to preserve our republican institutions, must not our Common Schools be elevated in character and increased in efficiency? And, in order to bring our schools up to the point of excellence demanded by the nature of our institutions, must there not be a special course of study and training to qualify teachers for their office? No other worldly interest presents any question comparable to these in importance.[5]

### Henry Barnard

A colleague of Horace Mann's in the common school movement, Henry Barnard (1811–1900) served as Secretary of the Connecticut State Board of Education from 1838 to 1842. Among his other formal contributions to education were his service as State Commissioner of the Public Schools in Rhode Island, 1845–1849, Chancellor of the University of Wisconsin, 1858–1860, and United States Commissioner of Education, 1867–1870.

[5] *Ibid.*, p. 103.

Barnard's significance as an educational leader was not confined to his role as an administrator, however. Over much of the nineteenth century he was the most prominent commentator on educational affairs in America. As a journalist and editor, he popularized public education through the *Connecticut Common School Journal* and the *American Journal of Education*. Through his writing and speaking, he kept Americans informed as to the progress and promise of the public school. He also introduced teachers to the ideas of European educational reformers such as Pestalozzi, Froebel, and Herbart.

Barnard's intellectual framework of education embraced four major currents: Christianity, capitalistic individualism, utilitarianism, and Americanism.[6] Barnard associated his entire educational program with Christianity. He opposed the free-thinking and materialistic skepticism of some of the proponents of non-sectarian common-school education. Because of his religious orientation, he felt that education should prepare Christian men and women. The Bible should be used to bring about good character; history and geography were deemed useful subjects in furthering the Christian commitment.

Like Mann's, Barnard's life coincided with the growth of American capitalism and industrialization. With the growth of cities and the increase in the urban working population came an increase of tenements, slum conditions, child labor, and more sharply felt economic class antagonisms. Barnard, however, espousing *laissez-faire* economic theory, felt that these social dislocations were necessary evils. The American school was to be definitely associated with the principles of economic individualism. Natural laws of supply and demand were operative in the economic realm; as a corollary, social competition was the best means of obtaining social progress.

Barnard's emphasis on a utilitarian curriculum was directly related to the continuing industrialization of American life. The growing tendency toward mass production required the preparation of a class of industrialists who could manage their business affairs intelligently and profitably. It also required a large body of workers who were capable of learning the skills involved in industrial productivity. These needs were essentially economic in character, and Barnard believed that a functional curriculum would satisfy them.

Barnard believed that the common school should further the ends of American patriotism as much as possible. Urging civic education, he stressed love of country, its traditions, heritage, and heroes.

[6] Curti, *Social Ideas*, pp. 139–68.

Barnard did not limit himself to theorizing, but also wrote about school practice. The ends of education implied more than mere mastery of the basic literary skills. Although a knowledge of writing and arithmetic was necessary, the proper objectives of education included good health, accurate observation, clear reflection, and the cultivation of noble attitudes. Further, emphasis should always be placed on the utilitarian aspects of education. The child should never suppose education to be merely a set of abstractions. In Barnard's *First Annual Report* as Secretary to the Connecticut Board of Common School Commissioners in 1838, he gave Connecticut teachers advice on subjects ranging from writing to religion.[7] The primary branches of learning should not be neglected, he wrote, since reading, writing, and arithmetic were the foundations of later schooling and a successful life. The most important subject was to be the English language, which included spelling, reading, speaking, grammar, and composition. Instead of being confined to long lists of words learned by repetition, spelling should be related deliberately to reading and writing. The practical uses of arithmetic should be stressed. Religious and moral instruction should also be taught.

Concerning teaching as a profession, Barnard warned against the confusion that could result from rapid teacher turnover. The loss of continuity, and therefore of time resulting from changing teachers, tended to retard the progress of the school, he pointed out. Condemning the practice of boarding teachers in the rural districts, Barnard suggested that the teacher be allowed a regular home of his own so that he could devote a part of his time to regular study. Like Mann, Barnard also urged more adequate teacher education, the establishment of normal schools, and increased financial compensation for teachers.

## CONCLUSION

The common school movement represented a significant stage in the development of the American Public school system. The solid establishment of basic, elementary, common-school education made possible the structure known as the American educational ladder. As a result of the pioneering work of Mann and Barnard, taxation for the support of public schools was enacted into law by various state legislatures. With this system to build on, public school education would eventually extend through the secondary level, and a complete system of publicly supported and controlled

---

[7] John S. Brubacher, *Henry Barnard on Education* (New York: McGraw-Hill Book Company, 1931). Brubacher provides a skillful introduction and editing of Barnard's *Annual Reports*.

educational institutions would be articulated. The concept and realization of the common school in America owe much to the theories and practice of such educational statesmen as Horace Mann and Henry Barnard.

## References

BRUBACHER, JOHN S. *Henry Barnard on Education*. New York: McGraw-Hill Book Company, 1931.

BURTON, WARREN. *The District School As It Was*. Boston: Lee and Shepard, 1897.

CREMIN, LAWRENCE. *The American Common School*. New York: Teachers College, Columbia University, 1951.

CURTI, MERLE. *The Social Ideas of American Educators*. New York: Littlefield, Adams, and Co., 1959.

FOSTER, FRANK C. "Horace Mann as Philosopher." *Educational Theory*, X (January, 1960), 9–25.

MANN, HORACE. *Lectures and Annual Reports on Education*. Cambridge: Cornhill Press of Boston, 1867.

THURSFIELD, RICHARD E. *Henry Barnard's American Journal of Education*. Baltimore: Johns Hopkins Press, 1945.

WILLIAMS, E. I. F. *Horace Mann, Educational Statesman*. New York: The Macmillan Company, 1937.

# SELECTIONS

*The first selection is the "First Annual Report of the Board of Education" of Massachusetts. After referring to the work of the Secretary of the Board, Horace Mann, the report calls attention to some of the specific problems which faced the common school of the state. As the report comments on construction of school buildings, school committees, teacher education, school libraries, and textbooks, the reader can see for himself the condition of common schools in Massachusetts as of 1837.*

# First Annual Report of the Board of Education

It is not the province of the Board of Education to submit to the Legislature, in the form of specific projects of law, those measures, which they may deem advisable for the improvement of the schools and the promotion of the cause of education. That duty is respectfully left by the Board, with the wisdom of the legislature and its committees, on whom it is by usage devolved. Neither will it be expected of the Board, on the present occasion, to engage in a lengthened discussion of topics, fully treated in their Secretary's report, to which they beg leave to refer, as embodying a great amount of fact, and the result of extensive observation skilfully generalized. The Board ask permission only to submit a few remarks on some of the more important topics connected with the general subject.

1. As the comfort and progress of children at school depend, to a very considerable degree, on the proper and commodious construction of schoolhouses, the Board ask leave to invite the particular attention of the Legislature to their Secretary's remarks on this subject. As a general observation, it is no doubt too true, that the schoolhouses in most of the districts of the Commonwealth are of an imperfect construction. It is apprehended that sometimes at less expense than is now incurred, and in other cases, by a small additional expense, schoolhouses

SOURCE: Horace Mann, *Lectures and Annual Reports on Education* (Cambridge, Mass.: Published for the Editor by the Cornhill Press of Boston, 1867), pp. 374–82. The first part of the report which deals with the appointment of the Secretary of the Board has been omitted.

much more conducive to the health and comfort, and consequently to the happiness and progress of children, might be erected. Nor would it be necessary, in most cases, in order to introduce the desired improvements, that new buildings should be constructed. Perhaps in a majority of cases, the end might be attained to a considerable degree, by alterations and additions to the present buildings. It is the purpose of the Secretary of the Board, as early as practicable, to prepare and submit a special report on the construction of schoolhouses. When this document shall be laid before them, it will be for the Legislature to judge, whether any encouragement can, with good effect, be offered from the school-fund, with a view to induce the towns of the Commonwealth to adopt those improvements in the construction of schoolhouses, which experience and reason show to be of great practical importance in carrying on the business of education.

2. Very much of the efficiency of the best system of school education depends upon the fidelity and zeal with which the office of a school-committee-man is performed. The Board deem it unneccessary to dilate upon a subject so ably treated by their Secretary. The difficulties to be surmounted before the services of able and faithful school-committee-men can be obtained, in perhaps a majority of the towns of the Commonwealth, are confessedly great and various. They can be thoroughly overcome only by the spirit of true patriotism, generously exerting itself toward the great end of promoting the intellectual improvement of fellowmen. But it is in the power of the Legislature to remove some of the obstacles, among which not the least considerable is the pecuniary sacrifice involved in the faithful and laborious discharge of the duties of the school committee. The Board have understood, with great satisfaction, that the subject has been brought before the House of Representatives. They know of no reason why the members of school committees should not receive a reasonable compensation, as well as other municipal officers, of whom it is not usually expected that they should serve the public gratuitously. There are none whose labors, faithfully performed, are of greater moment to the general well-being. The duties of a member of a school committee, if conscientiously discharged are onerous; and ought not to be rendered more so, by being productive of a heavy pecuniary loss, in the wholly unrequited devotion of time and labor to the public good.

3. The subject of the education of teachers has been more than once brought before the Legislature, and is of the very highest importance in connection with the improvement of our schools. That there are all degrees of skill and success on the part of teachers, is matter of too familiar observation to need repetition; and that these must depend, in no small degree, on the experience of the teacher, and in his formation under a good discipline and method of instructions in early life, may be admitted without derogating, in any measure, from the importance of natural gifts and aptitude, in fitting men for this as for the other duties of society. Nor can it be deemed unsafe to insist that, while occupations requiring a very humble degree of intellectual effort and attainment demand a long-continued training, it cannot be that the arduous and manifold duties of the instructor of youth should be as well performed without as with a specific preparation for them. In fact, it must be admitted, as the voice of reason and experience, that

institutions for the formation of teachers must be established among us, before the all-important work of forming the minds of our children can be performed in the best possible manner, and with the greatest attainable success.

No one who has been the witness of the ease and effect with which instruction is imparted by one teacher, and the tedious pains-taking and unsatisfactory progress which mark the labors of another of equal ability and knowledge, and operating on materials equally good, can entertain a doubt that there is a mastery in teaching as in every other art. Nor is it less obvious that, within reasonable limits, this skill and this mastery may themselves be made the subjects of instruction, and be communicated to others.

We are not left to the deductions of reason on this subject. In those foreign countries, where the greatest attention has been paid to the work of education, schools for teachers have formed an important feature in their systems, and with the happiest result. The art of imparting instruction has been found, like every other art, to improve by cultivation in institutions established for that specific object. New importance has been attached to the calling of the instructor by public opinion, from the circumstance that his vocation has been deemed one requiring systematic preparation and culture. Whatever tends to degrade the profession of the teacher, in his own mind or that of the public, of course impairs his usefulness; and this result must follow from regarding instruction as a business which in itself requires no previous training.

The duties which devolve upon the teachers even of our Common Schools, particularly when attended by large numbers of both sexes, and of advanced years for learners (as is often the case), are various, and difficult of performance. For their faithful execution, no degree of talent and qualification is too great; and when we reflect that in the nature of things only a moderate portion of both can, in ordinary cases, be expected, for the slender compensation afforded the teacher, we gain a new view of the necessity of bringing to his duties the advantage of previous training in the best mode of discharging them.

A very considerable part of the benefit, which those who attend our schools might derive from them, is unquestionably lost for want of mere skill in the business of instruction, on the part of the teacher. This falls with especial hardship on that part of our youthful population, who are able to enjoy, but for a small portion of the year, the advantage of the schools. For them it is of peculiar importance, that, from the moment of entering the school, every hour should be employed to the greatest advantage, and every facility in imparting knowledge, and every means of awakening and guiding the mind, be put into instant operation: and where this is done, two months of schooling would be as valuable as a year passed under a teacher destitute of experience and skill. The Board cannot but express the sanguine hope, that the time is not far distant, when the resources of public or private liberality will be applied in Massachusetts for the foundation of an institution for the formation of teachers, in which the present existing defect will be amply supplied.

4. The subject of district-school libraries is deemed of very great importance by the Board. A foundation was made for the formation of such libraries, by the

Act of 12th April, 1837, authorizing an expenditure by each district of thirty dollars, for this purpose, the first year, and ten each succeeding year. Such economy has been introduced into the business of printing, that even these small sums judiciously applied for a term of years will amply suffice for the desired object. To the attainment of this end, it is in the power of booksellers and publishers to render the most material aid. There is no reason to doubt, that if neat editions of books suitable for Common-School libraries were published and sold at a very moderate rate, plainly and substantially bound, and placed in cases well adapted for convenient transportation, and afterwards to serve as the permanent place of deposit, it would induce many of the districts in the Commonwealth to exercise the power of raising money for school libraries. A beginning once made, steady progress would in many cases be sure to follow. Where circumstances did not admit the establishment of a library in each district, it might very conveniently be deposited a proportionate part of the year in each district successively. But it would be highly desirable that each schoolhouse should be furnished with a case and shelves, suitable for the proper arrangement and safe-keeping of books. The want of such a provision makes it almost impossible to begin the collection of a library; and where such provision is made, the library would be nearly sure to receive a steady increase.

Although the Board are of opinion, that nothing would more promote the cause of education among us, than the introduction of libraries into our district schools, they have not deemed it advisable to recommend any measure looking to the preparation of a series of volumes, of which such a library should be composed, and their distribution, at public expense. Whatever advantages would belong to a library consisting of books expressly written for the purpose, obvious difficulties and dangers would attend such an undertaking. The Board deem it far more advisable to leave this work to the enterprise and judgment of publishers, who would, no doubt, find it for their interest to make preparations to satisfy a demand for district-school libraries in the way above indicated.

In this connection the Board would observe, that much good might unquestionably be effected by the publication of a periodical journal or paper, of which the exclusive object should be to promote the case of education, especially of Common-School education. Such a journal, conducted on the pure principles of Christian philanthropy, of rigid abstinence from party and sect, sacredly devoted to the one object of education, to collecting and diffusing information on this subject, to the discussion of the numerous important questions which belong to it, to the formation of a sound and intelligent public opinion, and the excitement of a warm and energetic public sentiment, in favor of our schools, might render incalculable service. The Board are decidedly of opinion, that a journal of this description would be the most valuable auxiliary which could be devised, to carry into execution the enlightened policy of the government, in legislating for the improvement of the schools, and they indulge a sanguine hope that its establishment will shortly be witnessed.

5. The subject of school-books is perhaps one of more immediate and pressing interest. The multiplicity of school-books, and the imperfection of many of them,

is one of the greatest evils at present felt in our Common Schools. The Board know of no way, in which this evil could be more effectually remedied, than by the selection of the best of each class now in use, and a formal recommendation of them by the Board of Education. Such a recommendation would probably cause them to be generally adopted; but should this not prove effectual, and the evil be found to continue, it might hereafter be deemed expedient to require the use of the books thus recommended, as a condition of receiving a share of the benefit of the school fund.

The foregoing observations are all that now occur to the Board of Education, as proper to be made to the Legislature, in connection with the improvement of our Common Schools. They beg leave to submit an additional remark on the subject of their own sphere of operations. It is evident, from the nature of the case, that much of the efficiency and usefulness of the Board must depend on the zeal and fidelity of its Secretary, and that it is all-important to command, in this office, the services of an individual of distinguished talent and unquestioned character. No other qualifications will inspire the confidence generally of the people; and without that confidence, it is impossible that his labors or those of the Board should be crowned with success. The Board ask permission to state, that they deem themselves very fortunate in having engaged the services of a gentleman so highly qualified as their Secretary, to discharge the interesting duties of his trust; and they respectfully submit to the Legislature, the expediency of raising his compensation to an amount, which could more fairly be regarded as a satisfactory equivalent for the employment of all his time. The Board also think, that a small allowance should be made for the contingent expenses of the Secretary in the discharge of his duties, such as postage, stationery, and occasional clerk-hire. It is just, however, to add, that this proposal for an increase of salary is made wholly without suggestion on the part of the Secretary.

In conclusion, the Board would tender their acknowledgments to their fellow-citizens, who, by attending on the meetings of the county conventions, or in any other way, have afforded their co-operation in the promotion of the great cause of popular education. At most of these meetings, permanent county conventions for the improvement of education have been organized. Spirited addresses have, in almost every case, emanated from the county meetings, well calculated to impart vigor and warmth to the public sentiment in reference to the cause of education. On the whole, the Board have reason to hope, that an impulse has been given to the public mind on the subject of education, from which valuable effects may be anticipated. It will be their strenuous effort, under the auspices of the Legislature, and as far as the powers vested in them extend, to encourage and augment the interest which has been excited, and they hope, as they shall acquire experience, that their labors will become more efficient. They do not flatter themselves that great and momentous reforms are to be effected at once. Where the means employed are those of calm appeal to the understanding and the heart, a gradual and steady progress is all that should be desired. The schools of Massachusetts are not every thing that we could wish, but public opinion is sound in reference to their improvement. The voice of reason will not be uttered in vain. Experience, clearly stated in its results, will command respect, and the Board entertain a confident opinion that the increased attention given to the subject will result in making our system of Common-School education fully worthy of the intelligence of the present day, and of the ancient renown of Massachusetts.

All which is respectfully submitted by

> EDWARD EVERETT,
> GEORGE HULL,
> JAMES G. CARTER,
> EDMUND DWIGHT,
> GEORGE PUTNAM,
> E. A. NEWTON,
> ROBERT RANTOUL, JUN.,
> JARED SPARKS.

*Boston, February 1, 1838.*

---

*In 1833, Warren Burton's slim volume,* The District School As It Was, *ap-. peared. The book recounts the trials and tribulations of a typical eighteenth-century American boy in the district school of New England. While the book is essentially a reminiscence, it presents a classic statement on the condition of education in the common school. In the student's preparation of the grammar lesson depicted here, the stress is placed on rote memorization with little attention to the content of the lesson. The ignorance of the teacher of any of the principles of educational pyschology is also evident.*

# Grammar—Young Lady's Accidence—Murray—Parsing—Pope's Essay

On my fifth summer, at the age of seven and a half, I commenced the study of grammar. The book generally used in our school by beginners, was called the *Young Lady's Accidence!* I had the honor of a new one. The *Young Lady's Accidence!* How often have I gazed on that last word, and wondered what it meant! Even now, I cannot define it, though, of course, I have a guess at its meaning. Let me turn this very minute to that oracle of definitions, the venerable Webster: "A small book containing the rudiments of grammar." That is it, then. But what an intelligible and appropriate term for a little child's book! The mysterious title,

SOURCE: Warren Burton, *The District School As It Was,* ed. Clifton Johnson (Boston: Lee and Shepard, 1897), pp. 34–41.

however, was most appropriate to the contents of the volume; for they were all mysterious, and that for years, to my poor understanding.

Well, my first lesson was to get the Parts of Speech, as they are called. What a grand achievement to engrave on my memory these ten separate and strange words! With what ardor I took my lesson from the mistress, and trudged to my seat! It was a new study, and it was the first day of the school, moreover, before the bashfulness occasioned by a strange teacher had subsided, and before the spirit of play had been excited. So there was nothing at the moment to divert me from the lofty enterprise.

Reader, let your mind's eye peep into that old school-house. See that little boy in the second high seat from the front, in home-made and home-dyed pea-green cotton jacket and trowsers, with a clean Monday morning collar turned out from his neck. His new book is before him on the bench, kept open by his left hand. His right supports his head on its palm, with the corresponding elbow pressed on the bench. His lips move, but at first very slowly. He goes over the whole lesson in a low whisper. He now looks off his book, and pronounces two or three of the first,—article, noun, pronoun; then just glances at the page, and goes on with two or three more. He at length repeats several words without looking. Finally, he goes through the long catalogue, with his eye fastened on vacancy. At length, how his lips flutter, and you hear the parts of speech whizzing from his tongue like feathered arrows!

There, the rigmarole is accomplished. He starts up, and is at the mistress's side in a moment. "Will you hear my lesson, ma'am?" As she takes the book he looks directly in her face, and repeats the aforementioned words loudly and distinctly, as if there were no fear of failure. He has got as far as the adverb; but now he hesitates, his eye drops, his lips are open ready for utterance, but the word does not come. He shuts them, he presses them hard together, he puts his finger to them, and there is a painful hiatus in his recitation, a disconnection, an *anti* to the very word he is after. "Conjunction," says the mistress. The little hand leaves the lips, at the same time that an involuntary "Oh!" bursts out from them. He lifts his head and his eye, and repeats with spirit the delinquent word, and goes on without hesitation to the end of the lesson. "Very well," says the teacher, or the hearer of the school; for she rather listened to than instructed her pupils. "Get so far for the next lesson." The child bows, whirls on his heel, and trips to his seat, mightily satisfied excepting with that one failure of memory, when that thundering word, conjunction, refused to come at his will. But that word he never forgot again. The failure fastened it in his memory forever. This pea-green boy was myself, the present historian of the scene.

My next lesson lagged a little; my third seemed quite dull; my fourth I was two days in getting. At the end of the week, I thought that I could get along through the world very well without grammar, as my grandfather had done before me. But my mistress did not agree with me, and I was forced to go on. I contrived, however, to make easy work of the study. I got frequent, but very short lessons, only a single sentence at a time. This was easily committed to memory, and would stay on till I could run up and toss it off in recitation, after which it did not trouble me more. The recollection of it puts me in mind of a little boy lugging in wood, a stick at a time. My teacher was so ignorant of the philosophy of mind, that she did not know that this was not as good a way as any; and indeed, she praised me for my smartness. The consequence was, that, after I had been through the book, I could scarcely have repeated ten lines of it, excepting the very first and the very last lessons. Had it been ideas instead of words that had thus escaped from my mind, the case would have been different. As it was, the only matter of regret was, that I had been forming a bad habit, and had imbibed an erroneous notion, to wit, that lessons were to be learned simply to be recited.

The next winter this Accidence was committed, not to memory, but to oblivion; for, on presenting it to the master the first day of the school, he told me it was old-fashioned and out of date, and I must have Murray's Abridgment. So Murray was purchased, and I commenced the study of grammar again, excited by the novelty of a new and clean and larger book. But this soon became even more dull and dry than its predecessor; for it was more than twice the size, and the end of it was at the most discouraging distance of months, if not of years. I got only half way through the verb this winter. The next summer I began the book again, and arrived at the end of the account of the parts of speech. The winter after, I went over the same ground again, and got through the rules of syntax, and felt that I had accomplished a great work. The next summer I reviewed the whole grammar; for the mistress thought it necessary to have "its most practical and important parts firmly fixed in the memory, before attempting the higher exercises of the study." On the third winter, I began to apply my supposed knowledge in the process of *passing*, as it was termed by the master. The very pronunciation of this word shows how little the teacher exercised the power of independent thought. He had been accustomed to hear parse called *pass*; and, though the least reflection would have told him it was not correct, that reflection came not, and for years the grammarians of our district school *passed*. However, it was rightly so called. It *was* passing, as said exercise was performed; passing over, by, around, away, from the science of grammar, without coming near it, or at least without entering into it with much understanding of its nature. Mode, tense, case, government, and agreement were ever flying from our tongues, to be sure; but their meaning was as much a mystery as the hocus pocus of a juggler.

At first we parsed in simple prose, but soon entered on poetry. Poetry—a thing which to our apprehension differed from prose in this only, that each line began with a capital letter, and ended usually with a word sounding like another word at the end of the adjoining line. But, unskilled as we all generally were in the art of parsing, some of us came to think ourselves wonderfully acute and dexterous nevertheless. When we perceived the master himself to be in doubt and perplexity, then we felt ourselves on a level with him, and ventured to oppose our *guess* to his. And if he appeared a dunce extraordinary, as was sometimes the case, we used to put ourselves into the *potential* mood pretty often, as we knew that our teacher could never assume the *imperative* on this subject.

The fact is, neither we nor the teacher entered into the writer's meaning. The general plan of the work was not surveyed, nor the particular sense of separate passages examined. We could not do it, perhaps from the want of maturity of mind; the teacher did not, because he had never been accustomed to anything of the kind in his own education; and it never occurred to him that he could deviate from the track, or improve upon the methods of those who taught him. Pope's *Essay on Man* was the parsing manual used by the most advanced. No wonder, then, that pupil and pedagogue so often got bewildered and lost in a world of thought like this; for, however well ordered a creation it might be, it was scarcely better than a chaos to them.

In closing, I ought to remark, that all our teachers were not thus ignorant of grammar, although they did not perhaps take the best way to teach it. In speaking thus of this department of study, and also of others, I have reference to the more general character of schoolmasters and schools.

# 5

# The Evolution of American Secondary Education

## INTRODUCTION

In the history of the evolution of American secondary education no single individuals stand out as do Henry Barnard and Horace Mann in the struggle to establish the common elementary school. Nor did the American high school emerge as a result of the same kind of simple, forthright arguments that were part of the struggle for elementary schools. The comprehensive high school was the result of a slow and painful process of evolution which only gradually defined it as the basic institution of American secondary education. This evolutionary process began with the import of the Latin Grammar school from Europe, continued with the appearance of the academy, and culminated in the public high school.

Although the struggle to establish publicly supported and controlled elementary education had been successful in most of the states by the time of the Civil War, public secondary schools did not emerge until the latter half of the nineteenth century. As the public high school rose in importance to become the dominant institution of secondary education, the famous ladder of American educational opportunity was completed. From that point on American youngsters could proceed from the pre-school kindergarten through the common elementary school to the high school, and eventually complete their education in the state college or university. The establishment of the public high school was therefore a crucial phase in American education, because it represented the completion of the basic public school system.

Although there are various ways of defining secondary education, ranging from the traditional strictly college preparatory to the more widely varied forms of contemporary adolescent education, for the purposes of this discussion secondary education will refer to those formal educational experiences, usually encountered during adolescence, which follow completion of elementary education.[1] This broad definition covers both comprehensive general studies and specialized vocational studies.

## CONCEPT OF THE EDUCATIONAL LADDER

The American educational "ladder" describes the single, articulated, and sequential system of schools open to all, regardless of social and economic class or religious affiliation. The ladder concept is the educational counterpart of the Jeffersonian-Jacksonian doctrines of equality of opportunity. In contrast to this educational egalitarianism, the European dual system differentiates secondary students into separate and discrete educational tracks with one set of schools for the leadership elite and another inferior group for the masses of the population.

To review the progress of the ladder concept in American education, three major periods in the history of secondary school development can be defined: first, the colonial period, dominated by the Latin Grammar school; second, the late eighteenth and early nineteenth centuries, dominated by the Academy; third, the late nineteenth and twentieth centuries, dominated by the public high school.

## DECLINE OF THE LATIN GRAMMAR SCHOOL

As indicated in the discussion of colonial education, the Latin Grammar schools provided college preparation for the upper classes. Attendance at the Latin Grammar school was necessary for admission to Harvard, Yale, and William and Mary. It was also recommended to those destined for ecclesiastical or political leadership, who studied the Roman and Greek classics which marked the man of education and breeding. As a result the Latin Grammar school lost its early humanism and came to offer a narrow curriculum based upon the ancient Greek and Latin writings.

Even before the American Revolution, such critics of the Latin Grammar school as Benjamin Franklin objected to the limited curriculum dominating secondary education. In 1749, Franklin had proposed an English Academy in Philadelphia that would offer a more realistic course of study to satisfy the contemporary needs of the people. At the same time a number of private venture schools appeared. These schools, usually conducted

[1] William M. French, *American Secondary Education* (New York: The Odyssey Press, 1957), p. 24.

by a single master, offered a wide range of subjects and skills such as modern languages, navigation, bookkeeping, and surveying. Although a number of the private venture schools were begun in commercial centers such as New York, Philadelphia, and Charleston, they were sporadic and usually short-lived.

After the American Revolution of 1776 and the beginning of the industrial revolution, the Latin Grammar school fell into disfavor. The popular quest was for a more utilitarian kind of secondary school that would prepare the student for the duties of republican citizenship and offer him a choice of vocations in an increasingly industrial society. The institution that emerged to fill this need was the academy.

## RISE OF THE ACADEMY

Although the academy was first introduced in the late eighteenth century, it reflected far more the social-cultural-economic *milieu* of the nineteenth century. According to Theodore Sizer, it was a social institution that typified the optimism of the American people during the enthusiastic but unrealistic period between the Revolution and the Civil War.[2]

The first half of the nineteenth century was a period of great faith in the possibilities of improving the human condition through social reform. The expansive liberalism that characterized this attitude fostered a climate in which the academies could provide increasing educational opportunities by means of open enrollment and relatively non-structured curricula. It was the age of the common man, of frontier individualism, and also of class mobility, for it was no longer necessary to own property in order to vote.

Economically the age was one of "free enterprise," the era of the individual entrepreneur and Jacksonian *laissez-faire*. The academy, privately controlled as it usually was, extended the spirit of the small entrepreneur into the field of education.

The great popularity of the academies was an outgrowth of the wave of spontaneous enthusiasm for formal education that took the form of an unorganized but nonetheless nationwide movement.[3] By 1855 there were 263,096 students in 6,185 instituions.[4]

The academy tended to replace or absorb the Latin Grammar school, because although it had no clear-cut design as the latter did, the academy

[2] Theodore R. Sizer, *The Age of the Academies* (New York: Bureau of Publications, Teachers College, Columbia University, 1964), p. 1.
[3] *Ibid.*, p. 12.
[4] *Ibid.*

met the educational needs of a civilization that was both frontier and industrial in character.

In many ways the academy synthesized the functions of the Latin Grammar school and the private venture school. Like the former it offered classical courses designed for college entrance. In addition, like the private venture school, it offered instruction in such practical subjects as accounting, bookkeeping, navigation, modern languages, and surveying, which were terminal courses for many students. The academies were attended chiefly by members of the rising middle class of businessmen, professionals, and entrepreneurs, and curricula were organized around their needs.

## Curricula and Administration of the Academy

Generally speaking, secondary school had four major responsibilities to meet. First, the rise of direct democracy, which resulted from the Revolution and the extension of suffrage, made it necessary for more people to be educated to take part in civic affairs. Second, commercial expansion and the industrial revolution created a demand for people skilled in such subjects as navigation, accounting, and modern languages. In the same way westward expansion of the frontier encouraged the study of surveying. College preparation remained, as it had always been, one of the perennial concerns of secondary education.[5] The American academies reflected these needs in the wide variety of courses they offered, usually under the heading of one of three basic curricula: classical (college preparatory); terminal (English); and normal (teacher education). Within the framework of these three major curricula there were a number of such hybrids as the classical-English, English-scientific, commercial-English, and normal-English. Because of the extreme *laissez-faire* educational context of the academy, there were probably as many varieties of curricular offerings as there were academies.

Circulars for different schools during this era promised the following courses: classics, Latin, Greek, English, oratory, composition, rhetoric, literature, French, Spanish, Portuguese, German, trigonometry, bookkeeping, accounting, surveying, geography, United States history, general history, logic, moral philosophy, astronomy, chemistry, drawing, religion, natural philosophy, geometry, algebra, needlework, phrenology, optics, geology, biology, botany, domestic science, and agricultural principles. (Even this list is far from exhaustive.)

With such a wide variety of courses to offer, the academies' energies

[5] French, *American Secondary Education*, p. 58.

were diffused. Some academies attempted to offer all of them, while others restricted themselves to only a few. Some of the teachers were college graduates and competent in their teaching areas, but others were charlatans, merely interested in a quick tuition fee. Methodology was based on the theory of mental discipline and the acquisition of factual information, and was carried out by drill, textbook memorization, recitation, and repetition. The lack of any common standards applied to education inevitably produced several patent weaknesses. There was chaotic proliferation without organization in course offerings, including numerous short courses in subjects sometimes taught for only a few weeks. There was no established system of accreditation for either teachers or schools. Some of these weaknesses were later inherited by the high school system that succeeded the academies.

The academies were private or semi-public schools controlled by independent, self-perpetuating boards of trustees. Although a few academies did receive local or state grants and subsidies from their inception, the trustees usually sustained the initial expenses of building the academy, hiring the staff, and attracting the students. The bulk of support came from the tuition fees paid by the students.

The prosperity of the academy coincided with a period of intense religious individualism. Denominations proliferated and tended to perpetuate themselves through education. Methodists, Episcopalians, Baptists, Roman Catholics, Presbyterians, Congregationalists, and other groups established their own academies in order to teach the principles of their particular religion, prepare students for college, and offer social and vocational education. Many small denominational colleges existing today were originally chartered as academies.

Some academies were downward extensions of state colleges and universities. Many colleges received charters from state legislatures but found no ready supply of adequately prepared students because of the sparseness of secondary education in their areas. For this reason some of them established secondary schools to prepare students for college entrance by offering basic literary skills and classical languages.

## Academy Decline

The Civil War eroded some of America's naive optimism. In the postwar period of the 1870's and 1880's, the rather unwieldy academies were increasingly replaced by the more stable institution of the public high school. According to Sizer, this trend was in large part attributable to the transition in America from a rural society to an urban one. The urban population was able to support an extensive public secondary school because it provided a larger tax base. By the beginning of the twentieth century, the country's economic basis had shifted from the individual to the corporate structure. As economic entrepreneurship gradually yielded to the corporation, the educational counterpart of entrepreneurship, the academy, also declined.[6] The public high school was better equipped to meet the new demands of the increasing city populations and fill the ranks of corporate industry.

## GROWTH OF THE HIGH SCHOOL

Although free high schools had existed in the United States since the founding of the English Classical School of Boston in 1821, it was not until the latter half of the nineteenth century that the high school was firmly established as the dominant institution of American secondary education. During the 1880's its numbers began to outrank the academy. According to the report of the United States Commissioner of Education for 1889–1890, there were 2,526 public high schools with an enrollment of 202,063 in contrast to the 94,391 students enrolled in 1,632 private secondary schools and academies.[7]

The rise of the high school was related to the socio-economic changes that had transformed the United States from a basically rural agrarian nation to an urban industrial one. The new urban life required that people be more highly trained, that they receive better vocational education, and that they concentrate on the specialized activities of an industrial society. One effect of such specialization was that children no longer had the same opportunity of direct experience with life as they had had in simpler rural communities. Urban society also tended to isolate them from direct participation in social life. As a result the schools came to perform the additional function of intermediary between the adult world and the child's world. What adolescents needed was an institution specifically designed to facilitate their introduction to participation in the adult world.

In addition to the shift from rural to urban life, the industrial revolution also stimulated exploration of new areas of knowledge and study. As a result, the basic literacy provided children by the common elementary school was no longer adequate preparation for their intelligent participation in an industrial society. The high school sought to provide broader educational opportunities for youth to be able to assimilate these expanding areas of knowledge.

[6] Sizer, *The Age of the Academies*, p. 41.

[7] Edward Krug, *The Shaping of the American High School* (New York: Harper & Row, 1964), p. 5.

However, the high school could not have come into existence as an upward extension of the educational ladder without the necessary foundation of the common elementary school, and, according to George S. Counts, could not have expanded as it did until the development of the latter was well advanced.[8] By the 1870's and 1880's, the existence of the common elementary school had become an accepted reality of American life.

The high school movement received additional impetus from the public's growing sensitivity to the needs of children and youth. Child labor legislation took adolescents out of the factories and mills and placed them in school. The greater educational opportunity resulting from compulsory attendance laws was considered a useful means of reducing juvenile delinquency and producing more worthy citizens.

Finally, industrialized urban society was able to support more extensive educational institutions than the rural one had. Mass production techniques created surplus wealth, making possible a larger base of taxation for spending on education.

The struggle to establish high school education for American youth was actually a continuation of the common school movement. The common school movement of the early nineteenth century had established the state's responsibility for tax-supported elementary education, and as the movement to extend that responsibility to the secondary level gained momentum the struggle was re-enacted. However, this time the arguments were raised in the courts rather than in the legislative assemblies.

Although several court cases are relevant to the legal establishment of taxation for high schools, the Kalamazoo Case of 1874 and the decision rendered by Justice Thomas C. Cooley of the Michigan State Supreme Court clearly established the precedent. A group of taxpayers of the Kalamazoo school district initiated a suit to prevent the board of education from levying a tax to support a high school. The claimants argued that the high school curriculum, which was primarily college preparatory, did not merit public support by taxation. Why, they asked, should the majority of taxpayers be coerced into paying for the education of the small minority that was college-bound?

Justice Cooley's decision to uphold the right of the Kalamazoo school district to tax the community for support of a high school was based on the state's obligation not only to provide elementary education, but also to maintain equal educational opportunity for all. Since the state was already maintaining public elementary schools and colleges, he ruled, it would be

[8] George S. Counts, *Secondary Education and Industrialism* (Cambridge: Harvard University Press, 1929), p. 26.

highly inconsistent for the state to fail to provide the interim stage whereby the student could move from elementary to higher education. Justice Cooley affirmed the right of the school board to tax for the support of this transitional institution.

The Cooley decision had the effect of encouraging state legislatures to pass laws permitting local boards to establish high schools. Later on, following much the same pattern as they had with elementary education, state legislatures first encouraged and then compelled the establishment of high schools. It was finally possible for a student to attend a complete sequence of educational institutions from kindergarten through elementary and high schools to the highest level a university could offer, all within the framework of publicly supported and controlled schools.

## Standardizing the Curriculum: The Committee of Ten

The American high school took shape during the period from 1880 to 1920, the same era that saw the basic American social and economic patterns shift from rural to urban orientation. In the confusion and conflict that marked the early years of the new institution's development, the most pressing question was that of whom to educate and how best to do it. Was it to be college preparatory, as had been traditionally true of secondary education? Or was the high school to be a terminal institution, specifically designed for those who would be concluding their formal education there? And should it therefore stress traditional college preparatory subjects, or offer more programs in manual, industrial, commercial, and vocational training?

At first the high school appeared to be in danger of repeating the history of its predecessor, the academy, in offering a multiplicity of ill-defined programs of instruction. Often within the same school could be found curricula with such titles as the ancient classical, the business commercial, the shorter commercial, the English terminal, the English science, and the scientific. The confusion caused by such lack of direction demanded solution if the high school was to become an integral step in the American educationl ladder.

To deal with this problem of standardization, the National Education Association established the Committee of Ten in 1892. The Committee was composed of representatives from five colleges and universities, one public school principal, two headmasters of private schools, United States Commissioner of Education William T. Harris, and Committee chairman Charles W. Eliot, President of Harvard University.[9] Since the majority of

---

[9] *Report of the Committee on Secondary School Studies* (Washington: Government Printing Office, 1893).

the Committee members were associated with higher education, it could be anticipated that its work would be oriented toward the college preparatory function of the high school.

Chairman Charles Eliot was an important leader in higher education, whose interests also extended to the fields of elementary and secondary education. He was concerned with improving the efficiency of the schools, making economic use of the time the students spent in school, and increasing their freedom of subject choice by the introduction of a system of electives. As head of the Committee, he vigorously guided its studies of the scope and function of secondary education. According to Krug, the Committee of Ten's policies developed around two of Eliot's basic concepts: earlier introduction of the fundamentals of several subjects in the upper elementary grades, and no differentiation between subjects or teaching of college preparatory and terminal students.[10]

The report of the Committee of Ten recommended eight years of elementary and four years of secondary education. For the high school, four separate curricula were recommended: classical, Latin-scientific, modern language, and English. While each curriculum included foreign language, mathematics, English, science, and history, the major differences were that the modern language curriculum permitted the substitution of modern languages for Latin and Greek and that the Latin-scientific emphasized mathematics and science.

Subjects appropriate to high school study were English and foreign languages such as Latin, Greek, German, French, and Spanish; mathematics such as algebra, geometry, and trigonometry; natural sciences such as descriptive astronomy, meteorology, botany, zoology, physiology, geology, and physical geography; physical sciences such as physics and chemistry. In addition, the intensive study of selected historical periods was recommended. The Committee further recommended that high school students study intensively a relatively small number of subjects for longer periods of time. Every subject was to be taught in the high school in the same way and to the same extent to each student regardless of his further educational aims.

The Report of the Committee of Ten is a revealing document in that it demonstrates the tendency of the higher institution, the college, to dominate the lower, the high school. Although the Committee stated that the high school did not exist exclusively for the purpose of college preparation, its report was more concerned with subject matter designed for college entrance. The Committee justified its orientation with the theory of

---

[10] Krug, *The Shaping of the American High School*, p. 17.

mental discipline. The recommended subjects, it claimed, could be used profitably by both the terminal and college preparatory students for training their powers of observation, memory, expression, and reasoning.[11]

## HIGH SCHOOL ACCREDITATION

The relationship of the high school to the college was a major problem of institutional articulation in the 1890's, and the aspect affording the greatest concern was that of entrance or admission requirements to the college. In 1895, the North Central Association was established with a combined membership of colleges and secondary schools for the purpose of establishing closer relations in the North Central states.[12]

In 1899, the National Education Association established the Committee on College Entrance Requirements. In an attempt to resolve the long-brewing conflict over the elective principle, which permitted the student to make his own choice of subjects, the Committee proposed a set of constant subjects, a core of courses to be required of all students without reference to their educational destination. The remainder of the program was to be elected by each student.[13] The Committee used the term "unit" to describe a subject acceptable for accreditation purposes. A subject studied for four or five periods a week for one school year in secondary school was defined as a "unit" of study. The constants recommended in the core group were four units of foreign languages, two of mathematics, two of English, one of history, and one of science.

In 1902 the Committee on Unit Courses of the North Central Association defined as acceptable a high school which required fifteen units of work for graduation. Each unit was defined as a course covering a school year of not less than thirty-five weeks, taught in four or five periods of at least forty-five minutes per week. Furthermore, all high school curricula and requirements for college entrance were to include as constants three units of English and two units of mathematics.[14]

In a manner similar to the North Central Association, other regional accreditation agencies were established: the New England Association, the Middle States Association, the Northwest Association, the Western Association, and the Southern Association. Historically, the accreditation

[11] French, *American Secondary Education*, pp. 113–14.
[12] Calvin O. Davis, *A History of the North Central Association of Colleges and Secondary Schools* (Ann Arbor: The North Central Association of Colleges and Secondary Schools, 1945), p. 7.
[13] Krug, *The Shaping of the American High School*, pp. 141–42.
[14] Davis, *A History of the North Central Association . . .* , p. 49.

associations have developed two alternatives to the problems of college entrance requirements. In the East, the College Entrance Examination Board established a system of examinations for college entrance. In the West, graduates of high schools which were accredited by the North Central Association were admitted to college by certification.[15]

## COMMISSION ON REORGANIZATION OF SECONDARY EDUCATION

In 1918, the National Education Association established the Commission on the Reorganization of Secondary Education to re-examine the scope and function of the high school. The Report of the Commission was significant for its recognition of the need for greater articulation of institutions at all levels of education. Under the leadership of chairman Clarence Kingsley, the Commission issued the famous "Cardinal Principles of Secondary Education," which listed the following as objectives of secondary education, although they were applicable to elementary and higher education as well: health, command of fundamental processes, worthy home membership, vocation, citizenship, worthy use of leisure, and ethical character. The major task of the high school was to translate the "Principles" into action.

The Commission also emphasized the function of the high school as an agent of social integration. In recommending the continuance of the comprehensive high school as part of the standard pattern of organization, the Commission expressed the belief that the public secondary school would bring students of varying racial, religious, ethnic, and economic backgrounds into the same institution. If specialized vocational, commercial, or college preparatory high schools were to replace the comprehensive high school, the Commission felt that the public secondary school could no longer perform its task of social integration.

To some observers, the "Cardinal Principles" did not seem to come to grips with the problems of industrial civilization. George S. Counts in *Secondary Education and Industrialism* said that the Commission left untouched the really vital questions raised by the development of an industrial civilization. What was lacking, he felt, was a carefully constructed social theory to guide the operation of the secondary school.[16]

During its development as a social institution a number of people proposed various programs for standardizing the high school in one way or another. Between 1880 and 1920 strong arguments were advanced in favor

[15] Krug, *The Shaping of the American High School*, p. 146.
[16] Counts, *Secondary Education and Industrialism*, pp. 51–52.

of maintaining the strictly college preparatory function of the high school. But equally eloquent pleas were tendered for developing the high school as a non-academically oriented terminal institution, "the people's college." Its shaping involved problems of curriculum construction, articulation in relation to other educational institutions, and accreditation.

During the period from 1880 to 1920, the American high school was primarily college preparatory, emphasizing Latin, modern foreign languages, mathematics, science, English, and history. However, a small group of educators, led by G. Stanley Hall, objected strongly to the domination of the high school by colleges. In numerous speeches and articles Hall denounced the tendency,[17] saying that the high school should be more concerned with the education of the adolescent. This group sought to extend the "child study" movement upward, regarding the high school as a natural extension from the common (elementary) school. Because of Hall's and others' efforts, some educators began to view the high school as an adolescent school rather than strictly college preparatory. Others, like David Snedden, launched the "social efficiency" movement. "Social efficiency," also a reaction against the high school's orientation toward college, was an assertion of social reform as defined by a utilitarian criterion. According to this group, the inclusion of any subject in the high school curriculum was justified only insofar as it prepared the student to be a citizen, earner, parent, and consumer.

## DEVELOPMENT OF THE
## COMPREHENSIVE HIGH SCHOOL

In 1880, the high school population was numbered at 110,277; by 1920 it was 2,382,542.[18] Despite the increased attendance, educators such as George S. Counts felt that the high school was still a selective institution. A close relationship existed between parental occupation and high school attendance. Furthermore, children of native-born parents attended in greater numbers than those of immigrant parents. In *The Selective Character of American Secondary Education*, Counts concluded that the high school was serving the upper socio-economic classes. He called for an extension of the quality of opportunity when he urged the opening of the doors of the high school to all students.[19]

William French in *American Secondary Education* found that the se-

[17] Krug, *The Shaping of the American High School*, pp. 84–85.
[18] French, *American Secondary Education*, p. 100.
[19] George S. Counts, *The Selective Character of American Secondary Education* (Chicago: The University of Chicago Press, 1922), p. 152.

lective character of the high school as it existed between 1880 and 1920 was reinforced by three factors: first, there was lacking a secondary education tradition among many of the immigrants from southern and eastern Europe; second, there were hidden costs in the form of books, supplies, transportation, lunches, and clothing; and third, in many rural districts the lack of a solid financial base impeded the establishment of the high school.[20]

In 1929 Counts called attention to the factors which were rapidly democratizing secondary education in the United States. These were the presence of more democratic social ideals, the extension of elementary education opportunities, the development of a more highly integrated society, the growing complexity of civilization, increasing overall wealth and income, and lower death and birth rates.[21]

By 1930, the comprehensive American high school was fairly well established as an institution enrolling adolescents from all kinds of backgrounds and offering an entire range of subjects. The increase in high school enrollments from 4,427,000 in 1930 to 9,619,000 in 1960 tells the story of its popular appeal. Despite the controversies which surrounded it as a social institution, the high school seemed to function as an agent of social and cultural integration, a place where students learned studies in common, mixed socially, and participated in common activities.

As a relatively new educational institution, the high school is still subjected to a vast amount of pressure by those who seek to use it for special purposes. In many instances, also, the high school has been forced to respond to the exigencies of the public temper. During World War I, patriotic pressures caused a drastic reduction in the number of people studying German as a foreign language. At the same time, rejections of inductees for military service due to physical disabilities stimulated programs of physical education. Also in 1917, the federal government sponsored the Smith-Hughes Vocational Education Act, which provided federal funds as grants-in-aid to states offering vocational studies. As an aftermath of World War II, high school educators concerned with the war's disruption of family life and the increase of juvenile delinquency introduced life adjustment programs into the curriculum. In the late 1950's, with the advent of the Russian space satellite Sputnik, critics began to accuse our high school program of being "watered-down" and pedagogically soft.

[20] French, *American Secondary Education*, pp. 101–2.
[21] George S. Counts, "Selection as a Function of American Secondary Education," *National Education Association Proceedings*, LXVII (1929), 597.

## The Conant Reports

In 1958, James B. Conant, former President of Harvard University, wrote a short book, *The American High School Today*, examining the contemporary condition of the American high school. In it he distinguishes between comprehensive and specialized high schools. While a comprehensive high school provided education for all the youth of a given district, a specialized high school provided either a vocational or an academic curriculum to selected students.[22] Conant then focuses his attention on the condition of the comprehensive high school.

In a comprehensive high school, more than half of the students terminated their fulltime education at graduation. For the terminal student, a variety of vocational programs was provided. For the college preparatory student, appropriate curricula were offered. A major educational objective in the comprehensive high school was the development of a democratic spirit and understanding between students with different intellectual abilities and goals.[23] The comprehensive high school sought to achieve three major aims: a general education for all future citizens, good elective programs for terminal students, and good college preparatory programs for the rest.

While generally satisfied with the genuinely comprehensive high school, Conant offered a program of twenty-one recommendations designed to improve the quality of American secondary education as a whole. He recommended a fully articulated counseling program which would aid the student in choosing elective courses corresponding to the student's interests, aptitudes, and achievement. He urged more individualized instruction so that programs might be fitted to the individual student's needs, and also suggested ability grouping by subject.

Conant recommended a core curriculum in which the general education requirements would be four years of English, three or four years of social studies, and at least one year of mathematics and science. The general educational requirements recommended for all students would occupy half the student's time; the remainder would be filled with appropriate elective programs.

In *The American High School Today*, Conant called for diversified programs that would develop marketable skills. In structuring their schools' vocational education programs, administrators were urged to assess the community's needs in terms of its employment situation. Pro-

[22] James B. Conant, *The American High School Today* (New York: McGraw-Hill Book Co., 1959), pp. 7–8.
[23] *Ibid.*, pp. 13–14.

grams should be offered in distributive education, agriculture, trade, and industry, depending upon their appropriateness to each community.

The rest of the recommendations in Conant's study urged scheduling increased time for English composition, special programs for slow readers, greater challenges for gifted students, and more offerings in science and foreign languages.[24]

Conant's findings and suggestions in *The American High School Today* were a reasoned assessment of the American comprehensive high school. Written during a time when American public secondary education was being sharply criticized, Conant's report presented a dispassionate and documented survey which indicated that the comprehensive high school was performing its task at least adequately. His recommendations were not presented in the form of attack but rather as constructive suggestions for improving the quality of instruction.

In 1961, Conant wrote *Slums and Suburbs*, which examined contemporary problems facing American education. He found that the metropolitan areas of the United States presented striking contrasts in both schools and residential areas, ranging from impoverished slums to wealthy suburbs. The suburban high school program was geared to the academic subjects necessary for college admission. On the other hand, the economically deprived slum high school concentrated on preparing students in vocational areas.[25] With the bifurcation of high schools in large metropolitan areas into these two widely divergent types, only in the moderately sized cities and in consolidated rural areas did the genuinely comprehensive high school remain, in which all students and curricula were contained within one school.

Conant's findings in *Slums and Suburbs* were revealing. Historically, the evolution of American public education has been in the direction of the single, sequenced educational ladder which would take the student from kindergarten to college. However, with the decline of the genuinely comprehensive high school in the large metropolitan areas and the emergence of high school programs based largely on socio-economic status, the principle of equal educational opportunity has been jeopardized. In time, the concept of the ladder could conceivably be replaced with a dual system of education containing one track for the upper socio-economic groups and a second track for the lower ones. Such a duality might split American society into two radically distinct groups without any uniting basis of commonly shared values. Further, such a tendency would actually

[24] *Ibid.*, pp. 44–76.
[25] James B. Conant, *Slums and Suburbs* (New York: McGraw-Hill Book Company, 1961).

be a regression toward the situation which the founders of the American public school system were seeking to avoid. In most large cities, problems of socio-economic segregation have been related to charges of *de facto* racial segregation, further aggravating the conditions of the high school.

## CONCLUSION

In conclusion, a study of the evolution of American secondary education shows that the development of the comprehensive public high school was and still is a slow and difficult process. Although many claims might be made for the American high school, perhaps the most significant one relates to the democratic ideal of equal opportunity. As the secondary school of all the people, the comprehensive high school is a necessary institutional link in the completion of the educational ladder. As the school for adolescents, it offers a proving ground for democratic experiences as students of various social, economic, and religious groups have the chance to share, participate, and learn in a common environment. In this way, the high school is an extension of the common school concept that is part of the unique American experience.

In a changing society, the high school, too, will have to change. The paramount tasks are to preserve its democratic comprehensiveness, maintain equality of educational opportunity, and provide a quality education for the children of all the people.

### References

Commission on Reorganization of Secondary Education. *Cardinal Principles of Secondary Education.* Washington, D. C.: U.S. Bureau of Education, Bulletin No. 35, 1918.

CONANT, JAMES B. *The American High School Today.* New York: McGraw-Hill Book Company, 1959.

———. *The Revolutionary Transformation of the American High School.* Cambridge: Harvard University Press, 1959.

———. *Slums and Suburbs.* New York: McGraw-Hill Book Company, 1961.

COUNTS, GEORGE S. *Secondary Education and Industrialism.* Cambridge: Harvard University Press, 1929.

———. *The Selective Character of American Secondary Education.* Chicago: University of Chicago Press, 1922.

DAVIS, CALVIN O. *A History of the North Central Association of Colleges and Secondary Schools.* Ann Arbor: The North Central Association of Colleges and Secondary Schools, 1945.

FRENCH, WILLIAM M. *American Secondary Education.* New York: The Odyssey Press, 1957.

KRUG, EDWARD A. *The Shaping of the American High School.* New York: Harper & Row Publishers, 1964.

National Education Association. *Report of the Committee of Ten on Secondary School Studies.* New York: American Book Company, 1894.

*Report of the Committee on Secondary School Studies.* Washington, D. C.: Government Printing Office, 1893.

SIZER, THEODORE R. *The Age of the Academies.* New York: Bureau of Publications, Teachers College, Columbia University, 1964.

# SELECTIONS

*Two documents, the* Report of the Committee on Secondary School Studies *and the* Cardinal Principles of Secondary Education, *were crucial in defining the nature and program of the high school as the secondary institution of American education. The Committee on Secondary School Studies, known as the Committee of Ten, was appointed by the National Educational Association in 1892. The Committee, guided by Chairman Eliot, submitted its report in 1893. The selections below illustrate the desire of the Committee that instruction in the subject areas begin at an earlier age, that more subjects be offered, and that the same methods of teaching be used for college preparatory and terminal students. Table I illustrates the four model curricula recommended by the Committee for high school students.*

# Report of the Committee on Secondary School Studies

Anyone who reads these nine reports consecutively will be struck with the fact that all these bodies of experts desire to have the elements of their several subjects taught earlier than they now are; and that the Conferences on all the subjects except the languages desire to have given in the elementary schools what may be called perspective views, or broad surveys, of their respective subjects—expecting that in later years of the school course parts of these same subjects will be taken up with more amplitude and detail. The Conferences on Latin, Greek, and the Modern Languages agree in desiring to have the study of foreign languages begin at a much earlier age than now,—the Latin Conference suggesting by a reference to European usage that Latin be begun from three to five years earlier than it commonly is now. The Conference on Mathematics wish to have given in elementary schools not only a general survey of arithmetic, but also the elements of algebra, and concrete geometry in connection with drawing. The Conference on Physics, Chemistry, and Astronomy urge that nature studies

SOURCE: *Report of the Committee on Secondary School Studies* (Washington: Government Printing Office, 1893), pp. 14–17, 46–47.

should constitute an important part of the elementary school course from the very beginning. The Conference on Natural History wish the elements of botany and zoology to be taught in the primary schools. The Conference on History wish the systematic study of history to begin as early as the tenth year of age, and the first two years of study to be devoted to mythology and to biography for the illustration of general history as well as of American history. Finally, the Conference on Geography recommend that the earlier course treat broadly of the earth, its environment and inhabitants, extending freely into fields which in later years of study are recognized as belonging to separate sciences.

In thus claiming entrance for their subjects into the earlier years of school attendance, the Conferences on the newer subjects are only seeking an advantage which the oldest subjects have long possessed. The elements of language, number, and geography have long been imparted to young children. As things now are, the high school teacher finds in the pupils fresh from the grammar schools no foundation of elementary mathematical conceptions outside of arithmetic; no acquaintance with algebraic language; and no accurate knowledge of geometrical forms. As to botany, zoology, chemistry, and physics, the minds of pupils entering the high school are ordinarily blank on these subjects. When college professors endeavor to teach chemistry, physics, botany, zoology, meteorology, or geology to persons of eighteen or twenty years of age, they discover that in most instances new habits of observing, reflecting, and recording have to be painfully acquired by the students,—habits which they should have acquired in early childhood. The college teacher of history finds in like manner that his subject has never taken any serious hold on the minds of pupils fresh from the secondary schools. He finds that they have devoted astonishingly little time to the subject; and that they have acquired no habit of historical investigation, or of the comparative examination of different historical narratives concerning the same periods or events. It is inevitable, therefore, that specialists in any one of the subjects which are pursued in the high schools or colleges should earnestly desire that the minds of young children be stored with some of the elementary facts and principles of their subject; and that all the mental habits, which the adult student will surely need, begin to be formed in the child's mind before the age of fourteen. It follows, as a matter of course, that all the Conferences except the Conference on Greek, make strong suggestions concerning the programmes of primary and grammar schools,—generally with some reference to the subsequent programmes of secondary schools. They desire important changes in the elementary grades; and the changes recommended are all in the direction of increasing simultaneously the interest and the substantial training quality of primary and grammar school studies.

If anyone feels dismayed at the number and variety of the subjects to be opened to children of tender age, let him observe that while these nine Conferences desire each their own subject to be brought into the courses of elementary schools, they all agree that these different subjects should be correlated and associated one with another by the programme and by the actual teaching. If the nine Conferences had sat all together as a single body, instead of sitting as de-

TABLE I

| Year | CLASSICAL — Three Foreign Languages (one modern) | | LATIN-SCIENTIFIC — Two Foreign Languages (one modern) | |
|---|---|---|---|---|
| I | Latin | 5 p. | Latin | 5 p. |
| | English | 4 p. | English | 4 p. |
| | Algebra | 4 p. | Algebra | 4 p. |
| | History | 4 p. | History | 4 p. |
| | Physical Geography | 3 p. | Physical Geography | 3 p. |
| | | 20 p. | | 20 p. |
| II | Latin | 5 p. | Latin | 5 p. |
| | English | 2 p. | English | 2 p. |
| | German (or French) begun | 4 p. | German (or French) begun | 4 p. |
| | Geometry | 3 p. | Geometry | 3 p. |
| | Physics | 3 p. | Physics | 3 p. |
| | History | 3 p. | Botany or Zoology | 3 p. |
| | | 20 p. | | 20 p. |
| III | Latin | 4 p. | Latin | 4 p. |
| | Greek | 5 p. | English | 3 p. |
| | English | 3 p. | German (or French) | 4 p. |
| | German (or French) | 4 p. | Mathematics (Algebra 2) (Geometry 2) | 4 p. |
| | Mathematics (Algebra 2) (Geometry 2) | 4 p. | Astronomy ½ yr. & Meteorology ½ yr. | 3 p. |
| | | 20 p. | History | 2 p. |
| | | | | 20 p. |
| IV | Latin | 4 p. | Latin | 4 p. |
| | Greek | 5 p. | English (as in Classical 2) (additional 2) | 4 p. |
| | English | 2 p. | German (or French) | 3 p. |
| | German (or French) | 3 p. | Chemistry | 3 p. |
| | Chemistry | 3 p. | Trigonometry & Higher Algebra or History | 3 p. |
| | Trigonometry & Higher Algebra or History | 3 p. | Geology or Physiography ½ yr. and Anatomy, Physiology & Hygiene ½ yr. | 3 p. |
| | | 20 p. | | 20 p. |

TABLE I (*cont.*)

| Year | Modern Languages<br>Two Foreign Languages<br>(both modern) | | English<br>One Foreign Language<br>(ancient or modern) | |
| --- | --- | --- | --- | --- |
| I | French (or German) begun | 5 p. | Latin, or German or French | 5 p. |
| | English | 4 p. | English | 4 p. |
| | Algebra | 4 p. | Algebra | 4 p. |
| | History | 4 p. | History | 4 p. |
| | Physical Geography | 3 p. | Physical Geography | 3 p. |
| | | 20 p. | | 20 p. |
| II | French (or German) | 4 p. | Latin, or German or French | 5 or 4 p. |
| | English | 2 p. | English | 3 or 4 p. |
| | German (or French) begun | 5 p. | Geometry | 3 p. |
| | Geometry | 3 p. | Physics | 3 p. |
| | Physics | 3 p. | History | 3 p. |
| | Botany or Zoology | 3 p. | Botany or Zoology | 3 p. |
| | | 20 p. | | 20 p. |
| III | French (or German) | 4 p. | Latin, or German or French | 4 p. |
| | English | 3 p. | English (as in others 3) (additional 2) | 5 p. |
| | German (or French) | 4 p. | | |
| | Mathematics (Algebra 2) (Geometry 2) | 4 p. | Mathematics (Algebra 2) (Geometry 2) | 4 p. |
| | Astronomy ½ yr. & Meteorology ½ yr. | 3 p. | Astronomy ½ yr. & Meteorology ½ yr. | 3 p. |
| | History | 2 p. | History (as in the Latin-Scientific 2) (additional 2) | 4 p. |
| | | 20 p. | | 20 p. |
| | French (or German) | 3 p. | Latin, or German or French | 4 p. |
| | English (as in Classical 2) (additional 2) | 4 p. | English (as in Classical 2) (additional 2) | 4 p. |

91

TABLE I (cont.)

| IV | German (or | | Chemistry | 3 p. |
|---|---|---|---|---|
| | French) | 4 p. | Trigonometry & | |
| | Chemistry | 3 p. | Higher Algebra | 3 p. |
| | Trigonometry & | | History | 3 p. |
| | Higher Algebra 3 | | Geology or Physi- | |
| | or History 3 | 3 p. | ography ½ yr. | |
| | Geology or Physi- | | and Anatomy, | |
| | ography ½ yr. and | | Physiology, & | |
| | Anatomy, | | Hygiene ½ yr. | 3 p. |
| | Physiology, & | | | 20 p. |
| | Hygiene ½ yr. | 3 p. | | |
| | | 20 p. | | |

tached and even isolated bodies, they could not have more forcibly expressed their conviction that every subject recommended for introduction into elementary and secondary schools should help every other; and that the teacher of each single subject should feel responsible for the advancement of the pupils in all subjects, and should distinctly contribute to this advancement.

On one very important question of general policy which affects profoundly the preparation of all school programmes, the Committee of Ten and all the Conferences are absolutely unanimous. Among the questions suggested for discussion in each Conference were the following:

7.   Should the subject be treated differently for pupils who are going to college, for those who are going to a scientific school, and for those who, presumably, are going to neither?

8.   At what age should this differentiation begin, if any be recommended?

The 7th question is answered unanimously in the negative by the Conferences, and the 8th therefore needs no answer. The Committee of Ten unanimously agree with the Conferences. Ninety-eight teachers intimately concerned either with the actual work of American secondary schools, or with the results of that work as they appear in students who come to college, unanimously declare that every subject which is taught at all in a secondary school should be taught in the same way and to the same extent to every pupil so long as he pursues it, no matter what the probable destination of the pupil may be, or at what point his education is to cease. Thus, for all pupils who study Latin, or history, or algebra, for example, the allotment of time and the method of instruction in a given school should be the same year by year. Not that all the pupils should pursue every subject for the same number of years; but so long as they do pursue it, they should all be treated alike. It has been a very general custom in American high schools and academies to make up separate courses of study for pupils of supposed different destinations, the proportions of the several studies in the different courses being various. The principle laid down by the Conferences will, if logically carried out, make a great simplification in secondary school programmes. It will lead to each subject's being treated by the school in the same way by the year for all pupils, and this, whether the individual pupil be required to choose between courses which run through several years, or be allowed some choice among subjects year by year.

---

*The Commission on the Reorganization of Secondary Education of the National Education Association made its report in 1918. In urging the reconstruction of the high school program, the Commission attempted to define the aims and purposes of secondary education. The result of this deliberation was the* Cardinal Principles of Secondary Education, *which became the basis of the program for the American secondary school.*

# Cardinal Principles of Secondary Education

This commission, therefore, regards the following as the main objectives of education: 1. Health. 2. Command of fundamental processes. 3. Worthy home-membership. 4. Vocation. 5. Citizenship. 6. Worthy use of leisure. 7. Ethical character.

The naming of the above objectives is not intended to imply that the process of education can be divided into separated fields. This can not be, since the pupil is indivisible. Nor is the analysis all-inclusive. Nevertheless, we believe that distinguishing and naming these objectives will aid in directing efforts; and we hold that they should constitute the principal aims in education.

## THE ROLE OF SECONDARY EDUCATION
## IN ACHIEVING THESE OBJECTIVES

The objectives outlined above apply to education as a whole—elementary, secondary, and higher. It is the purpose of this section to consider specifically the role of secondary education in achieving each of these objectives.

For reasons stated in Section X, this commission favors such reorganization that secondary education may be defined as applying to all pupils of approximately 12 to 18 years of age.

SOURCE: *Cardinal Principles of Secondary Education: A Report of the Commission on the Reorganization of Secondary Education, Appointed by the National Education Association* (Washington: Government Printing Office, 1918), pp. 10–16.

1. *Health.* Health needs can not be neglected during the period of secondary education without serious danger to the individual and the race. The secondary school should therefore provide health instruction, inculcate health habits, organize an effective program of physical activities, regard health needs in planning work and play, and cooperate with home and community in safe-guarding and promoting health interests.

To carry out such a program it is necessary to arouse the public to recognize that the health needs of young people are of vital importance to society, to secure teachers competent to ascertain and meet the needs of individual pupils and able to inculcate in the entire student body a love for clean sport, to furnish adequate equipment for physical activities, and to make the school building, its rooms and surroundings, conform to the best standards of hygiene and sanitation.

2. *Command of fundamental processes.* Much of the energy of the elementary school is properly devoted to teaching certain fundamental processes, such as reading, writing, arithmetical computations, and the elements of oral and written expression. The facility that a child of 12 or 14 may acquire in the use of these tools is not sufficient for the needs of modern life. This is particularly true of the mother tongue. Proficiency in many of these processes may be increased more effectively by their application to new material than by the formal reviews commonly employed in grades seven and eight. Throughout the secondary school, instruction and practice must go hand in hand, but as indicated in the report of the committee on English, only so much theory should be taught at any one time as will show results in practice.

3. *Worthy home-membership.* Worthy home-membership as an objective calls for the development of those qualities that make the individual a worthy member of a family, both contributing to and deriving benefit from that membership.

This objective applies to both boys and girls. The social studies should deal with the home as a fundamental social institution and clarify its relation to the wider interests outside. Literature should interpret and idealize the human elements that go to make the home. Music and art should result in more beautiful homes and in greater joy therein. The coeducational school with a faculty of men and women should, in its organization and its activities, exemplify wholesome relations between boys and girls and men and women.

Home-membership as an objective should not be thought of solely with reference to future duties. These are the better guaranteed if the school helps the pupils to take the right attitude toward present home responsibilities and interprets to them the contribution of the home to their development.

In the education of every high-school girl, the household arts should have a prominent place because of their importance to the girl herself and to others whose welfare will be directly in her keeping. The attention now devoted to this phase of education is inadequate, and especially so for girls preparing for occupations not related to the household arts and for girls planning for higher institutions. The majority of girls who enter wage-earning occupations, directly from the high school remain in them for only a few years, after which home making becomes their life-long occupation. For them the high-school period offers the only assured opportunity to prepare for that lifelong occupation, and it is during this period that they are most likely to form their ideals of life's duties and responsibilities. For girls planning to enter higher institutions—our traditional ideals of preparation for higher institutions are particularly incongruous with the actual needs and future responsibilities of girls. It would seem that such high-school work as is carefully designed to develop capacity for, and interest in, the proper management and conduct of a home should be regarded as of importance at least equal to that of any other work. We do not understand how society can properly continue to sanction for girls high-school curriculums that disregard this fundamental need, even though such curriculums are planned in response to the demands made by some of the colleges for women.

In the education of boys, some opportunity should be found to give them a basis for the intelligent appreciation of the value of the well-appointed home and of the labor and skill required to maintain such a home, to the end that they may cooperate more effectively. For instance, they should understand the essentials of food values, of sanitation, and of household budgets.

4. *Vocation.* Vocational education should equip the individual to secure a livelihood for himself and those dependent on him, to serve society well through his vocation, to maintain the right relationships toward his fellow workers and society, and, as far as possible, to find in that vocation his own best development.

This ideal demands that the pupil explore his own capacities and aptitudes, and make a survey of the world's work, to the end that he may select his vocation wisely. Hence, an effective program of vocational guidance in the secondary school is essential.

Vocational education should aim to develop an appreciation of the significance of the vocation to the community, and a clear conception of right relations between the members of the chosen vocation, between different vocational groups, between employer and employee, and between producer and consumer. These aspects of vocational education, heretofore neglected, demand emphatic attention.

The extent to which the secondary school should offer training for a specific vocation depends upon the vocation, the facilities that the school can acquire, and the opportunity that the pupil may have to obtain such training later. To obtain satisfactory results those proficient in that vocation should be employed as instructors and the actual conditions of the vocation should be utilized either within the high school or in cooperation with the home, farm, shop, or office. Much of the pupil's time will be required to produce such efficiency.

5. *Civic education* should develop in the individual those qualities whereby he will act well his part as a member of neighborhood, town or city, State, and Nation, and give him a basis for understanding international problems.

For such citizenship the following are essential: A many-sided interest in the welfare of the communities to which one belongs; loyalty to ideals of civic righteousness; practical knowledge of social agencies and institutions; good judgment as to means and methods that will promote one social end without defeating others; and as putting all these into effect, habits of cordial cooperation in social undertakings.

The school should develop the concept that the civic duties of men and women, while in part identical, are also in part supplementary. Differentiation in civic activities is to be encouraged, but not to the extent of loss of interest in the common problems with which all should cope.

Among the means for developing attitudes and habits important in a democracy are the assignment of projects and problems to groups of pupils for cooperative solution and the socialized recitation whereby the class as a whole develops a sense of collective responsibility. Both of these devices give training in collective thinking. Moreover, the democratic organization and administration of the school itself, as well as the cooperative relations of pupil and teacher, pupil and pupil, and teacher and teacher, are indispensable.

While all subjects should contribute to good citizenship, the social studies—geography, history, civics, and economics—should have this as their dominant aim. Too frequently, however, does mere information, conventional in value and remote in its bearing, make up the content of the social studies. History should so treat the growth of institutions that their present value may be appreciated. Geography should show the interdependence of men while it shows their common dependence on nature. Civics should concern itself less with constitutional questions and remote governmental functions, and should direct attention to social agencies close at hand and to the informal activities of daily life that regard and seek the common good. Such agencies as child-welfare organizations and consumers' leagues afford specific opportunities for the expression of civic qualities by the older pupils.

The work in English should kindle social ideals and give insight into social conditions and into personal character as related to these conditions. Hence the emphasis by the committee on English on the importance of a knowledge of social activities, social movements, and social needs on the part of the teacher of English.

The comprehension of the ideals of American democracy and loyalty to them should be a prominent aim of civic education. The pupil should feel that he will be responsible, in cooperation with others, for keeping the Nation true to the best inherited conceptions of democracy, and he should also realize that democracy itself is an ideal to be wrought out by his own and succeeding generations.

Civic education should consider other nations also. As a people we should try to understand their aspirations and ideals that we may deal more sympathetically and intelligently with the immigrant coming to our shores, and have a basis for a wiser and more sympathetic approach to international problems. Our pupils should learn that each nation, at least potentially, has something of worth to contribute to civilization and that humanity would be incomplete without the contribution. This means a study of specific nations, their achievements and possibilities, not ignoring their limitations. Such a study of dissimilar contributions in the light of the ideal of human brotherhood should help to establish a genuine internationalism, free from sentimentality, founded on fact, and actually operative in the affairs of nations.

6. *Worthy use of leisure.* Education should equip the individual to secure from his leisure the recreation of body, mind, and spirit, and the enrichment and enlargement of his personality.

This objective calls for the ability to utilize the common means of enjoyment, such as music, art, literature, drama, and social intercourse, together with the fostering in each individual of one or more special avocational interests.

Heretofore, the high school has given little conscious attention to this objective. It has so exclusively sought intellectual discipline that it has seldom treated literature, art, and music so as to evoke right emotional response and produce positive enjoyment. Its presentation of science should aim, in part, to arouse a genuine appreciation of nature.

The school has failed also to organize and direct the social activities of young people as it should. One of the surest ways in which to prepare pupils worthily to utilize leisure in adult life is by guiding and directing their use of leisure in youth. The school should therefore, see that adequate recreation is provided both within the school and by other proper agencies in the community. The school, however, has a unique opportunity in this field because it includes in its membership representatives from all classes of society and consequently is able through social relationships to establish bonds of friendship and common understanding that can not be furnished by other agencies. Moreover, the school can so organize recreational activities that they will contribute simultaneously to other ends of education, as in the case of the school pageant or festival.

7. *Ethical character.* In a democratic society ethical character becomes paramount among the objectives of the secondary school. Among the means for developing ethical character may be mentioned the wise selection of content and methods of instruction in all subjects of study, the social contacts of pupils with one another and with their teachers, the opportunities afforded by the organization and administration of the school for the development on the part of pupils of the sense of personal responsibility and initiative, and above all, the spirit of service and the principles of true democracy which should permeate the entire school—principal, teachers, and pupils.

Specific consideration is given to the moral values to be obtained from the organization of the school and the subjects of study in the report of this commission entitled "Moral Values in Secondary Education." That report considers also the conditions under which it may be advisable to supplement the other activities of the school by offering a distinct course in moral instruction.

# 6

# The Evolution of American Higher Education

## INTRODUCTION

Higher education in the twentieth century has experienced phenomenal growth, as more and more Americans attend institutions of higher learning than ever before in the nation's history. Mixed emotions of unrest, uncertainty, enthusiasm, and zeal have accompanied this evolution from the quiet exclusive ivy colleges to the modern multiversity's combination of teaching, research, service, and scholarship.

While American institutions of higher learning now range from small liberal arts colleges with only a few hundred students to the great state universities with enrollments of tens of thousands, all of these colleges and universities share a common heritage. This chapter seeks to trace the development of higher learning in America from its origins in the colonial and early national periods through the founding of the state and land grant colleges to the modern university of the twentieth century.

## THE COLONIAL COLLEGE

In the English-speaking colonies of North America, the patterns of higher education originally followed those of the two major English universities, Oxford and Cambridge. Attended by the sons of wealthy families, the English universities offered liberal arts education and the professional studies of law, medicine, and theology, of which the latter was most highly respected. In addition to educating scholars, lawyers, doctors, and theologians, Oxford and Cambridge were expected to prepare the cultured, well-rounded "gentleman." Higher education as practiced in England was class-based and designed for the elite, not for the masses of population.

The English university, like most of the other institutions of higher education in Western Europe, derived its basic structure from the medieval universities of Paris, Salerno, and Bologna. Their essential curriculum was liberal arts as contained in the trivium of grammar, rhetoric, and logic, and the quadrivium of music, astronomy, geometry, and mathematics. Latin was the language of instruction. After completing the liberal studies, the medieval student specialized in one of the professional areas: theology, law, or medicine. The methodology used in the medieval university was the kind of scholasticism developed by Abelard and Saint Thomas Aquinas.

The Renaissance of the fourteenth and fifteenth centuries emphasized the importance of humanistic studies. The scholars of this period stressed Greek and Ciceronian Latin as the languages of the educated man. With the advent of the Protestant Reformation religion became the dominant force as various sects sought to use higher education as a means of building doctrinal commitment by training an educated ministry. The colonial conception of higher education, as transmitted to the New World from England, was derived from the scholasticism of the medieval university, the classical emphasis of Renaissance humanism, and the educational zeal of the Protestant Reformation.

The Puritans of Massachusetts emphasized the necessity of safeguarding the Church in the New World through the tutelage of an educated ministry. Because of their influence, on October 28, 1636, the Massachusetts General Court enacted the legislation which created Harvard College, and at the same time appropriated an initial endowment of £400 for its support. Harvard's original curriculum consisted of the same traditional liberal arts that had been offered in the medieval universities. The function of the college in the clergy's education was evidenced by the emphasis placed on the ancient languages of Hebrew, Greek, and Latin, which were needed for scriptural scholarship. The foundation upon which the entire program of studies rested was Calvinist theology.

In the colonial South, the plantation-owning class of Southern gentlemen sent their sons to England for higher studies in the humanities and professional training. In Virginia, demand for an institution of higher learning led to the royal charter establishing the College of William and Mary in 1693. Thomas Jefferson's interest in higher education later contributed to the reorganization of William and Mary's curriculum in 1779 to include natural philosophy, mathematics, law, anatomy, medicine, moral philosophy, fine arts, and modern languages.

In the Middle Atlantic colonies, Princeton was chartered in 1746 in New

Jersey as the educational institution of the Presbyterians. King's College, which became Columbia, was chartered in 1754 to serve the Anglicans of New York, but it soon acquired a reputation for being tolerant in admission and liberal in curriculum. The University of Pennsylvania was chartered in 1779.

By the early eighteenth century Harvard was beginning to be influenced by the liberal thought that eventually characterized the dominant commercial class of Boston. Theological discussion at the college bore the imprint of Deism. As a protest against Harvard's liberal theology, more orthodox Congregationalists established their own institution at New Haven in 1701 to preserve the established religious doctrines, and Cotton Mather persuaded Elihu Yale to supply the first endowment. By the outbreak of the American Revolution, Dartmouth in New Hampshire, Brown in Rhode Island, and Rutgers in New Jersey were also established colleges in North America.

Although each of the colonial colleges had its own particularities, they all required that applicants for admission be versed in Latin and Greek. These requirements sustained the Latin Grammar school as the only secondary institution that supplied the classical language preparation considered so important by the colleges. In addition, Hebrew was also offered by the colleges because it aided study of the Holy Scripture. The eighteenth-century colonial college curriculum resembled the following:

First Year:    Latin, Greek, logic, Hebrew, and rhetoric.
Second Year:  Greek, Hebrew, logic, and natural philosophy.
Third Year:   Natural philosophy, metaphysics, and moral philosophy.
Fourth Year:  Mathematics, and review in Latin, Greek, logic, and natural philosophy.[1]

Enrollment in the colonial colleges was small and came from the economically and socially favored classes. Financial support was meager and the quest for funds always a problem. Despite the authoritarianism exercised by the institutions, the students even then complained about food, lodging, and the quality of instruction.

## EARLY NATIONAL PERIOD

Although institutions of higher learning were neglected during the Revolutionary War, the success of the American cause stimulated enthusiasm for a uniquely American form of education. The establishment of a na-

[1] Frederick Rudolph, The American College and University: A History (New York: Alfred A. Knopf, 1962), pp. 25–26.

tional university under federal auspices was proposed during the debates in the Constitutional Convention. Although Washington, Jefferson, and Madison supported it, the proposal was defeated. Throughout his career Washington continued to urge the establishment of such an institution. His first Inaugural Address referred to it, and his will contained a bequest to be used in financing one. Jefferson unsuccessfully pleaded the same cause during his administration, too.

Though a national university was not established, the early period following independence witnessed an enthusiasm for the founding of colleges. Private colleges continued to function, and numerous state colleges were chartered in the west and south as well. While the colleges on the Atlantic seaboard shifted away from strict adherence to the religious orthodoxy of their founders, the new denominational colleges that followed in the wake of frontier settlement maintained the Protestant commitment to train an educated ministry.

The early state colleges were usually located in small towns. Many of the locations were not easily accessible and were determined by political expediency rather than by carefully considered planning. College preparatory schools were usually lacking, and the colleges often had to maintain their own secondary departments. Libraries, staff, and facilities were weak. Usually, after a brief burst of educational enthusiasm, the relationship between state legislatures and the state colleges was poor.

The University of Virginia, chartered in 1819, was one of the first major institutions to deviate in organization, control, and curriculum from the older pattern of higher education found in the private colonial college. The University of Virginia exemplified several factors typical of the state university: first, public control and support; second, a scientific rather than a classical curriculum; third, student election of subjects rather than a prescribed course of study; fourth, a high level of instruction; fifth, nonsectarianism.[2] These factors could be found to varying degrees in most of the state-established and state-maintained universities such as Indiana, founded in 1820, Michigan, 1837, Wisconsin, 1848, and others prior to the Civil War.

### Denominational Colleges

In addition to the state governments, the various religious denominations established institutions of higher education. As the frontier moved west, ministers of the various religious denominations often accompanied

[2] John S. Brubacher, "A Century of the State University," in William Brickman and Stanley Lehrer, eds., *A Century of Higher Education: Classical Citadel to Collegiate Colossus* (New York: Society for the Advancement of Education, 1962), pp. 70–71.

the migration of their congregations. Frequently, ministers and priests led the westward advance as missionaries, and some of them stayed to serve the small towns which soon dotted the Midwest and West.

The religious revivals that swept the country during the first half of the nineteenth century created waves of evangelistic ardor. One of the characteristics of revivalism was the way the exercises reflected the religious commitments of each preacher. Because of this religious personalism, many small groups split away from their parent denominations during the pre-Civil War period. Two factors operated to involve the religious denominations in higher education: first, American Protestants, like their European counterparts, usually valued an educated ministry, and even denominations at first suspicious of "too much education" came to agree with them; second, the proliferation of religious groups brought about a competition between them. The denominational college was a popular means of educating the faithful and of building religious commitment in both the ministry and the congregation. However, the college did not restrict itself to religious education but also offered the liberal and practical subjects. Furthermore, many of these small colleges had to prepare their own students at the secondary level, which stimulated the growth of the academies. Presbyterians, Congregationalists, Roman Catholics, Methodists, Lutherans, Christian Disciples, Baptists, Episcopalians, Quakers, and Mormons were among the sects which founded a number of small liberal arts colleges.[3]

## The Dartmouth College Case

As the number of colleges increased and the states became involved in higher education, it was necessary that the private colleges' independence from state control be guaranteed; the precedent was set in the famous Dartmouth College case of 1819. The controversy over the control of Dartmouth College developed from the intense political rivalry between the Federalists, who controlled Dartmouth's board of trustees, and the Jeffersonian Democratic-Republicans, who controlled the New Hampshire state legislature. In 1816 the Democratic-Republican majority in the legislature attempted to take control of Dartmouth, change the charter, annul the original provisions, and establish a new institution called the University of New Hampshire. The Federalist-controlled board of trustees contended that the action of the state legislature was unconstitutional. Daniel Webster argued the case before the United States Supreme Court and

[3] For a discussion of the evolution of denominational higher education, see Allan O. Pfnister, "A Century of the Church-Related College," in Brickman and Lehrer, *A Century of Higher Education.*

won a decision favorable to the board of trustees affirming the original charter. According to Chief Justice John Marshall, the charter granted by King George III was of contractual nature; and under the United States Constitution, the binding force of contracts could not be impaired. In his decision Marshall upheld the sanctity of the Constitution's contract clause and applied it to the Dartmouth case, restoring the college to the board of trustees and returning it to its earlier status as a private educational institution.

The Dartmouth College decision of 1819 had far-reaching significance for both educational and national development. It protected the continued existence of the independent, privately controlled college, and ended state efforts to establish control over such institutions by legislative action. Concerning national enterprise, the Dartmouth decision established the precedent for the inviolability of the commercial contract. At the same time it strongly sanctioned the duality of higher education in the United States, which has produced two great academic systems, one private and the other state-supported. Further, the Dartmouth case illustrated the intimate relationship between education and national life. No institution, not even higher education, can escape political and social conflict. Educational institutions are related to and affected by other political, social, economic, and religious institutions.

## NEW STATE UNIVERSITIES

As a result of the combined effects of the Dartmouth College decision's protection of private higher education and the demands of the westward-moving population, new state universities were established in the early nineteenth century. As such western areas as the Northwest Territory and the Louisiana Purchase were organized and then admitted as states, their respective governments sought to establish their own state universities; their efforts were encouraged by the federal government's policy of granting land from the national domain for education.

The precedent of land grants for education had been established by the Ordinances of 1785 and 1787, which were enacted by the Continental Congress prior to the ratification of the Constitution.[4] The Ordinance of 1785 reserved the sixteenth section of each township of the Northwest Territory for education, and the Ordinance of 1787 expressed a federal commitment to encourage "schools and the means of education." The use

---

[4] The reader is referred to Chapter III, "Early Federal Period" for a more detailed treatment of the Ordinances of 1785 and 1787 and their general provisions for land grants to education.

of the abundant frontier land as a source of financial aid to education was an obvious step for the national government to take since it did not require increased taxation.

The establishment of state universities was further encouraged by the federal land grant policy, which granted two townships of land for institutions of higher learning to each state as it entered the Union. Ohio was the first to benefit from this policy, and the Ohio Enabling Act, which contained a provision for land grants to higher education, set a pattern that was followed by other states as they were admitted to the Union. During the 1850's this precedent was cited in the arguments favoring the adoption of a system of land grant colleges and universities. Although several state universities already benefited from the income derived from grants of land by the federal government, it was not until after the enactment of the Morrill Act in 1862 that the "land grant" colleges and universities were established specifically to further agricultural and industrial studies.

## Land Grant Institutions

In addition to the land grant provisions contained in the various enabling acts under which states were admitted to the Union, by the middle of the nineteenth century the federal government had also become involved in a number of special educational activities related to higher education.[5] These projects were intended to achieve specific objectives rather than serve as aid to higher education in general. The military academies at West Point and Annapolis, for instance, were established to train army and naval officers and contribute directly to the national defense. In 1857, Columbia Institute for the Deaf, later named Gallaudet College, was established with federal assistance. After the Civil War, Howard University was established to provide higher education for the newly freed Negroes. These various ventures of the federal government into higher education were not parallel movements, but they were all aimed at solving particular educational problems. The policy of specific areas of assistance was followed until the 1960's when general programs of aid to education were enacted by Congress.

The movement in behalf of the land grant college and university dur-

---

[5] For additional reading related to the federal government's role in education, see Hollis P. Allen, *The Federal Government and Education* (New York: McGraw-Hill Book Company, 1950); Richard G. Axt, *The Federal Government and Financing Higher Education* (New York: Columbia University Press, 1952); Homer D. Babbidge and Robert M. Rosenzweig, *The Federal Interest in Higher Education* (New York: Columbia University Press, 1962).

ing the 1850's represented a phase of American educational history which again reflected the interaction of growing social, economic, and political pressures upon education. The land grant movement, culminating in the Morrill Act of 1862, is a clearcut example of education as a civilizational instrument intimately related to social forces.

During the first half of the nineteenth century, the exclusive emphasis on classical and professional curricula inherited from the European tradition continued to dominate American colleges. Farmers' and laborers' pleas for agricultural and industrial instruction and research were ignored by the established colleges and universities, as higher education continued to lag behind the needs of a pioneer people on the verge of a great technological revolution.

Allan Nevins, in *The State Universities and Democracy*, wrote that the quest for equal opportunity was the motivating force behind the land grant college movement.[6] This equalitarian impulse echoed the earlier appeals of Horace Mann and Henry Barnard for educational democracy. The farmers and laborers who were members of the agricultural and industrial organizations of the 1850's and 1860's believed that genuine equality of opportunity depended on an education which would facilitate improvement of their economic condition. Although the common school had contributed to economic and social mobility in an earlier period, public elementary education by itself was an inadequate guarantee of mobility in an era of increasing technological specialization. Finding the existing liberal arts colleges unresponsive to their needs, the members of the agricultural and industrial organizations believed that a new institution of higher education was required. Thus, a coalition of farmer, laborer, and industrialist formed to advance the cause of the land grant college.

The idea of the industrial college was first developed by Jonathan Baldwin Turner, who in the early 1850's outlined a plan for a state industrial university in Illinois and asked the federal government for a land grant to be used to establish it. Turner believed that such an institution would help the working classes understand the technological age. In 1853, the Illinois legislature petitioned Congress to endow such a system.[7] Following the example of the earlier land grants to the states, Justin S. Morrill, a Vermont Congressman, introduced a land grant act to encourage agricultural and mechanical instruction without excluding the other scientific and classical studies. Morrill's act encompassed three broad goals:

[6] Allan Nevins, *The State Universities and Democracy* (Urbana: University of Illinois Press, 1962), p. 17.

[7] *Ibid.*, p. 14.

protest against the domination of higher education by the classics; development of practical instruction at the collegiate level; and vocational preparation of the agricultural and industrial classes.

The passage of the First Morrill Act in 1862 represented the culmination of a legislative struggle that extended back five years. When Congress initially passed it, President Buchanan, a strict interpreter of the Constitution, vetoed it. When the bill returned to the President's office in 1862, the more liberal Abraham Lincoln willingly gave his signature. The Morrill Act granted each state 30,000 acres of public land for each Senator and Representative it had in Congress according to the apportionment of the census of 1860.[8] The income from this land was to support at least one college whose primary purpose was agricultural and mechanical instruction. In states lacking adequate acreage of public land, the grant was given in federal scrip, i.e., certificates based upon the public domain which could be sold by the state. The proceeds which accrued were then used to establish the land grant college. It is significant that the federal government, in the case of the Morrill Act, extended the context of federal aid to higher education from the concept of the specifically directed grant to the more general purpose of aiding agriculture and industry.

The Second Morrill Act, passed in 1890, provided a direct cash grant of $15,000, to be increased annually to a maximum of $25,000, for the support of land grant colleges and universities. This Act also provided for similar institutions for Negroes in states prohibiting their enrollment in existing land grant institutions. It should be noted that the federal government attached requirements to this aid specifying that land grant colleges provide instruction in agricultural and mechanical subjects and in military training. As the United States emerged as a world power, it was becoming more aware of the need for a larger body of trained military officers than could be provided by the military academies. This provision strengthened the Reserve Officer Training Corps.

Although the Morrill Acts resulted from many pressures, they were essentially a response to the rapid industrial and agricultural growth of the United States in the latter half of the nineteenth century. Agricultural societies and workingmen's associations had recruited the support of higher learning to advance this technological revolution still further.

The growth of the land grant colleges in the post-Civil War era coincided with the Populist movement in American politics. After enjoying prosperity during the war the farmers of the 1870's and 1880's faced de-

[8] Benjamin F. Andrews, *The Land Grant of 1862 and the Land-Grant College* (Washington: Government Printing Office, 1918), pp. 7–8.

clining prices, deflated currency, and periodic agricultural depressions. Hoping to improve their economic and political position, the agricultural-ists banded together in a number of societies such as the Grange and the Farmers' Alliances. By the late 1880's and 1890's, significant numbers of farmers formed the agriculturalist political coalition called the Populist Party. The equal educational opportunity provided by the land grant col-leges was a corollary to the Populists' demands that American economic and political life be made more democratic. Although American Populism had its strength among the farmers and was a last major assertion of rural interests against the growing urbanization of the United States, the busi-ness and industrial interests, though opposed to agrarian radicalism, also supported the land grant college movement as an invaluable instrument in industrializing America. Although the farmers and industrialists cooper-ated in urging a practical curriculum suited to popular needs, agricultural interests dominated. They exerted strong pressures on the land grant col-leges established in rural areas to develop a "science of agriculture."

Since the passage of the First Morrill Act over a hundred years ago, land grant institutions have been established throughout the United States. In a number of states, these agricultural and mechanical colleges have become part of the state university. Examples of such universities are Maine, founded in 1865, Illinois and West Virginia in 1867, California in 1868, Nebraska in 1869, Ohio State in 1870, and Arkansas in 1871. More recent examples are the University of Puerto Rico, founded in 1903, and the University of Hawaii, founded in 1907. In addition to the land grant colleges connected with universities there were also a numer of agricul-tural and mechanical colleges established as separate institutions, such as Purdue University, founded in 1869, the Agricultural and Mechanical Col-lege of Texas in 1871, and the Alaska Agricultural College and School of Mines in 1922. Seventeen southern states established separate land grant colleges for Negroes under the provisions of the Second Morrill Act of 1890. As this partial listing illustrates, there were great differences in the character and location of the land grant institutions.

In *American Higher Education,* Brown and Mayhew have referred to the similarities and diversities among land grant colleges and universities. For example, land grant colleges emphasize agriculture as a blending of the scientific and practical. They also provide areas of study that are closely related to agriculture, such as home economics and veterinary medicine. Maintaining their commitment to industry, the colleges stress technology, engineering, and applied science. In addition to their agricul-tural and industrial programs, these schools provide instruction in the liberal arts and sciences and in teacher education. Many of them have developed large extension programs as well to make education available to as many people as possible in each state.[9]

Since land grant institutions serve particular needs of the people in each state, they have developed differences. Some land grant universities have become great research centers by developing a full complex of graduate and professional schools. For example, the faculties of the University of California at Berkeley, the University of Wisconsin, and the University of Illinois include distinguished scholars and scientists engaged in research and scholarship. Several land grant universities are among the highest in the number of graduate and professional degrees granted. In contrast to these research centers, some of the Negro land grant colleges concentrate much of their effort on vocational, technical, and remedial instruction.[10] The land grant concept as it was developed over a hundred years ago is still dynamic; today it has been extended to urban life. As the nation has changed, the land grant colleges and universities have changed with it.

## FORMATION OF THE UNIVERSITY

The history of American higher education is the story of long, continuous interaction between transplanted European concepts and the American environment. For example, the liberal arts college was derived from the English system and was primarily concerned with undergraduate instruction. It granted a bachelor's degree which marked the recipient as a generally educated non-specialist.

The modern American university has resulted from the imposition of the German graduate school upon the four-year undergraduate college. The nineteenth-century German universities, which emphasized *Lehrfreiheit und Lernfreiheit,* freedom to teach and freedom to learn, had a great influence on American higher education between the Civil War and World War I. Universities such as Berlin, Halle, Gottingen, Bonn, and Munich encouraged scholarly research. A university's graduate faculty, whose members usually held doctorates of philosophy, would guide the research by the instructional methods of seminar, laboratory, and lecture.

In the late nineteenth century many American professors completed their education with a period of residence in a German university. Upon their return to the United States, they sought to transform American

[9] Hugh S. Brown and Lewis B. Mayhew, *American Higher Education* (New York: The Center for Applied Research in Education, 1965), pp. 26–27.

[10] *Ibid.,* p. 24.

higher education into the German pattern. For example, Daniel Coit Gilman of Johns Hopkins and Charles W. Eliot of Harvard worked to make their institutions centers of graduate study and research.[11] The Johns Hopkins University, founded in Baltimore in 1876, became the prototype of the American university inspired by its German counterpart. Here instruction took the form of lectures to large groups and seminars in which a professor and a limited number of graduate students pursued advanced study and research. The methods of Johns Hopkins were emulated by the graduate schools at Harvard, Yale, Columbia, Princeton, and Chicago.[12] Abraham Flexner, a noted student of higher education also inspired by the German university, urged scholars and scientists to be conscious of four major concerns: the conservation of knowledge and ideas; the interpretation of knowledge and ideas; the search for truth; the training of students to carry on this work.[13] Thus, the German emphasis on scholarship and research came to dominate the American university as the graduate faculty devoted themselves to the pursuit of truth and the advancement of knowledge.

The American university took shape and reached its present state of definition in the late nineteenth century. The focal point of the university was the undergraduate college of liberal arts and sciences, which eventually came to be surrounded by the graduate college and the professional schools of law, medicine, agriculture, education, engineering, nursing, social work, theology, dentistry, commerce, and other specialized areas.

This period also saw a tremendous expansion of the undergraduate curriculum. Libraries were enlarged as instruction in science increased, the study of modern languages was introduced, and English, American history, economics, and political science were gradually included. Preprofessional courses, and later whole programs, were introduced at the expense of the general liberal arts studies. Under the prompting of President Eliot of Harvard, the elective system became popular.

Two major developments of modern higher education in the United States have been the rapid increase in student enrollment and the extensive expansion of the curriculum. Although college enrollments grew steadily throughout the late nineteenth and early twentieth centuries, the largest increase occurred during the post-World War II era. The regular curriculum expanded to include larger numbers of professional, specialized, and technical courses than had ever been dreamed of during the

[11] *Ibid.*, p. 29.
[12] Abraham Flexner, *Universities: American, English, German* (New York: Oxford University Press, 1930), pp. 73–74.
[13] *Ibid.*, p. 6.

nineteenth century. Today the modern university catalogue often includes programs in business administration, nuclear physics, animal husbandry, and hotel and restaurant management, along with the general education courses of the liberal arts and sciences. As with the secondary schools, a great deal of controversy has revolved around the nature of the college curriculum.

Robert Hutchins, in *Higher Learning in America*, 1936, attacked the confusion in American higher education.[14] For Hutchins, three major factors contributed to this state of affairs: love of money, a false conception of democracy, and a false notion of progress. He accused the modern university of selling its soul to the shifting fancies of donors, students, big business, football-oriented alumni, and politicians. Opposing what he called the "service station" institution, Hutchins argued for a university whose sole purpose was the pursuit of intellectual truth. Hutchins' work was a critique of higher education alleging that the American university had yielded to the pressure of a perverted sense of utility which regarded the art of money-making as the most desirable knowledge to acquire. Furthermore, over-specialization had caused scholars to concentrate too narrowly and exclusively, thus limiting communication in the university instead of making it a community of scholars. Finally, a certain amount of anti-intellectualism had developed from the emphasis on the purely utilitarian at the expense of theoretical and speculative studies. Hutchins believed that a knowledge of the theoretical was essential to the fulfillment of man's rational nature. He wanted to remove the sources of confusion and distraction and center the focus of the university on the pursuit of truth.

Some critics have viewed Hutchins' critique of higher education as advocating an ivory tower kind of retreat that would isolate the scholar and the university from the business of actual living in the everyday world. Rather than concentrating on solely intellectual pursuits, they feel, the college and university should meet the demands of the modern world and provide education in the specialized technologies which belong to the scientific age. The debate over the purposes and value of higher learning in American life will undoubtedly continue for some time.

## EMERGENCE OF THE MULTIVERSITY

Clark Kerr, former President of the University of California, has stated that the American university has experienced two great transformations. The first occurred during the latter years of the nineteenth century when the land grant movement and German intellectualism combined to pro-

[14] Robert M. Hutchins, *Higher Learning in America* (New Haven: Yale University Press, 1936).

duce the form of the university that we know. The second transformation has occurred since World War II.[15] Since 1945, the American university has been called upon to educate masses of students and to engage in federally sponsored research related to the national interest. According to Kerr:

> By the end of this period, there will be a truly American university, an institution unique in world history, an institution not looking to other models but serving, itself, as a model for universities in other parts of the globe. This is not said in boast. It is simply that the imperatives that have molded the American university are at work around the world.[16]

In 1963 Kerr described the University of California as an institution having a total operating budget of nearly half a billion dollars; spending nearly $100 million for construction; employing over 40,000 persons; maintaining operations in over 100 locations; conducting projects in more than 50 foreign nations; offering 10,000 courses in its catalogues, and envisioning a predicted enrollment of 100,000 students.[17] Such an institution as that described by Kerr no longer fitted the inherited pattern of the university as a single community of scholars and students. It was instead a series of communities and activities united by a common name, governing board, and related purposes into a new institution which Kerr termed the "multiversity." He said of it:

> The multiversity is an inconsistent institution. It is not one community but several—the community of the undergraduate and the community of the graduate; the community of the humanist, the community of the social scientist, and the community of the scientist; the communities of the professional schools; the community of all the nonacademic personnel; the community of the administrators. Its edges are fuzzy—it reaches out to alumni, legislators, farmers, businessmen, who are all related to one or more of these internal communities. As an institution, it looks far into the past and far into the future, and is often at odds with the present. It serves society almost slavishly—a society it also criticizes, some times unmercifully. Devoted to equality of opportunity, it is itself a class society. A community, like the medieval communities of masters and students, should have common interests; in the multiversity, they are quite varied, even conflicting. A community should have a soul, a single animating principle; the multiversity has several—some of them quite good, although there is much debate on which souls really deserve salvation.[18]

[15] Clark Kerr, *The Uses of the University* (Cambridge, Mass.: Harvard University Press, 1963), pp. 86–87.
[16] *Ibid.*
[17] *Ibid.*, p. 8.
[18] *Ibid.*, pp. 18–19.

Since the multiversity is composed of a number of communities of interest, it has not been easy to govern. As an institution approaches the stage of definition, new relationships and power balances must be formed. As California's president, Kerr found several competitors for power in the multiversity: first, the students who, through the elective system, affect which areas and disciplines the university will develop; second, the faculty who have achieved some authority over admissions, course approval, examinations, degree-granting, faculty appointments, and academic freedom; third, public authorities, such as the board of trustees, the state department of finance, the governor, and the legislature, who are authorized to make detailed reviews of organization and expenditures; fourth, organizations that exert informal pressures on the multiversity, such as agricultural and business organizations, trade unions, public school groups, and mass media; fifth, the administration, which has become a prominent feature of the multiversity. As the institution grows in size, administration becomes a more formal and distinct function.[19]

One of the most acute problems faced by modern American higher education today is the tremendous increase in college enrollments. In the fifteen years from 1949 to 1964, college enrollments almost doubled: in 1949, 2,445,000 students were enrolled; by 1964 this number had increased to 4,988,000, a 96 per cent increase. According to Thornton, the increase in college enrollment suggests that students are remaining in college for a longer period of time; that the rate of student withdrawal prior to graduation is decreasing; that a larger number of persons beyond the usual college age of 18–21 are enrolling; and that a greater proportion of the college-age population are enrolled in degree programs.[20] T. R. McConnell, a noted student of higher education, has predicted that by 1970 the enrollment in post-high school education programs will be at least seven million and possibly as high as eleven million persons.[21]

The present large enrollment and the predicted increases will severely test institutions of higher education. With great masses of students to be educated, expenditures, construction, faculty, libraries, and other college and university needs must also increase if educational opportunities are to be maintained. In order to allocate their resources as efficiently as possible, some of the states have turned to expert planning to meet these problems. Some states have already created, and others are planning, extensive

[19] Ibid., pp. 20–28.

[20] James W. Thornton, The Community Junior College (New York: John Wiley and Sons, 1966), pp. 7–8.

[21] T. R. McConnell, A General Pattern for American Public Higher Education (New York: McGraw-Hill Book Company, 1962), p. 2.

systems of junior colleges to handle the increasing student population. The federal government has enacted legislation to assist both students and institutions. The development of master plans, the growth of the junior college, and the increased federal activity will be discussed in greater detail later in this chapter.

In a democratic society, quantitative and qualitative problems are interrelated; thus the basic problem is that educational opportunities must be made available to larger numbers of people without reducing educational quality. A complex society such as ours needs individuals who are expertly prepared in engineering, medicine, science, education, the professions, and the creative arts. According to McConnell, the social sciences and humanities are as necessary as the sciences and technology for the maintenance of the democratic process:

> . . . a modern democratic society must have a large body of citizens who possess a deep understanding of the problems of modern life; who are devoted to the purposes and ideals of free society; and who will take a responsible and enlightened part in public affairs, both national and international.[22]

## Master Plans

The historic decentralization and lack of coordination of American higher education have produced great variation in administrations, size, organization, faculties, educational programs, and standards of institutions. No common pattern exists among the more than 1,300 degree-granting schools, colleges, and universities.[23] This lack of coordination has, according to McConnell, had two unfortunate results: failure to provide the kind of education that would most fully capitalize on our human resources and most adequately meet our varied civic, cultural, and industrial needs; and inefficient and uneconomical use of the financial resources available to higher education.[24]

Although most states recognize the need for coordinating their higher educational resources, a number of problems complicate their planning. Large population shifts to the urban areas have changed the focus of educational needs. In many states, the original state colleges and universities were located in small towns, and at some distance from the major cities. Recently, some of the large cities have established branches of their state university to meet their own growing educational needs. For example, the University of Illinois at Chicago Circle was opened in 1965 as a degree-

---

[22] *Ibid.*, p. 53.
[23] *Ibid.*, pp. 2–3.
[24] *Ibid.*, p. 136.

granting undergraduate institution to serve the Chicago area. This branch is nearly one hundred years younger than its parent institution, the University of Illinois, located in Urbana. Chicago Circle and similar commuter colleges and universities in other states represent the much delayed extension of the land grant principle to the large cities. These institutions have developed in response to the urban areas' demand for educational opportunities equal to those provided by the older institutions in the rural areas. Nonresident students and faculty who live elsewhere in the city commute daily to and from the college or university. Meanwhile, the existing private and denominational colleges and universities, which have hitherto served exclusively the higher educational needs of many of the cities, have often opposed the establishment of new public institutions unless some role is provided for the private institutions as well. Thus, the problems of planning and financing higher education are compounded for both the state legislatures and the educational institutions.

To meet the problems of higher education, many of the states and public colleges and universities have cooperated to devise master plans for future development. California has led in this movement; in 1959, a Coordinating Council for Higher Education was established by its state legislature. The Council, composed of three representatives each from the University of California, the state colleges, the public junior colleges, the private institutions, and the general public (the latter appointed by the governor), was given the function of advising the governing boards of the institutions and state officials on the following matters: budgetary review and requests for capital outlay of the university and state college systems; interpretation of functional differentiations in the publicly supported institutions and recommendation of desirable changes in higher education programs; planning for the orderly growth of higher education and recommendations concerning needs and locations of new facilities and programs.[25]

Through planning and coordination, California has articulated a state system of public higher education composed of junior colleges, state colleges, and the University of California. The junior colleges offer instruction through but not beyond the fourteenth grade level in courses that can be used for transfer to higher institutions, in vocational and technical fields, and in general arts courses. The state colleges provide undergraduate and graduate instruction through the master's degree in liberal arts and sciences, in applied fields, in teaching, and in the professions. The University of California is the primary state-supported academic agency

[25] *Ibid.*, pp. 152–53.

for research. It provides undergraduate and graduate instruction in the liberal arts and sciences, teaching, and the professions. Among the public institutions of higher education in California, the University has sole jurisdiction in law, medicine, dentistry, veterinary medicine, and architecture. It has sole authority to award the doctorate in all fields of learning, with the exception that in some areas it may award a joint doctorate with the state colleges.[26]

The state of Illinois has also developed a master plan for higher education. The Illinois legislature authorized the Illinois Commission of Higher Education to devise a plan for the unified administration of all state-controlled institutions of higher education. The Commission's report, *A Master Plan for Higher Education in Illinois*, 1964, contained the following recommendations: first, the development of colleges and universities to serve commuter students; second, the clear definition of two-year colleges as part of higher education by providing them with increased state support and a separate state board for planning and coordination; third, expansion of technical and semi-technical education programs to serve educationally disadvantaged youth; fourth, development of research and graduate programs; fifth, more extension and adult education programs; sixth, a greater number of qualified faculty, better use of outstanding teachers, and more extensive use of modern instructional techniques; seventh, a better enrollment balance between upper- and lower-level classes at state universities, which will improve lower-level standards and will free needed faculty and facilities for more upper-level and graduate work; eighth, rational priorities in construction so that current programs will be better housed, and also so that there will be places for all students without over-building; ninth, greater use of existing physical facilities through high standards and careful planning as to the use of space and the scheduling of more classes in late afternoon and evening hours; tenth, authorization of the Board of Higher Education to plan, but not to administer, all public education in Illinois.[27]

The California and Illinois master plans represent the efforts of only two of the states which have embarked upon coordination of higher education. In addition, formal coordinating agencies were established in Wisconsin and Texas in 1955, and in Utah in 1959. Voluntary boards were established in Ohio in 1939 and in Indiana in 1951. New York adopted its own master plan in 1950. These efforts at coordination and the adoption of

[26] *Ibid.*, pp. 155–56.
[27] Board of Higher Education, *A Master Plan for Higher Education in Illinois* (Springfield, Ill.: Board of Higher Education, 1964), p. 19.

master plans will undoubtedly continue to be important means of structuring higher education.

## JUNIOR COLLEGES

The California and Illinois master plans for higher education, as well as that of New York, provide for the extensive development of junior or community colleges. Since the two-year junior college is the most recent institutional development in American higher education, its definitive history has yet to be written. In the period from 1850 to 1920, several university presidents argued that the first two years of the American liberal arts college did not properly belong to higher education, but should be treated as part of secondary education. Presidents Henry A. Tappan of Michigan, William W. Follwell of Minnesota, William Rainey Harper of Chicago, and David Starr Jordan of Stanford urged that the first two years of undergraduate education be offered elsewhere than in the existing four-year college.[28] These men were not especially interested in initiating a new collegiate institution, but merely wanted to free their universities from what they considered secondary education in order to devote more time to graduate instruction and research. It was President Harper of the University of Chicago who in 1892 took the initiative and separated the first two and last two years of instruction into what were called the Academic College and the University College. In 1896, these titles were changed to the "junior college" and the "senior college." For Harper, the junior college was essentially an extension of the high school.[29]

As an institution, however, the junior college did not win immediate widespread support. Administrators still tended to approach the concept of a separate two-year college somewhat cautiously. The pioneer venture in establishing the junior college was made in 1901 in Joliet, Illinois, with the founding of the Joliet Junior College. Under the direction of Superintendent J. Stanley Brown, high school graduates were encouraged to take post-graduate work without additional tuition.[30] Although Brown's primary aim was to provide courses which would enable students to enter four-year colleges with advanced standing, terminal courses quickly became part of the program as well. In imitation of the venture at Joliet, junior colleges were established throughout the nation.

During the 1920's, 1930's, and 1940's, the number of junior colleges

[28] Thornton, *The Community Junior College*, pp. 46–48.
[29] *Ibid.*, p. 47.
[30] Elbert K. Fretwell, Jr., *Founding Public Junior Colleges* (New York: Bureau of Publications, Teachers College, Columbia University, 1954), pp. 11–12.

steadily increased, for various reasons. During this period, however, the junior college growth did not provide the relief for the university that Harper and Jordan had anticipated. Some four-year colleges retrenched their programs to two years during the depression period in order to survive. Some technical high schools and institutes were converted to junior colleges. In these and similar instances, junior colleges were being formed from schools already in operation, rather than being founded from the beginning as institutions specifically designed to relieve the overextended universities. Nevertheless, they steadily increased in number: in 1922 there were 207 junior colleges enrolling more than 16,000 students; in 1939, 575 junior colleges, and in 1958, 667.[31] By 1964, there were 700 two-year colleges in the United States whose combined enrollment totaled in excess of 1,000,000 students.[32]

As with any new institution, it was difficult at first to define the function of the junior college. As indicated, the two-year college was first conceived by university presidents as a means of diverting the responsibility for educating first- and second-year undergraduates to other institutions. According to this concept, the junior college would offer general liberal arts courses. In 1925, the American Association of Junior Colleges expanded its definition of the institution by stating that its members would offer two years of collegiate instruction of a quality equivalent to the first two years of a four-year college. In addition, the junior college curriculum would serve the social, civic, religious, and vocational needs of the community in which the college was located.[33] Despite this multifaceted definition of its function, the aims of the junior college were ill-defined, and differences of opinion persisted. Were liberal arts and sciences to be offered, or were semi-professional, terminal programs to be set up? As in the case of the high school, the institution that evolved combined both functions.

During the late 1920's and 1930's, junior colleges began to place greater emphasis on vocational and technical training programs. These programs were usually classified as terminal programs since they were the student's culminating experience in an institution of formal education. One of the most extensive programs of terminal or semi-professional education was introduced at the Los Angeles Junior College, which offered fourteen separate terminal programs in 1929, its inaugural year.[34] Other

---

[31] Leland L. Medsker, *The Junior College: Progress and Prospect* (New York: McGraw-Hill Book Company, 1960), p. 12.
[32] Thornton, *The Community Junior College*, p. 45.
[33] *Ibid.*, p. 51.
[34] *Ibid.*, p. 52.

junior colleges throughout the country also increased the number of terminal programs they offered.

A number of factors were at work in the growing emphasis on semiprofessional and technical education. In 1917 Congress passed the Smith-Hughes Act, which provided federal aid for vocational education. Although this legislation was primarily intended for such programs in the secondary schools, the incentives it provided encouraged vocational education in junior colleges in states where they were considered an extension of secondary education. During the 1920's a large numbers of educators subscribed to the doctrine of social efficiency, which held that each subject of study could be justified only in terms of its contribution to economic and social utility. During the depression of the 1930's, widespread unemployment stimulated vocational education as many individuals sought to improve their occupational skills. Since World War II, automation has required higher levels of technical competence.[35] Additional leisure time has also encouraged more adult study programs.

Today's junior college, or community college, is a multifunctional institution. It still provides the first two years of collegiate studies, upon completion of which students may transfer to four-year institutions. The student living at home and working part-time may thus obtain a relatively inexpensive education. The junior college has responded to the need in America for technically trained individuals who can perform subprofessional services. It provides adult education by offering vocational, adult, and liberal arts courses. As a community college, it is a cultural, educational, and civic center for the people in the area which it serves. The term "community college" indicates the close relationship between the college and the community.

In many of the states which have adopted master plans for higher education the junior college is a vital component of the state educational system, providing the first two years of education to students who later transfer to other four-year colleges. This has alleviated some of the pressures of massive student enrollment which has strained four-year college facilities. The junior college has also provided college education for many students who might have otherwise lacked the opportunity. As it becomes part of the articulated system of higher education, the purpose for which it was conceived is being realized.

California, having the largest junior college system, enrolls the largest number of students. The first enabling legislation in California for junior college establishment came in 1907 when the legislature authorized the

[35] *Ibid.*, p. 53.

offering of post-graduate courses by high school districts. In 1917, the first state aid legislation was passed. In 1921, the legislature authorized the formation of junior college districts.[36] *The Master Plan for Higher Education in California, 1960–1975* proposed diversion of part of the future enrollment from the state colleges and universities to the public junior colleges. It recommended that 50,000 students who would otherwise enter the state colleges and university in 1975 be diverted to the junior colleges.[37] The presence of an extensive junior college system has facilitated a selective state college and university policy without denying any student the opportunity for higher education.

Florida has also developed an extensive system of junior colleges. In 1955 its state legislature provided funds for junior colleges already existing and authorized appointment of a community college council to make recommendations for future junior college development. In 1956, it strongly recommended establishment of a system of community colleges to provide a broad range of educational programs. In 1957, it enacted laws to improve the programs of existing junior colleges and establish additional institutions to serve the growing population.

In addition to California and Florida, New York and Texas have major junior college systems. Other states, such as Illinois, have either begun or are planning to establish their own.

## FEDERAL AID TO HIGHER EDUCATION

After World War II the federal government reaffirmed its commitment to the realization of equal educational opportunity by demonstrating a heightened interest in higher education. In addition, higher education was also becoming an instrument of power nationally. However, federal interest in higher education was not new, as a brief review of the government's record indicates. The Morrill Act of 1862 granted land for the establishment of agricultural and mechanical colleges. The Second Morrill Act of 1890 granted funds to support college instruction in specified areas. Before that, in 1887, the Hatch Act established agricultural experiment stations. The Smith-Lever Act of 1914 created the Agricultural Extension Service. During the New Deal period of the 1930's, universities were involved in programs established by the Works Progress Administration, the National Youth Administration, and the Civilian Conservation Corps. During World War II, universities participated in the Engineering, Science, and Management War Training Program. The Servicemen's Re-

---

[36] Medsker, *The Junior College*, p. 210.
[37] McConnell, *American Public Higher Education*, p. 114.

adjustment Act, known as the GI Bill, was passed in 1944 to provide education for returning veterans, 7,800,000 of whom received benefits at a cost totaling $14.5 billion.[38] The law was extended to provide for Korean War veterans as well.

Although the federal government has a long record of providing aid to higher education, the post-World War II era has seen sustained and intensified programs of assistance that have no precedents. Educational historians have begun to feel that the successful ascent of the Soviet space satellite Sputnik exerted a profound effect upon American education. Popular reaction to the Soviet space success contributed to a climate of concerned congressional opinion that favored increased federal expenditure in education. In 1958, the National Defense Education Act was passed to stimulate studies in science, foreign languages, and mathematics. The Act was again extended in 1964. NDEA titles made loans available to college students; financially assisted improvement in science, mathematics, and modern language instruction; supported guidance, counseling and testing programs, and vocational education; and encouraged research and experimentation in educational media. This legislation not only aided higher education, but benefited all educational levels.

Although the NDEA was an extensive commitment of federal support to education, many observers felt that it was still inadequate. On January 23, 1963, President Kennedy called attention to the problems facing higher education:

> Now a veritable tidal wave of students is advancing inexorably on our institutions of higher education, where the annual costs per student are several times as high as the cost of a high school education, and where these costs must be borne in large part by the student or his parents. Five years ago the graduating class of the secondary schools was 1.5 million; 5 years from now it will be 2.5 million. The future of these young people and the nation rests in large part on their access to college and graduate education. For this country reserves its highest honors for only one kind of aristocracy—that which the Founding Fathers called "an aristocracy of achievement arising out of a democracy of opportunity." [39]

President Kennedy's urgent plea for aid to higher education revealed a skillful blending of the quantitative and the qualitative dimensions in education. The phrase "a democracy of opportunity" demonstrated his determination to provide greater access to institutions of higher learning

---

[38] Sidney W. Tiedt, *The Role of the Federal Government in Education* (New York: Oxford University Press, 1966), p. 25.

[39] John F. Kennedy, *Message from the President of the United States Relative to a Proposed Program for Education* (H.R. No. 54, January 29, 1964), p. 5.

for more students. His use of the term "an aristocracy of intellect" reflected his resolution that, despite increased enrollments, American higher education would maintain its standards of excellence.

Under President Kennedy's auspices the National Education Improvement Act of 1963 was introduced as an omnibus bill to provide general aid to education. Those areas of the act which touched upon higher education provided for an extension of the NDEA student loan program, liberalization of the payment plan, and more graduate fellowships. To expand and improve higher education, it proposed loans to public and nonprofit institutions for construction of academic facilities, construction and expansion of college and university libraries, development of graduate centers, and facilities for teaching modern foreign languages. Although the National Education Improvement Act was not passed, several parts of it were enacted as separate pieces of legislation, including the Higher Education Facilities Act of 1963. In focusing attention on the need for increased facilities in that area, President Kennedy said:

> The long-predicted crisis in higher education facilities is now at hand. For the next fifteen years, even without additional student aid, enrollment increases in colleges will average 340,000 each year. If we are to accommodate the projected enrollment of more than 7 million college students by 1970—a doubling during the decade—$23 billion of new facilities will be needed, more than three times the quantity built during the preceding decade. This means that, unless we are to deny higher education opportunities to our youth, American colleges and universities must expand their academic facilities at a rate much faster than their present resources will permit.[40]

The Higher Education Facilities Act of 1963 provided a program of grants to institutions of higher education for the construction of academic facilities. Congress appropriated $230,000,000 for each of the years 1963 to 1966 inclusive. For the years 1967 and 1968, Congress was to determine the amount of appropriations. Any institution of higher education was eligible for a construction grant for an academic facility. This unique feature of the Act made private and church-related institutions eligible for aid. However, construction in religious institutions was limited to facilities for instruction or research in the natural or physical sciences, mathematics, modern foreign languages, engineering, or library use.

The Higher Education Act of 1965, enacted during the Johnson administration, was a major piece of legislation authorizing federal expenditures for community service and continuing education programs; college library

[40] *Ibid.*, p. 7.

assistance and library training and research; aid to developing institutions which could potentially contribute to higher education, but which were still struggling for survival; and student assistance, by offering grants to qualified high school graduates of exceptional financial need who would otherwise be unable to attend an institution of higher learning.

Assessing the federal contribution to higher education, one can easily see that education is still closely related to broad social, political, and economic needs, both foreign and domestic. The international uncertainties of the post-World War II era have underscored the public's realization that knowledge as an instrument of power is directly related to the national interest. Research in science and technology has contributed greatly to the United States military potential. American universities have produced experts who have established educational programs in developing nations. Peace Corps volunteers have been trained on the campuses of many American colleges and universities. Domestically, the results of scholarly research have contributed to economic expansion, medical breakthroughs, and improved social conditions. Certain features of the federal assistance programs to higher education, such as the educational opportunity grants, are particularly concerned with the war on poverty.

## STUDENT UNREST

A discussion of contemporary higher education would be incomplete without some reference to the student unrest which has characterized many colleges and universities in the 1960's. During the academic year of 1965 national attention focused on the University of California campus at Berkeley when some students engaged in a dispute with the university administration over campus political activity. Some students even questioned the adequacy of the University as an educational institution. Some observers have referred to the unrest at Berkeley and at other institutions as a sign of alienation. In describing student life in the multiversity, former President Kerr of the University of California said:

> The multiversity is a confusing place for the student. He has problems of establishing his identity and a sense of security within it. But it offers him a vast range of choices, enough literally to stagger the mind. In this range of choices he encounters the opportunities and the dilemmas of freedom. The casualty rate is high. The walking wounded are many. Lernfreiheit —the freedom of the student to pick and choose, to stay or move on—is triumphant.[41]

[41] Kerr, *Uses of the University*, p. 42.

In *Education at Berkeley,* the Select Committee on Education of the University of California's Academic Senate reported the students' sense of being involved in a great national and international development, which had reached a state of crisis in higher education. The major reasons for this crisis were characterized as the changing role of the university in modern society, the proliferation of knowledge, the growth of population and the change in social expectations, and the emergence of a new generation of students. All of the major elements composing a university—teachers, students, knowledge, and society—were in an unprecedented state of change. The great task of the modern university, said the *Report,* was the very complex one of preserving integrity and stability while accepting change.[42]

To combat student feelings of impersonality and alienation on the large campus, the Select Committee made specific recommendations. It advocated increased use of seminars, tutorials, and preceptorials, and student advice in academic policy-making. Problem-oriented courses were recommended rather than the introductory survey course. The major aim was to achieve a more sensitive adaptation of the student's opportunities to his needs. The Select Committee saw no necessary conflict between the teaching and the research functions of the university. The close interpenetration of teaching and research should create a sense of ultimate unity and coherence.[43]

While it is still too early to assess the student unrest of the 1960's, a general comment might be made. When institutions change and social patterns are altered, there are always manifestations of unrest. Sometimes it is symptomatic of needed reconstruction. As the *Report* of the Select Committee states, the modern university faces the task of preserving its integrity and commitment while accepting the challenge of change.

Higher learning in the United States was a product of both transplanted European and native American concepts. While the colonial college served the upper social classes, the state university served to extend equality of educational opportunity to all who were capable of attaining it. The classical curriculum gradually gave way to a number of curricula including not only liberal but professional and technical studies as well. The land grant policy of the federal government, particularly as set forth in the Morrill Acts, broadened the concept of higher education to include mechanical and agricultural programs. Despite the contributions of the state and federal governments to higher education, college and universities

[42] Charles Muscatine et al., *Education at Berkeley: Report of the Select Committee on Education* (Berkeley: University of California Printing Department, 1966), pp. 3–4.
[43] *Ibid.*, pp. 4–7.

have not been exclusively public institutions. A healthy pluralism flourishes in the area of higher education as numbers of private and denominational colleges and universities continue to fulfill specific needs of various groups in the United States. In both public and private institutions of higher education research and teaching are combined now.

## CONCLUSION

American higher education has a number of problems to deal with in the next few years. To maintain and improve the current quality of education it must examine the purposes, functions, and results of its facilities and methods. It must also face the prospect of increasing enrollments in the decades ahead, and the consequent need for additional laboratories, libraries, and teachers in order to accommodate the influx. As enrollments increase, there have been fears that the teacher-student relationship might be depersonalized at the higher level and the student reduced to a mere number in the complex of the multiversity setting. Efforts to use the technologies of education, so that teachers have time to meet and work with students, need to be pursued in order to inhibit the tendency toward impersonality. The unsolved problem of the future is to provide a quality education to increasing numbers of students, and at the same time to advance scholarship and research into the frontiers of knowledge.

## References

ALLEN, HOLLIS P. *The Federal Government and Education.* New York: McGraw-Hill Book Company, 1950

ANDREWS, BENJAMIN F. *The Land Grant of 1862 and the Land-Grant College.* Bulletin No. 13. Washington: Government Printing Office, 1918.

AXT, RICHARD G. *The Federal Government and Financing Higher Education.* New York: Columbia University Press, 1952.

BABBIDGE, HOMER D., and ROSENZWEIG, ROBERT M. *The Federal Interest in Higher Education.* New York: Columbia University Press, 1962.

Board of Higher Education. *A Master Plan for Higher Education in Illinois.* Springfield, Ill.: Board of Higher Education, 1964.

BRICKMAN, WILLIAM F., and LEHRER, STANLEY, eds. *A Century of Higher Education: Classical Citadel to Collegiate Colossus.* New York: Society for the Advancement of Education, 1962.

BROWN, HUGH S., and MAYHEW, LEWIS B. *American Higher Education.* New York: The Center for Applied Research in Education, Inc., 1965.

BRUBACHER, JOHN S., and RUDY, WILLIS. *Higher Education in Transition: An American History: 1636–1956.* New York: Harper & Row, Publishers, 1958.

BRUNNER, HENRY S. *Land-Grant Colleges and Universities, 1862–1962.* Washington: United States Government Printing Office, 1962.

BUTTS, R. FREEMAN. *The College Charts Its Course:Historical Cnceptions and Current Proposals.* New York: McGraw-Hill Book Company, 1939.

DANFORTH, EDDY, JR. *College for Our Land and Time: The Land Grant Idea in American Education.* New York: Harper & Row, Publishers, 1956.

FLEXNER, ABRAHAM. *Universities: American, English, German.* New York: Oxford University Press, 1930.

FRETWELL, ELBERT K., JR. *Founding Public Junior Colleges.* New York: Bureau of Publication, Teachers College, Columbia University, 1954.

*Higher Education Act of 1965.* Public Law 89–329, 89th Cong., H.R. 9567, November 8, 1965.

*Higher Education Facilities Act of 1963.* Public Law 88-204, 88th Cong., H.R. 6143, December 16, 1963.

HOFSTADTER, RICHARD, and HARDY, C. DEWITT. *The Development and Scope of Higher Education in the United States.* New York: Columbia University Press, 1952.

KENNEDY, JOHN F. *Message from the President of the United States Relative to a Proposed Program for Education, and a Draft of a Bill to Strengthen and Improve Educational Quality and Educational Opportunities in the Nation.* House of Representatives Document, No. 54, January 29, 1963.

KERR, CLARK. *The Uses of the University.* Cambridge, Massachusetts: Harvard University Press, 1963.

MCCONNELL, T. R. *A General Pattern for American Public Higher Education.* New York: McGraw-Hill Book Company, Inc., 1962.

MEDSKER, LELAND L. *The Junior College: Progress and Prospect.* New York: McGraw-Hill Book Company, Inc., 1960.

MUSCATINE, CHARLES, et al. *Education at Berkeley: Report of the Select Committee on Education.* Berkeley: University of California Printing Department, 1966.

NEVINS, ALLAN. *The State Universities and Democracy.* Urbana, Ill.: University of Illinois Press, 1962.

ROSS, EARLE D. *Democracy's College: The Land Grant Movement in the Formative Stage.* Ames, Iowa: Iowa State College Press, 1942.

RUDOLPH, FREDERICK. *The American College and University: A History.* New York: Alfred A. Knopf, 1962.

TEWKSBURY, DONALD G. *The Founding of American Colleges and Universities Before the Civil War.* New York: Bureau of Publications, Teachers College, Columbia University, 1932.

THORNTON, JAMES W. *The Community Junior College.* New York: John Wiley and Sons, 1966.

THWING, CHARLES F. *A History of Higher Education in America.* New York: Appleton, 1906.

TIEDT, SIDNEY W. *The Role of the Federal Government in Education.* New York: Oxford University Press, 1966.

# SELECTIONS

*The Dartmouth College case of 1819 represents a significant decision of the Supreme Court in the area of higher education. The case grew out of a controversy between the president and board of trustees of Dartmouth against the state legislature of New Hampshire over the control of the college. The decision of Chief Justice John Marshall on behalf of the trustees' right to independent control served to protect both the existence of the private college against state encroachment and the sanctity of contract as guaranteed by the Constitution.*

## The Dartmouth College Case

This court can be insensible neither to the magnitude nor delicacy of this question. The validity of a legislative act is to be examined, and the opinion of the highest law tribunal of a state is to be revised; an opinion which carries with it intrinsic evidence of the diligence, of the ability, and the integrity with which it was formed. On more than one occasion this court has expressed the cautious circumspection with which it approaches the consideration of such questions, and has declared that in no doubtful case would it pronounce a legislative act to be contrary to the constitution. But the American people have said, in the constitution of the United States, that "no state shall pass any bill of attainder, ex post facto law, or law impairing the obligation of contracts." In the same instrument they have also said "that the judicial power shall extend to all cases in law and equity arising under this constitution." On the judges of this court, then, is imposed the high and solemn duty of protecting, from even legislative violation, those contracts which the constitution of our country has placed beyond legislative control, and, however irksome the task may be, this is a duty from which we dare not shrink. . . .

It can require no argument to prove that the circumstances of the case constitute a contract. An application is made to the crown for a charter to incorporate a religious and literary institution. In the application it is stated that large contributions have been made for the object, which will be conferred on the corporation as soon as it shall be created. The charter is granted, and on its faith the

SOURCE: *The Trustees of Dartmouth College v. William H. Woodward*, 4 Wheaton, U.S. 518, 4 L. ed 629.

126

property is conveyed. Surely in this transaction every ingredient of a complete and legitimate contract is found. . . .

That education is an object of national concern, and a proper subject of legislation, all admit. That there may be an institution founded by government, and placed entirely under its immediate control, the officers of which would be public officers, amenable exclusively to government, none will deny. But is Dartmouth College such an institution? Is education altogether in the hands of government? Does every teacher of youth become a public officer, and do donations for the purpose of education necessarily become public property, so far that the will of the legislature, not the will of the donor, becomes the law of the donation? These questions are of serious moment to society, and deserve to be well considered. . . .

Almost all eleemosynary corporations, those which are created for the promotion of religion, of charity, or of education, are of the same character. The law of this case is the law of all. In every literary or charitable institution, unless the objects of the bounty be themselves incorporated, the whole legal interest is in trustees, and can be assessed only by them. The donors or claimants of the bounty, if they can appear in court at all, can appear only to complain of the trustees. In all other situations they are identified with, and personified by, the trustees, and their rights are to be defended and maintained by them. Religion, charity, and education are, in the law of England, legatees or donees, capable of receiving bequests or donations in this form. They appear in court, and claim or defend by the corporation. Are they of so little estimation in the United States that contracts for their benefit must be excluded from the protection of words which, in their natural import, include them? Or do such contracts so necessarily require new modeling by the authority of the legislature that the ordinary rules of construction must be disregarded in order to leave them exposed to legislative alteration?

All feel that these objects are not deemed unimportant in the United States. The interest which this case has excited proves that they are not. The framers of the constitution did not deem them unworthy of its care and protection. They have, though in a different mode, manifested their respect for science by reserving to the government of the Union the power "to promote the progress of science and useful arts by securing, for limited times, to authors and inventors the exclusive right to their respective writings and discoveries." They have so far withdrawn science and the useful arts from the action of the state governments. Why, then, should they be supposed so regardless of contracts made for the advancement of literature as to intend to exclude them from provisions made the security of ordinary contracts between man and man? No reason for making this supposition is perceived. . . .

In the view which has been taken of this interesting case, the court has confined itself to the right possessed by the trustees, as the assignees and representatives of the donors and founders, for benefit of religion and literature. Yet it is not clear that the trustees ought to be considered as destitute of such beneficial interest in themselves as the law may respect. . . .

But the court has deemed it unnecessary to investigate this particular point, being of opinion, on general principles, that in these private eleemosynary institutions the body corporate, as possessing the whole legal and equitable interest, and completely representing the donors, for the purpose of executing the trust, has rights which are protected by the constitution.

It results from this opinion that the acts of the legislature of New Hampshire which are stated in the special verdict found in this case, are repugnant to the constitution of the United States, and that the judgment on this special verdict ought to have been for the plaintiffs. The judgment of the state court must therefore be

*Reversed.*

---

*The Morrill Act of 1862 is one of the crucial documents in the evolution of American higher education. The Act resulted from the pressure of political, social, and economic forces to extend the concept of equality of educational opportunity to higher education. The Morrill Act was introduced by United States Representative Justin Morrill of Vermont and signed in 1862 by President Abraham Lincoln. The text of the Act follows.*

# Morrill Land-Grant Act of 1862

An Act Donating public lands to the several States and Territories which may provide colleges for the benefit of agriculture and the mechanic arts.

*Be it enacted by the Senate and House of Representatives of the United States of America in Congress assembled,* That there be granted to the several States, for the purposes hereinafter mentioned, an amount of public land, to be apportioned to each State a quantity equal to 30,000 acres for each Senator and Representative in Congress to which the States are respectively entitled by the apportionment under the census of 1860: *Provided,* That no mineral lands shall be selected or purchased under the provisions of this act.

Sec. 2. *And be it further enacted,* That the land aforesaid, after being surveyed, shall be apportioned to the several States in section or subdivisions of sections, not less than one-quarter of a section; and wherever there are public lands in a State subject to sale at private entry at $1.25 per acre, the quantity to which said State shall be entitled shall be selected from such lands within the

SOURCE: Benjamin F. Andrews, *The Land Grant of 1862 and the Land-Grant College* (Washington: Government Printing Office, 1918, *Bulletin,* 1918, No. 13), pp. 7–8.

limits of such State; and the Secretary of the Interior is hereby directed to issue to each of the States in which there is not the quantity of public lands subject to sale at private entry at $1.25 per acre to which said State may be entitled under the provisions of this act land scrip to the amount in acres for the deficiency of its distributive share, said scrip to be sold by said States and the proceeds thereof applied to the uses and purposes prescribed in this act, and for no other use or purpose whatsoever: *Provided*, That in no case shall any State to which land scrip may thus be issued be allowed to locate the same within the limits of any other State or of any territory of the United States; but their assignees may thus locate said land scrip upon any of the unappropriated lands of the United States subject to sale at private entry at $1.25 or less an acre: *And provided further*, That not more than one million acres shall be located by such assignees in any one of the States: *And provided further*, That no such location shall be made before one year from the passage of this act.

Sec. 3. *And be it further enacted*, That all the expenses of management, superintendence, and taxes from date of selection of said lands previous to their sales and all expenses incurred in the management and disbursement of moneys which may be received therefrom shall be paid by the States to which they may belong, out of the treasury of said States, so that the entire proceeds of the sale of said lands shall be applied, without any diminution whatever, to the purposes hereinafter mentioned.

Sec. 4. *And be it further enacted*, That all moneys derived from the sale of the lands aforesaid by the States to which the lands are apportioned, and from the sales of land scrip hereinbefore provided for, shall be invested in stocks of the United States or of the States, or some other safe stocks, yielding not less than 5 per centum upon the par value of said stocks; and that the moneys so invested shall constitute a perpetual fund, the capital of which shall remain forever undimished, except so far as may be provided in section fifth of this act, and the interest of which shall be inviolably appropriated by each State which may take and claim the benefit of this act to the endowment, support, and maintenance of at least one college, where the leading object shall be, without excluding other scientific and classical studies and including military tactics, to teach such branches of learning as are related to agriculture and the mechanic arts in such manner as the legislatures of the States may respectively prescribe in order to promote the liberal and practical education of the industrial classes in the several pursuits and professions in life.

Sec. 5. *And be it further enacted*, That the grant of land and land scrip hereby authorized shall be made on the following conditions, to which, as well as to the provisions hereinbefore contained, the previous assent of the several States shall be signified by legislative acts:

*First.* If any portion of the fund invested as provided by the foregoing section, or any portion of the interest thereon, shall by any action or contingency be diminished or lost, it shall be replaced by the State to which it belongs, so that the capital of the fund shall remain forever undiminished; and the annual interest shall be regularly applied without diminution to the purposes mentioned in the fourth section of this act, except that a sum, not exceeding 10 per centum upon the amount received by any State under the provisions of this act, may be expended for the purchase of lands for sites or experimental farms whenever authorized by the respective legislatures of said States;

*Second.* No portion of said fund, nor the interest thereon, shall be applied, directly or indirectly, under any pretense whatever to the purchase, erection, preservation, or repair of any building or buildings;

*Third.* Any State which may take and claim the benefit of the provisions of this act shall provide, within five years, at least not less than one college, as prescribed in the fourth section of this act, or the grant to such State shall cease; and said State shall be bound to pay the United States the amount received of any lands previously sold, and that the title to purchasers under the States shall be valid;

*Fourth.* An annual report shall be made regarding the progress of each college, recording any improvements and experiments made, with their costs and results, and such other matters, including State industrial and economical statistics, as may be supposed useful; one copy of which shall be transmitted by mail free, by each to all the other colleges which may be endowed under the provisions of this act, and also one copy to the Secretary of the Interior;

*Fifth.* When lands shall be selected from those which have been raised to double the minimum price in consequence of railroad grants, they shall be computed to the States at the maximum price, and the number of acres proportionally diminished;

*Sixth.* No State, while in a condition of rebellion or insurrection against the Government of the United States, shall be entitled to the benefit of this act;

*Seventh.* No State shall be entitled to the benefits of this act unless it shall express its acceptance thereof by its legislature within two years from the date of its approval by the President.

Sec. 6. *And be it further enacted,* That land scrip issued under the provisions of this act shall not be subject to location until after the first day of January, 1863.

Sec. 7. *And be it further enacted,* That land officers shall receive the same fees for locating land scrip issued under the provisions of this act as are now allowed for the location of military bounty land warrants under existing laws: *Provided,* That maximum compensation shall not be thereby increased.

Sec. 8. *And be it further enacted,* That the governors of the several States to which scrip shall be issued under this act shall be required to report annually to Congress all sales made of such scrip until the whole shall be disposed of, the amount received for the same, and what appropriation has been made of the proceeds.

Approved, July 2, 1862.

# 7

## The Evolution of American
## Teacher Education

### INTRODUCTION

With the institutional growth of the American educational system and widespread popular acceptance of publicly supported and publicly controlled schools, a parallel interest in teacher education developed. The leaders of both the common school and high school movements realized that the success of the "ladder concept" in education depended on an available supply of qualified teachers. Educational statesmen such as Mann and Barnard urged the establishment of institutions to train teachers. This chapter deals with the evolution of American teacher education from the pioneer writings of Samuel Hall in the 1830's to the clearly defined programs offered today. The development of normal schools, teachers' colleges, and professional education as a discipline are integral phases in the history of teacher education.

### COLONIAL AND EARLY NATIONAL PERIODS

During the colonial period, teachers varied greatly in their personal and educational qualifications. As explained in an earlier chapter, colonial education was administered through vernacular schools, and secondary and higher institutions. The vernacular school was designed for the masses, the Latin Grammar school and colonial college for the leadership classes. Coinciding with this early bifurcation, there was also a sharp differentiation among the teachers themselves. Teachers in the lower schools were often poorly educated and possessed, at best, only a rudimentary knowledge of the basic skills of reading, writing, and arithmetic. Some of them were bond-servants; others were students of the ministry or the law who kept school to support themselves until they were able to enter their preferred profession.

Teacher selection and certification varied from colony to colony. In New England, school committees certified the appointment of the teacher with the approval of the town minister. In the parochial schools of the middle colonies, the society or the church that supported the school approved his appointment. In the southern plantation areas, tutors were selected by individual families for their own employment. Generally speaking, the certification of the elementary teacher was based primarily on the candidate's religious and political orthodoxy, and after that on his skill in teaching reading, writing, arithmetic, and religion.

The master of the Latin Grammar school, for whom a knowledge of Latin and Greek was necessary, was usually a college graduate. A respected member of the colonial community, he was accorded a higher social distinction than the lowly elementary teacher.

During the Revolution the emphasis on the war effort diverted attention from educational efforts to the pressing task of defeating the English army. Whatever money was available was applied to the military needs of the Continental Army rather than toward maintaining or building new schools. In the unsettled political and social conditions that followed the Revolution, the most immediate problem was the establishment of the Republic, and education continued to be neglected. As interest in schools was eclipsed, the status and training of teachers also declined. It was not until the common school revival of the early nineteenth century that the training of teachers was seriously undertaken.

## THE COMMON SCHOOL AND TEACHER EDUCATION

During the first half of the nineteenth century, elementary education became significant again in the United States in the form of the common school system. The proponents of universal education realized that the success of public education depended upon a body of qualified teachers. Among the first to contribute to the literature of teacher education in the United States was a Congregational minister, Samuel Hall, who conducted a private academy for the preparation of teachers. In 1830 he became head of the normal department at Phillips Andover Academy, where he lectured on the "art of teaching." His book, *Lectures to School-Masters on Teaching*, 1833, reveals the condition of elementary education in New England during the early years of the nineteenth century.

Hall first surveyed the weaknesses plaguing the common school itself. Political and religious divisions within school districts weakened the community support necessary for good schools. Many communities were unwilling to finance their schools adequately and supply them with needed equipment. The wealthy classes enrolled their children in private schools and neglected the common school. Hall also found serious deficiencies in the qualifications of many teachers.[1] He believed that improved teacher education would aid the common school movement, and urged the establishment of institutions devoted to teacher preparation in the necessary branches of literature, the science of teaching, and the modes of school government.[2]

The table of contents of Hall's book indicates his conception of a "science of education." Among the topics he treated are: the importance, character, and usefulness of common schools; obstacles to their usefulness; qualifications of teachers; management and government of a school; teaching of spelling, reading, arithmetic, geography, English grammar, writing, history, and composition; gaining the attention of students; location and construction of school houses; beginning the first day of school.[3]

In his discussion of teacher qualifications, Hall mentioned seven major attributes: first, common sense: the ability to appraise conditions realistically, and through judgment and discrimination to exercise propriety; second, uniformity of temper; third, a capacity to understand and gauge character; fourth, decision of character: pursuit of a uniform course without dissuasion from action he judges correct; fifth, affection for the respect and good will of the students; sixth, just, moral discretion; seventh, the necessary literary qualifications: reading, spelling, writing, grammar, arithmetic, geography, and American history.[4]

In writing about the early history of teacher education, Henry Barnard noted four significant pamphlets which appeared in 1825: Thomas H. Gallaudet's "Plan of a Seminary for the Education of Instructors of Youth"; James Carter's "Essays on Popular Education," containing a particular examination of the schools of Massachusetts, and an "Outline of an Institution for the Education of Teachers"; and Walter R. Johnson's "Observations on the Improvement of Seminaries of Learning." [5] In addition

---

[1] Samuel Hall, *Lectures to School-Masters on Teaching* (Boston: Carter, Hendee and Co., 1833), pp. 20–21.

[2] *Ibid.*, p. vi.

[3] *Ibid.*, pp. x–xii.

[4] *Ibid.*, pp. 33–35.

[5] Henry Barnard, *Normal Schools, and Other Institutions, Agencies, and Means Designed for the Professional Education of Teachers* (Hartford: Case, Tiffany, and Company, 1851), p. 7.

to these indications of concern with the problems, Governor De Witt Clinton urged the New York legislature to study the best methods of securing highly trained common school teachers.

Among the proponents of teacher education during the era of common school revival, James G. Carter deserves special interest. As a member of the Massachusetts legislature, Carter had joined Horace Mann in advocating the common school cause. Convinced that instruction could be improved only by competent teachers, he urged that they be prepared in normal schools devoted exclusively to teacher education. Carter made a fourfold recommendation which he believed should be followed in establishing normal schools:

1. Selection of a board of commissioners to represent the public interests in teacher education.

2. Appointment of a principal, as head of the normal school, and of a staff of assistant professors to prepare the prospective teachers.

3. Establishment of a library of books on the science of education.

4. Establishment of a demonstration school for children of different ages pursuing various studies.

Carter stressed the establishment of a model school as part of the normal school. In the model school, the prospective teacher could gain needed experience in actual teaching:

> After the young candidate for an instructor, therefore, has acquired sufficient knowledge for directing those exercises and teaching those branches which he wishes to profess, he must then begin his labors under the scrutinizing eyes of one who will note his mistakes of government and faults of instruction, and correct them. The experienced and skillful professor of the science will observe how the mind of the young teacher acts upon that of the learner. He will see how far and how perfectly they understand each other, and which is at fault if they do not understand each other at all.[6]

As a member of the Massachusetts legislature, Carter also sponsored the bills creating the State Board of Education. Horace Mann, who was named first secretary of the Board in 1837, saw the normal school as a new instrument for the advancement of humanity. He was convinced that the existence of the common school was dependent upon the success of the normal school.[7]

[6] James G. Carter, "Outline of an Institution for the Education of Teachers," 1825, in Barnard, *Normal Schools*, pp. 78–81.

[7] Charles Harper, *A Century of Public Teacher Education* (Washington: National Education Association, 1939), p. 22.

As a result of the groundwork laid by Carter and Mann, Governor Edward Everett of Massachusetts signed the bill authorizing the establishment of three normal schools in the towns of Lexington, Barre, and Bridgewater. These early schools offered a curriculum consisting of reading, writing, grammar, arithmetic, geography, spelling, composition, vocal music, drawing, physiology, algebra, philosophy, methodology, and Scriptural reading. As Massachusetts had been the leader in the common-school revival, it also came to lead in teacher education.

## ADOPTION OF THE NORMAL SCHOOL

Other states imitated the pattern which Massachusetts had set. New York first attempted unsuccessfully to educate teachers for the common schools in the existing academies. By 1844, however, New York's legislature had authorized a normal school for the "instruction and practice of teachers of common schools." The New York State Normal School was established at Albany. David Perkins Page, the head of the school, significantly contributed to teacher education by stressing training in both theory and practice. His book, *Theory and Practice of Teaching or the Motives and Methods of Good School-Keeping*, 1847, became a standard work in teacher education.[8] Page stressed the idea of practice teaching in a model school, believing teacher education to be inadequate without a period of actual teaching experience under classroom conditions.

Henry Barnard, like Horace Mann, recognized the reciprocal relationship between the success of the common school and that of the normal school. In the *Connecticut Common School Journal*, he compiled a body of educational literature called *Normal Schools, and Other Institutions, Agencies, and Means Designed for the Professional Education of Teachers*, 1851, which included a number of articles, essays, and other writings dealing with teacher education. In this work he summarized the weaknesses impeding the normal school movement in the United States: students were accepted by normal schools without proper preparation and without sufficient testing of their aptitude for teaching; the majority of pupils did not remain in the normal schools long enough to be adequately prepared in subjects and in methods; there were few endowments or scholarships available to aid qualified students financially; there was a lack of trained normal school professors; and the normal schools tried to accomplish more than their means permitted.[9]

[8] David P. Page, *Theory and Practice of Teaching or the Motives and Methods of Good School-Keeping* (New York: A. S. Barnes and Co., 1885).
[9] Barnard, *Normal Schools*, p. 8.

The midwestern and western states quickly followed the eastern states in the establishment of normal schools. By 1875, the normal school was accepted throughout the United States. State governments established normal schools by acts of legislature, determined their number, and contributed to the construction of a physical plant. Location of the school was usually determined by spirited bidding among interested communities, one of whom would often donate a site for the school.

The course of studies in the normal school was customarily given over a two-year period. The curriculum consisted of a review of the basic common school subjects, lectures on schoolkeeping, and experience in practice teaching in a model school under the direction of the normal school's faculty.

Although normal school programs of teacher education were criticized frequently, these institutions advanced the idea of professional preparation for teachers. Their very existence disputed the common American notion that anyone could teach. They also served as a transitional institution which later developed into the teacher's college. The faculties of the normal schools produced a professional literature which promoted the evolution of a theoretical framework for education. The model school became a distinctive characteristic of teacher education. Perhaps one of the most important contributions of the normal school was the concept that teacher preparation was intimately related to the needs of the public school and the public welfare.

## Transition to Teachers College

In the post-Civil War era, colleges and universities gradually recognized the importance of teacher education. The development of the high school as a public secondary institution contributed to this belated recognition. Increasing high school enrollments at the turn of the century also created a greater demand for qualified secondary school teachers. By then, two other changes were already taking place to fill the need: the normal schools were evolving from two-year institutions into four-year degree-granting colleges, and a small number of colleges and universities were establishing chairs of pedagogy. However, some academic traditionalists in the colleges and universities still resisted the entry of professional education into higher education. Where education was first accepted, it was not given the status of an independent discipline but was included as a part of the department of philosophy or psychology. Despite the opposition of traditionalists in the liberal arts, colleges and universities slowly added departments or colleges of education. In 1873, the University of Iowa established the first permanent chair of pedagogy; Wisconsin University followed in 1879, Indiana and Cornell in 1886, and in 1892 Teachers College became a part of Columbia University. By 1900, colleges and universities had assumed responsibility for teacher education.

As the colleges and universities entered the field of teacher education, the normal schools were becoming teachers' colleges. According to Woodring, by 1900 the growing number of high schools enabled many normal schools to require a high school diploma for admission. Between 1911 and 1920, nineteen state normal schools became teachers' colleges; by 1930, sixty-nine had made the transition.[10] The transformation usually included the following steps: raising the entrance requirements to include high school graduation; enriching the curriculum by adding liberal arts subjects to the courses on professional education and methodology; lengthening the program of studies from two to four years; including work in the theory of education; securing the privilege to grant degrees through state legislative action; and improving faculties. After World War II, many state legislatures permitted teachers' colleges to shift their status to that of the general purpose college, which could grant degrees in other fields besides professional education.

## PROFESSIONAL EDUCATION

There is considerable controversy today concerning the most desirable program of teacher preparation. Much of it centers around the nature and status of the teaching profession. The question of the professional status of teachers is partly left over from archaic conceptions about teaching. The commonly held belief that an extended period of teacher training is unnecessary,[11] which was attacked by George Counts in *The Social Foundations of Education*, originated during frontier times when untutored farmers organized schools. As areas of knowledge became increasingly sophisticated, however, more than mere training in literacy became necessary.

In 1890, the Superintendent of Schools in New York, Andrew Draper, addressed himself to the problem of improving the professional status of teachers. He found that education had been prevented from becoming a recognized profession by the ease with which one could obtain the right to teach, the laxity of conditions governing teacher employment, the de-

[10] Paul Woodring, "A Century of Teacher Education," in William Brickman and Stanley Lehrer, eds., *Century of Higher Education* (New York: Society for the Advancement of Education, 1962), p. 158.

[11] George S. Counts, *The Social Foundations of Education* (New York: Charles Scribner's Sons, 1934).

mands placed on normal schools to restrict themselves primarily to candidates for elementary work, and the small number of teachers who were trained graduates.[12] To improve the quality of teaching and to elevate its status, Draper outlined a program of professional preparation which embraced educational psychology, philosophy of education, history of education, and educational methodology. In urging broad scholarship, he said:

> . . . a teaching profession cannot be established on a basis which only covers the work of the common schools. The mere knowledge that is to be conveyed to the child is not all that is required on the part of the teacher. A teaching profession will be controlled by the same inexorable laws as hedge about the other professions. In advance of professional training there must be a scholarship foundation, adequate in extent, and sufficiently well laid to place individual teachers, not a few, but all of them, on an equal footing, and in comfortable relations with the ministers and physicians, and architects and engineers, and which will make sure that the mental equipment of the collective body is at no disadvantages in comparison with that of the entire body of persons composing the other professions.[13]

The work of Draper and other educational leaders contributed to the emergence of a body of professional literature which examined both the theoretical and practical aspects of education. During the 1880's and 1890's, American educators were stimulated by the pedagogical treatises of the German philosopher, Johann Herbart, whose work is discussed more fully later in this book. Herbart had attempted to structure a teaching methodology according to psychological principles. The American Herbartians, led by Frank and Charles McMurry, Charles De Garmo, C. C. Van Liew, and Elmer Brown, introduced Herbart's concepts of apperception, correlation, concentration, cultural epochs, and interest to American teachers. The Herbartians contributed to the enrichment of the elementary school curriculum by including literature, history, and nature study as a part of the school's program. They also wrote textbooks on teaching methods which were widely used in teacher education. In 1892, the National Herbartian Society was organized to advance the study of education as a discipline.

In the scientific movement in education, the development of statistical methods for measurement and testing was greatly aided by E. L. Thorndike's work, *An Introduction to the Theory of Mental and Social Measure-*

---

[12] Andrew S. Draper, *A Teaching Profession: An Address Before the Massachusetts State Teachers' Association, at Worcester, Massachusetts, November 28, 1890* (Albany: Weed, Parsons, and Co., 1890), p. 5.

[13] *Ibid.*, p. 10.

*ments*, 1904. J. M. Rice contributed to scientific measurement as well, with his tests designed to study spelling achievement.

As systems of education expanded and school districts grew larger, professional educators found themselves involved in intricate problems of school administration. Problems of supervision, administration, public relations, financing, and school law led to special courses in school government.

In addition to the improvements in the scientific and administrative aspects of education, its history and philosophy continued to be taught as part of the fundamental knowledge necessary to student teachers. These courses were designed to explore the most basic problems of the profession, such as the aims and purposes of education, the function of the school, and the relationship of the school to society.

## PATTERNS OF TEACHER EDUCATION

In the twentieth century, teacher education programs assumed definite patterns. Several tendencies contributed to this formalization. For one thing, the evolution of the public high school required the services of a growing number of secondary school teachers, who had to be educated. Second, as a result of the work of G. Stanley Hall and the later progressive education movement there was an increased sensitivity toward the nature of the child, which made the preparation of elementary school teachers particularly important. Third, the National Education Association and other interested organizations had been working to professionalize education, and the research of numerous scholars had created a body of educational literature which helped to make the public more aware of the needs of the public schools. While the structured programs of teacher education were a vast improvement over the chaos of the nineteenth century, tremendous variations in their quantity and quality still existed from one state to another and even from one institution to another.

The general format that emerged consisted of four major areas: a certain number of general education courses required of all students; second, a sequence of depth courses, which for prospective secondary school teachers would be in a major subject area such as English or history, and for elementary school teachers would emphasize the range of subjects and skills taught in the elementary school; third, a number of professional education courses such as history, philosophy, or sociology of education, educational psychology, and teaching methods; and fourth, a number of laboratory experiences with children and youth which would culminate in a period of supervised student teaching.

All teacher education programs now include a general education requirement which usually takes up between a third and a half of the total four-year bachelor's degree program. The courses are usually in the areas of English composition and literature, social sciences and history, physical and biological sciences and mathematics. In addition, most colleges and universities require a foreign language. There may also be specific institutional requirements such as those found in Roman Catholic colleges and universities, which usually require work in philosophy and theology. The student's choice of elective subjects fills out his individual program.[14] Although the general education requirement is found in all teacher education programs, it varies a great deal in quality. Some institutions have developed well-thought-out programs of general education, while others have programs of poor quality which consist merely of accumulating numbers of credit hours in something vaguely labeled "liberal arts."

In the second area of teacher education, that of specialization, the preparation of elementary teachers usually differs from that of secondary school teachers. As a specialization its most accurate description would be "elementary education." The courses, which correspond to the subjects and skills taught in the elementary school such as language arts, mathematics, social studies, the sciences, music, art, and physical education, are conventionally organized under such headings as the teaching of reading, the teaching of art, materials and methods in the teaching of language arts, children's literature, and others directly related to the elementary school.[15] Throughout the years, there have been recurrent attacks criticizing the specialized preparation of the elementary school teacher as being devoid of intellectual content. Its defenders, however, contend that it provides the most practical preparation for elementary school teaching.

The subject matter specialization of the secondary school teacher has also been controversial. In conventional programs, the high school teacher generally concentrates on subjects required in secondary education. For example, he majors in English, French, mathematics, history, chemistry, or another academic department, and takes professional education courses related to the teaching of his subject in the high school. The quality of academic majors also varies institutionally. While some institutions rigidly prescribe the course content of each major, others are flexible and require only a minimum number of hours in the subject. The high school teacher occupies the often difficult position of being both a subject matter specialist and a teacher of adolescents. Furthermore, he is often caught

[14] Walter K. Beggs, *The Education of Teachers* (New York: The Center for Applied Research in Education, Inc., 1965), pp. 26–27.

[15] *Ibid.*, pp. 30–32.

in a cross-fire between liberal arts professors and professional educators. The conventional teacher education program contains a professional education sequence known as the Social and Psychological Foundations of Education, which includes courses in the history and philosophy of education, sociology of education, educational psychology, growth and development and often in tests and measurements. In addition to the foundational courses, various courses are offered in educational methodology and in the use of audio-visual aids. The purpose of teaching the social, historical, and philosophical foundations of education is to give the student perspective into his profession and to relate the school to other social institutions. Philosophy of education is designed to go to the very heart of the process, examining the broad aims and purposes of education. Educational psychology deals with the learning process, the motivation of students, and evaluation of their progress. In methodological courses the prospective teacher learns to plan and organize instructional units. Like other aspects of his preparation, the teacher's professional foundation contains tremendous qualitative variations. In many instances, little correlation is made between the underlying theory and the actual practice of teaching. Critics allege that a great deal of material in the sequence is duplicated. To the teacher whose practice is guided by theory, as distinguished from the teacher who is a mere craftsman, a carefully constructed program in the foundations of education is indispensable.

A vital element in the usual pattern of a teacher's education is laboratory experience, in which he observes teaching situations and actually begins to teach. For example, the candidate may visit schools to observe a variety of situations and participate in community activities related to education. But the crucial phase of the laboratory experiences, and of the whole teacher education program, is the practice teaching in a classroom. The student teacher is given the opportunity to demonstrate his ability under the guidance of the co-operating teacher, who should be a very competent classroom practitioner, and the supervisor, a college professor of education, who should be an expert on educational methods in the student teacher's area of specialization. While some colleges and universities maintain laboratory schools for this purpose, the student is usually assigned to a public school for periods which may range from six weeks to an entire semester. Although most teachers find student teaching to be the most valuable part of their preparation, the quality of the experience depends on the quality of the school to which the student teacher is assigned and on the competence of the co-operating teacher and the supervisor under whom he practices.

While the foregoing description of regular programs of teacher education has necessarily been oversimplified, an account of this kind is necessary for an understanding of the present problems. It is also important to remember that the conventional pattern emérged neither quickly nor smoothly; its evolution began with a haphazard piecing together of courses in the early nineteenth century normal schools, and continues today. Second, over 1,100 colleges and universities offer teacher education, and each one has its own peculiarities and requirements. It is hoped that this brief explanation of teacher education programs will provide the reader with the background needed to understand something of the controversies of the 1950's and the "revolution in teacher education" which has occurred in the 1960's.


## PATTERNS OF TEACHER CERTIFICATION

The patterns of teacher certification, the granting of a license to prospective teachers attesting to some degree of competence, have been closely related to teacher education. As public education became more common and more important in the nineteenth century, a number of governmental agencies assumed control of teacher certification. As described earlier, during the eighteenth century religious and political conformity were more important requirements than pedagogical competence. By the nineteenth century, districts, towns, townships, and counties were all licensing teachers, and a confusing number of certificates existed. Such licensing agencies usually administered some kind of examination to determine the competence of applicants for teaching positions who lacked educational preparation or experience. Generally, normal school graduates were certificated without examination.

In the latter half of the nineteenth century, state superintendents or departments of education took over the function of teacher certification. Gradually, each state developed its own licensing program through which it controlled who entered the teaching profession. While this was a vast improvement over certification being granted by numerous local agencies, each state still applied its own set of qualifications.

The requirement of public schools that teachers possess bachelor's degrees appeared only very late in the nineteenth century. In 1896, Utah was the first state to require a degree for high school teaching. Gradually, other states followed. By 1920, ten states required a college degree for secondary school certification. By 1950, every state required it as a standard qualification of the beginning high school teacher.[16] Elementary teaching

16 *Ibid.*, p. 50.

lagged behind; only after World War II did the majority of states require the bachelor's degree for any kind of initial certification.[17] California was first, in 1963, requiring a minimum of five years of college for any standard teaching credentials; other states have followed since then.

Although state patterns for teacher certification have become increasingly complex, there is still little real uniformity among the states. The nature of professional preparation varies as do the number and kinds of certificates granted, and the duration of their validity. Despite differences, the following practices are common: centralization of certification authority in state departments of education; issuance of certificates for definite subjects or specified grade levels; minimum requirement of a bachelor's degree for certification; and requirement of specific courses in professional education and a definite number of courses in the teaching field.

The complexities of teacher certification have been severely criticized. In 1946, the National Education Association established the National Commission on Teacher Education and Professional Standards (the TEPS Commission), which was to continually reexamine teacher selection, recruitment, preparation, certification, in-service training, and general advancement of educational standards. Through the efforts of this Commission and other professional education organizations, the National Council for Accreditation of Teacher Education (NCATE) was established in 1952 to accredit programs of teacher education offered by colleges and universities. Upon invitation, NCATE evaluates each institution meeting the following criteria: first, it must already have been accredited by the proper regional accrediting agency and by the appropriate state department of education; second, it must be a non-profit institution of higher learning offering not less than four years of college work leading to the bachelor's degree; third, it must offer a four-year curriculum for the preparation of either elementary or secondary teachers, or both, or offer graduate programs in education.[18] Sponsors of NCATE procedures advocate the Council as a national organization for the evaluation and accreditation of qualified teacher education programs. The states would then automatically license all graduates who have successfully completed the accredited programs. By 1965, twenty-four states had agreed to accept NCATE accreditation for teacher certification, which has significantly contributed to the tendency to centralize teacher certification. NCATE detractors allege that it is inflexible and has overemphasized requirements not justified by research.

[17] *Ibid.*, pp. 50–51.
[18] *Ibid.*, pp. 74–75.

## The Conant Report

In the 1950's and 1960's, considerable criticism was directed against both the existing patterns of teacher education and the confusion which seemed to prevail in teacher certification. In 1961, the Carnegie Corporation, a private fund concerned with the improvement of teacher education, subsidized a study of teacher preparation and certification by James B. Conant, former president of Harvard University. Conant's analysis of teacher education and certification patterns, as well as his recommendations, were published in 1963 in *The Education of American Teachers*.[19]

In preparing his book, Conant visited seventy-seven institutions in twenty-two states. As he surveyed certification patterns, he analyzed the teacher education systems of the sixteen most populous states and conducted interviews with teachers, administrators, professors, students, and laymen. Finding the situation a rapidly changing one, he concluded that "no two states have adopted exactly the same requirement." In recommending a major overhauling of certification procedures, Conant suggested that the states require only that teacher candidates: 1) possess a bachelor's degree from a legitimate college or university; 2) submit evidence of successful student teaching under direction of college and public school personnel in a practice-teaching situation approved by the state department of education; 3) possess an endorsed teaching certificate from the college or university attesting to their competence to teach a designated field or grade level.[20]

The major impact of Conant's recommendations was to place the responsibility for certification on the institution that prepared the teacher. The college or university would attest that the prospective teacher had the academic, professional, and administrative qualifications to teach a specified area or subject, thus confining the specific preparation of the teacher to that institution. The state's responsibility would be to determine whether the candidate had performed successfully in the given teaching situation.

Conant concluded that practice teaching was the essential professional course in teacher education. He urged the creation of a position of "clinical professor," a master teacher who periodically taught at the same level as the candidates whom he supervised. The "clinical professor" would be chiefly responsible for supervision, for teaching courses in methodology,

[19] James B. Conant, *The Education of American Teachers* (New York: McGraw-Hill Book Company, 1963).
[20] *Ibid.*, p. 60.

for guiding the student teachers toward instructional materials, and for the planning and conducting of instruction.[21]

Conant's *The Education of American Teachers* carried numerous recommendations and criticisms of the extant patterns of teacher education and certification, which were widely disseminated and generated intense discussion. While it is too early to adequately assess the impact of the report, it seems unlikely that the major reconstruction Conant has advocated will be accepted. However, certain of his proposals have contributed to the emphasis on higher academic standards and to the creation of teaching internships which characterized the trends in teacher education in the 1960's.

## REVOLUTION IN EDUCATION: THE CRITICISM OF THE 1950'S

During the 1950's, a great debate was waged which focused public and professional attention on the quality of American education. Some critics of the public school program contended that educational standards had been lowered by a "soft pedagogy" engendered by progressive and life adjustment theorists. Defenders of public education challenged the critics by contending that the American public school system was educating more students at a higher level of quality than had ever been attempted anywhere in the world. In the light of subsequent events it already appears that that decade will mark a major watershed in American educational history. Like other major developments in this field, such as the common school and the high school, the debate of the 1950's was related to major social, political, economic, and international trends. Some examination of the climate of opinion during that period may serve to set the debate in perspective.

The precipitating factor in focusing public attention on education was the Soviet success in space. The launching of Sputnik in 1957 also launched a barrage of criticism against the quality of American education. Critics such as Admiral Hyman G. Rickover compared European and American education and found American education inadequate.[22] Rickover and others alleged that American public schools were failing to recognize academically talented students. They urged greater emphasis

[21] *Ibid.*, p. 62.
[22] H. G. Rickover, *Education and Freedom* (New York: E. P. Dutton and Company, 1959).

on mathematics and science in order to meet the Soviet challenge and to improve the academic quality of American education.

The post-World War II era brought profound social and economic changes. Automation demanded greater technological skills. Some critics accused public education of failing to properly educate people to cope with technological change. Critics such as Max Rafferty placed the onus for this failure on the influence of progressive education and the life adjustment movement, which he alleged had undermined the intellectual vitality of American education.[23]

The educational debate involved a number of charges and counter-charges in the long feud between liberal arts professors and professional educators. According to Woodring, teacher education in the United States followed two distinctive traditions: First, the liberal arts or academic concept of teacher education, which regards the purpose of education as the transmission of knowledge and intellectual discipline, has long dominated college teacher education and has considerably influenced the preparation of secondary school teachers. The other view of professional education, which emphasizes the growth of the whole child, originated in the normal schools and the teachers' colleges. This concept has strongly influenced elementary-school teaching and has also influenced secondary education somewhat by its attention to adolescent development. The patterns of teacher education that developed during the twentieth century were an unhappy merger of these two traditions.[24]

After the Supreme Court's anti-segregation decision in *Brown v. the Board of Education of Topeka* in 1954, equality of educational opportunity for Negroes and other minority groups became a nationwide concern. Attention was focused on the conditions of the culturally disadvantaged in both urban and rural slums. Civil rights leaders and others demanded an urgent reassessment of schools and their educational programs.

During the early 1950's, the arguments raised by these and other critics of the public school program and the counter-arguments of its defenders reached a fever peak. Some of the major faults found were that American public schools had deteriorated in quality, as non-intellectual programs of life adjustment and progressivism had weakened the hitherto rigorous intellectual disciplines of mathematics, science, and foreign languages that had characterized American education in the past; that neglect of academically gifted students in the public schools had resulted in

[23] For a recent statement of Rafferty's view see Max Rafferty, *What They Are Doing to Your Children* (New York: New American Library, 1963).

[24] Paul Woodring, *New Directions in Teacher Education* (New York: The Fund for the Advancement of Education, 1957), pp. 17–18.

a generally mediocre level of education; that concentration on education courses in teacher preparation had resulted in growing incompetence on the part of American teachers; and that western European systems of education were intellectually superior to the programs offered in American schools.

Professional educators, public school administrators, and teachers met the attack of the critics and challenged the validity of their arguments. Comparisons of American public education to western European educational systems were not valid since they were entirely different. The critics had ignored the fact that only a very small percentage of western Europeans attended academic schools because of rigorously administered procedures of selection which denied equality of educational opportunity to most of the population. The defenders claimed that American schools in the post-World War II era were educating more children than ever before in the nation's history. Although it might be true that educational facilities were taxed by the large numbers of students, this was not the fault of teachers or educators. Rather, more money was needed to improve facilities and increase the number of available teachers. The educators also claimed that the critics of professional education were ignorant of research in educational psychology, instructional media, and educational innovations. Finally, advocates of the American system contended that the open enrollment of public schools guaranteed equality of educational opportunity and that attention to the interests and needs of the learner reflected sound educational practices.

In the course of the controversy a number of harsh and unjustified charges were brought against the public schools. In various ways, the educational profession was used as a scapegoat to blame for many of the nation's ills. However, near the end of the 1950's, the whole subject was more dispassionately examined. While the debate had produced tensions, it had also brought about a climate of opinion in both the public and professional minds in which reconstruction of the patterns of American teacher education could profitably take place.

## Re-evaluation and Progress

The changes that came about during the late 1950's and early 1960's have been described by numerous educators as constituting a "revolution in American education." Many agencies worked together to bring them about. Both the federal government and private corporations supported projects to improve teacher preparation through changes in content and curricula; and professional educators and academic professors cooperated in educational experimentation. In assessing the progress that resulted, Francis Keppel, former U.S. Commissioner of Education, has spoken of two kinds of revolution, the quantitative and the qualitative. The first was the expansion of education to include every child in America. This part of the revolution began in the common elementary school, reached upward to the high school, and is now being extended to higher education. The second is the improvement in quality as well as equal educational opportunity to all Americans.[25]

In the years after World War II, American education faced acute challenges in both respects. In the early 1950's, the wartime babies' entrance into the schools created unprecedented pressures on the educational system. Facing a serious shortage of teachers and classrooms, the schools were forced to resort to double sessions held in emergency facilities. To cope with the overflow, more buildings, classrooms, and teachers were made available as educational expenditures increased. Near the end of the 1950's, public and professional concern shifted to the problems of providing quality education.[26] Educators began to develop new programs of teacher education designed to increase teacher competence, and they experimented with new instructional patterns. Advances were made in the harnessing of technology for educational purposes. Foundations such as the Fund for the Advancement of Education and the Carnegie Corporation encouraged research, analysis, and experimentation in teacher education. The federal government, through its Office of Education, supported the preparation of new material to be taught in the arts, languages, composition, social studies, and the vocational studies. The National Science Foundation supported experimentation in developing new mathematical, biological, and physical science curricula.[27]

Since the changes begun ten years ago continue to affect the contemporary educational situation, it is difficult to put them into historical perspective. Their implications have not yet completely penetrated the American educational system. However, three recent developments in teacher preparation are significant: the inauguration of the breakthrough programs by the Fund for the Advancement of Education; the growing federal involvement in teacher education; and the innovations being made in education today.

[25] Francis Keppel, *The Necessary Revolution in American Education* (New York: Harper & Row, Publishers, 1966), p. 1.
[26] Ronald Gross and Judith Murphy, eds., *The Revolution in the Schools* (New York: Harcourt, Brace & World, Inc., 1964), pp. 74–75.
[27] Keppel, *Revolution in American Education*, p. 114.

## "BREAKTHROUGH PROGRAMS"

In 1951 the Ford Foundation established an independent philanthropic organization called the Fund for the Advancement of Education, which has supported a number of experimental programs in American schools and colleges designed to improve teacher education.[28] While the Fund has sponsored a number of projects to improve educational management and financing, promote equalization of educational opportunity, and encourage use of educational technology, its greatest efforts have been directed toward a breakthrough in the conventional patterns of teacher education.

To encourage such a change, programs supported by the Fund have pointed the way toward new approaches in preparing liberal arts graduates for teaching careers. The breakthrough originally began with grants to twenty-eight colleges and universities.[29] The programs were carried out in two carefully planned stages. Initial grants were used for experimental programs designed to identify the desirable characteristics of teacher education. As major features of good teacher education the Foundation's Report of 1954–1956 cited the following: 1) a liberally educated teacher; 2) a scholarly knowledge of the subject to be taught; 3) development of insights into child psychology, learning processes, and the purpose of education, which were best cultivated through seminars related to the problems of the inexperienced teacher; and 4) apprentice teaching through internships.[30] Then, in the late 1950's and the 1960's, a concerted effort was made at a real breakthrough as the Fund made available an additional series of large grants for extensive experiments based on the new patterns.

While the Ford Foundation has invested over seventy million dollars in stimulating experimentation in teacher education, the new programs did not merely seek to solve problems of quantity but were based on definite philosophical foundations. In *New Directions in Teacher Education* Paul Woodring examined the qualitative aspect of teacher preparation in the United States. He criticized the "inconsistent trend toward teacher specialization" which, while stressing such specialties as physical education, guidance, or audio-visual aids, lost sight of the general purpose of

[28] Woodring, *New Directions*, pp. 3–4.

[29] James C. Stone, *The Breakthrough in Teacher Education* (San Francisco: Jossey-Bass, Inc., 1968).

[30] *Ibid.*

education.[31] For him, the primary task of quality education was to focus on the meaning and purpose of formal education:

Quality is meaningless until we can decide what is good; progress is meaningless unless we know which way is forward. All value judgments about education must rest upon an educational philosophy which, in turn, must rest upon a philosophy of man and his place in the universe.[32]

Compounding the philosophical problems confronting American education, both the theory and practice of education were vastly complicated by the rapid social changes of the twentieth century. At crucial stages in the growth of education, the introduction of new media and the creation of new areas of specialization have occurred at such a prodigious rate that they have prevented the development of a consistent philosophy which might bring order and harmony to the profession as a whole.

Woodring's critique indicated that the solution seemed to lie in the direction of requiring a broader liberal education for all teachers and school administrators. During the period of professional education greater attention should be devoted to educational philosophy, so that each teacher and administrator might see beyond the limitations of his specialty and place it in the total educational perspective. According to Woodring, the liberally educated teacher will be able to see his subject in this broader perspective.[33]

## Master of Arts in Teaching

During the late 1950's and the 1960's, the Master of Arts in Teaching emerged as an academic degree that was developed from various "Fifth Year" programs. Although the concept of the "fifth year" had originated at Harvard in 1936, it did not receive significant national attention until after World War II. The Harvard approach then gained renewed prominence in light of the acute teacher shortage and the controversies surrounding conventional patterns of teacher education. The "fifth year" program at Harvard was the first to be supported by the Fund for the Advancement of Education. The Master of Arts in Teaching became the major component in the Fund's breakthrough programs.

The majority of the almost two hundred "fifth year" pre-service teacher education programs were established after 1950. Although they varied in detail, they all emphasized a strong liberal arts content, inten-

[31] Woodring, New Directions, p. 10.
[32] Ibid., p. 4.
[33] Ibid., pp. 10–11.

sive subject matter specialization, concentrated professional education sequences, and carefully supervised practice teaching, usually in the form of subsidized internships. The teacher internship, a crucial part of the breakthrough programs, differed from the conventional student teaching situation in that the internship was a paid teaching assignment holding the intern legally accountable for his instruction. While the student-teaching experience was conventionally the culminating experience in the older pattern, the subsidized internship was designed as the central integrating experience in the newer breakthrough program. The typical "fifth year" program was designed to attract liberal arts graduates who lacked undergraduate preparation in professional education. Although called a "fifth year," the concentrated postgraduate preparation varied in length from a six-week summer term to two full academic years. While it led variously to a graduate degree or a teaching certificate, the Master of Arts in Teaching has become the degree most frequently awarded.

According to Woodring, the Master of Arts in Teaching represents a synthesis of the positive features of the conventional Master of Arts and Master of Education degrees. MAT programs are usually planned jointly by the faculties of arts and science and of professional education and are designed for secondary teachers who need both professional preparation and scholarly competence.[34] Woodring has asserted that the Master of Arts in Teaching was probably the first program for the preparation of secondary teachers to recognize that high school teaching was distinct from both elementary and college teaching. The MAT concept rejected both the notion that academic scholarship was the only essential for successful teaching and the view that the high school teacher's preparation should be similar to that of the elementary teacher.[35]

The Graduate Internship Teacher Education Program of the School of Education of the University of California at Berkeley, inaugurated in 1956, was an experiment conducted to increase the supply of secondary-school teachers and to improve the conventional pattern of their preparation at the same time. This experiment rested on several premises which also underlay most of the later breakthrough programs: 1) joint responsibility of the university and the public schools for teacher preparation; 2) cooperation between the education and academic departments within the university; 3) emphasis on the relationship between theory and practice;

[34] *Ibid.*, p. 46.
[35] Paul Woodring, "The Need for a Unifying Theory of Teacher Education," in Elmer R. Smith, ed., *Teacher Education: A Reappraisal* . . . (New York: Harper & Row, Publishers, 1962), pp. 147–48.

4) emphasis on the need for experimental and multiple programs within an institution.[36]

Admission to the Berkeley program was restricted to college graduates who had had little or no course work in professional education. The interns were required to have a teaching contract for public school positions which they would hold the following fall. Thus, the internship provided a year of full-time public-school teaching experience. Before embarking on the year's teaching, the interns enrolled in a summer program of teaching and related seminars which provided early direct experience with classroom situations. An important feature of the internship program was the deliberate interrelationship of theory and practice which sought to avoid the bifurcation that characterized some conventional programs of teacher education. The basic method of instruction was the seminar and conference rather than the lecture.[37]

The Master of Arts in Teaching Program of the University of Chicago, which enrolled its first students in 1960, is still another example of the trend toward the "fifth year" degree. In this program three basic features stood out: increased subject matter competence, a strong theoretical foundation in professional education, and extended practice teaching. Since these features appear in many MAT programs, it will be helpful to examine the University of Chicago program more closely.

MAT programs usually require that the student enroll in a number of graduate courses in the field of subject matter specialization. The University of Chicago program emphasized that prospective secondary school teachers should do a substantial amount of graduate work in the teaching field under the guidance of competent research scholars. The basic assumption was that effective teaching required a solid body of knowledge in the subject as well as an understanding of the methods of inquiry by which knowledge in the field is discovered, tested, revised, and extended.[38] To relate theory to practice, the Chicago program stressed seminars to give the prospective teacher an opportunity to work with scholars conducting philosophical, historical, and psychological inquiry into the learning processes and into the function of educational institutions. The major contribution of the seminars was to develop general theoretical

[36] James C. Stone and Clark N. Robinson, *The Graduate Internship Program in Teacher Education* (Berkeley and Los Angeles: University of California Press, 1965), pp. 5–7.

[37] *Ibid.*, p. v.

[38] Hugo E. Beck, "The Teacher-Scholar: A Two-Year Program," in National Commission on Teacher Education and Professional Standards, *Changes in Teacher Education: An Appraisal* (Washington: National Education Association of the United States, 1964), pp. 113–15.

principles on which specific practices could be built. To develop teaching proficiency, an extended experience in teaching was included.[39]

## Impact of Breakthrough Programs

The breakthrough programs represented one significant innovative approach to restructuring American teacher education. They were designed to broaden the context of teacher education so that there might be a number of alternative patterns of preparation in addition to the conventional one discussed earlier. Since the programs were experimental, it is difficult to assess completely the impact they will have on American teacher education. However, with experiments of any kind, whether social, political, economic, or educational, there comes a time to evaluate past action and to plot the future course. James Stone, Director of Teacher Education at the University of California at Berkeley, has surveyed the programs supported by the Ford Foundation, and commented on their major accomplishments and deficiencies.[40]

A significant accomplishment of the breakthrough program has been the high quality of students attracted to and graduating from them. Prior to their admission the students were specially recruited and selected, then carefully guided through the program. New sources of teacher supply were also discovered among groups not usually interested in the conventional curricula. While the old programs had appealed to liberal arts graduates in general, such particular groups as housewives, older men, and returning military personnel were attracted to the new ones. Graduates of breakthrough programs also tended to remain in educational work.[41]

Stone found that the new programs emphasized increased subject matter content as a part of teacher education. Funds were used to introduce innovative instructional techniques and materials into the teaching of academic subject matter such as history, English, mathematics, science, and other disciplines usually offered in the secondary curriculum. The programs also extended the period for teacher preparation through the master's degree. Since public school staffs co-operated directly with college professors in pre-service teacher education, the alliance between the high school and the college was strengthened. School principals and supervisors were given a role in selecting, assigning, and evaluating the interns. Stone regarded these features of the breakthrough programs as con-

[39] Ibid.
[40] Stone, Breakthrough, p. 167.
[41] Ibid., pp. 167–69.

structive achievements of the experiment to improve teacher education.[42]

While he viewed the venture as basically successful, Stone found several deficiencies in it as well. One major weakness was the attempt by some institutions to plan more projects than could be realistically accomplished in the allotted space of time. Some of the projects failed to utilize the latest educational innovations. For example, no more than fifteen per cent of the interns worked with such new techniques as team teaching, educational television, and programmed learning. In some situations, "internship" was merely a new label for the conventional student teaching experience. Since the programs were geared to secondary education, little experimentation was carried on in elementary schools.[43] In some of the professional education seminars, and in a number of breakthrough programs, Stone found a wide discrepancy still existing between theory and practice.[44]

## FEDERAL INVOLVEMENT IN
## TEACHER EDUCATION

The same forces which activated the interest of the private corporations in teacher education also stimulated federal involvement. Through the National Defense Education Act, passed in 1958 and extended in 1964, funds were made available to upgrade the background of teachers in the areas of science, mathematics, foreign languages, counseling, and guidance. In teaching foreign languages, the aim shifted from a mere reading knowledge of the language to the more comprehensive goal of understanding, writing, and speaking it as well. Russian and Chinese were added to the usual French and Spanish. Utilization of tape recorders permitted students to hear the language spoken by natives. The increase of foreign language laboratory installations from 46 in 1958 to more than 7,000 in 1965 was encouraged substantially by NDEA funds.[45]

In his educational message of 1962, President Kennedy advised Congress of the significant advances being made in the discovery and transmission of knowledge. While the special institutes of the National Science Foundation and the Office of Education were instrumental in keeping teachers up-to-date, he felt that the opportunities for attending these institutes were still too limited and needed improving. Further, President Kennedy felt that there was a definite need for higher standards in teacher

---

[42] *Ibid.*, pp. 172–74.
[43] *Ibid.*, pp. 177–78.
[44] *Ibid.*, pp. 181–82.
[45] Keppel, *Revolution in American Education*, p. 128.

education, in both course content and instructional methods. He urged that teacher education institutions be given federal assistance in examining and improving their programs.[46] The President felt that:

> . . . the key to educational quality is the teaching profession. About 1 out of every 5 of the nearly 1,600,000 teachers in our elementary and secondary schools fails to meet full certification standards for teaching or has not completed 4 years of college work. Our immediate concern should be to afford them every possible opportunity to improve their professional skills and their command of the subjects they teach.[47]

Although Kennedy encouraged general aid to education legislation, it was not enacted as a program until 1965, when President Johnson proposed aid to elementary, secondary, and higher education, both private and public. The passage of the Johnson legislation revealed a shift in the congressional attitude toward school assistance. In the past, Congress had been inclined to enact specific programs rather than general aid legislation. The more successful bills were those designed to improve a specific type of instruction, such as vocational education under the Smith-Hughes Law, or mathematics and science under the National Defense Education Act. The Elementary and Secondary Education Act of 1965, which represented the first general coverage legislation to be voted for elementary and secondary schools, contained the following provisions: Title I, "Federal Assistance for Local Educational Agencies for the Education of Children of Low-Income Families," was designed to assist schedules of school construction and the development of special programs to aid educationally deprived children. Title II proposed to correct the inadequacies of teaching materials with a five-year program designed to make books and other printed materials available to school children. These funds were allotted to the purchase of library books, textbooks, periodicals, magnetic tapes, phonograph records, and other materials. Title III provided for the establishment of model schools, pilot programs, and community centers designed to supplement the offerings of local school systems in such areas as continuing adult education, guidance and counseling, remedial instruction, special educational services, enriched academic programs, and health. Title IV stressed improvement of educational research, the dissemination of information to teachers and teacher training institutions, and the establishment of regional educational laboratories. Title V was in-

---

[46] John F. Kennedy, *Message from the President of the United States Relative to an Educational Program*, H. R. Document No. 330 (Washington: U.S. Government Printing Office, Feb. 6, 1962), p. 5.

[47] *Ibid.*, pp. 4–5.

tended to help state departments of education administer the new programs.

In the 1960's, the federal government decided to finance educational research and development on a scale unprecedented in American history. The implications of this decision were felt not only by teacher education but throughout the whole discipline. First, the long-standing debate between proponents and opponents of federal aid to education began to subside. The passage of the Act of 1965 seemed to indicate clearly that Congress had indeed determined to assist American education. Second, education became recognized as a national responsibility. Presidential addresses and congressional legislation revealed the concern of the federal government for the quantity and quality of American education. Third, federal responses had shifted from specific aid or emergency programs to general aid. The scope of federal assistance had also broadened from concentration upon higher education to embrace all levels of education.

## EDUCATIONAL INNOVATIONS

During the late 1950's and early 1960's, concerted efforts were made to revolutionize means of instruction. Basic to the instructional revolution was the thorough investigation of the learning process, from which conclusions were drawn as to the most efficient use of the new educational technology. New administrative and organizational patterns were devised to carry out those changes in the schools that would facilitate the new instructional methods. Francis Keppel, former Commissioner of Education, has referred to education as America's largest industry. In the mid-1960's, there were 123,000 schools, 55 million school pupils and college students, nearly 2.4 million teachers, 100,000 administrators and supervisors, and 144,000 public school board members. While the total cost of education was thirty-nine billion dollars annually, less than one-half of one per cent of the national educational expenditure was being devoted to research to improve the process.[48] Despite this weakness, some major innovations were made in the 1960's.

Gross and Murphy have examined the major factors in the educational revolution. Scholars and scientists conducted research which led them to a profound understanding of the basic structure of their disciplines. This analysis helped define the necessary elements of a subject and construct a teaching strategy based upon that structure. Subsequent curricular and

[48] Keppel, *Revolution in American Education*, p. 121.

methodological revisions led to the "new" mathematics, physics, and biology. The financial contributions of private foundations such as Ford and Carnegie created an impetus of urgency and responsibility. Experimental psychologists such as B. F. Skinner and Jerome S. Bruner also advanced the educational revolution, Skinner by his contributions to the programmed learning movement, and Bruner by introducing the concepts of "structure," "intuition," and "discovery." School administrators and classroom teachers found an essential link by implementing the innovations in school practices and by bridging the tenuous gap between theory and practice.[49]

The curricular and instructional revolution of the 1960's naturally had ramifications in teacher education. Many experiments such as the breakthrough program were designed with the intention of training prospective teachers in the use of the new technology. Although new courses have been designed in the use of educational television, programmed learning, and the "new mathematics," only minor inroads were made into the structure of the conventional patterns. Even the breakthrough programs suffered from this weakness.

Before the major implications of the educational innovations of the 1960's are discussed, some description of the new patterns is in order. Team teaching, one of the first innovations to attract widespread attention in educational circles, has been defined as:

> . . . an effort to improve instruction by the reorganization of personnel in teaching. Two or more teachers are given responsibility, working together, for all, or a significant part of the instruction of the same group of students.[50]

As a cooperative form of organization, administration, and instruction, this method enables two or more teachers with complementary academic strengths who work on a "regular and purposeful basis to plan, to prepare, to present, and to evaluate learning experiences." [51] One anticipated outcome is that teachers and students may develop special areas of competence and be able to use these assets most advantageously.

Woodring has suggested that the team concept will also alter conventional teacher education programs in that classroom teachers will need less specialized training but a more thorough grasp of the whole educational process. While not needing to be highly proficient in all subjects,

[49] Gross and Murphy, *Revolution in the Schools*, p. 2.
[50] Judson T. Shaplin, "Team Teaching," in *Ibid.*, p. 93.
[51] Melvin P. Heller, "Team Teaching: Professionalism for Professionals," *Catholic High School Quarterly Bulletin*, XXIII, 4 (January, 1966), 1.

the teacher should have the broadest kind of liberal education and a professional knowledge of the learner and the learning process. Finally, all teachers will need to be educated to work effectively as team members.[52] The implementation of the team teaching concept requires new arrangements of space and time. Larger time sequences are needed for instruction. Classroom space must be arranged to accommodate larger groups for part of the day and smaller groups at other periods.

Educational television is an example of the successful instructional use of the new technology. Early in the 1950's educators began to experiment with educational television. In 1957, Alexander J. Stoddard initiated the National Program in the Use of Television in the Schools which was financed by the Ford Foundation's Fund for the Advancement of Education. In 1961, the six-state Midwest Program on Airborne Television Instruction, located at Purdue University, began to broadcast lessons to schools and colleges from high-flying airplanes. A major open circuit effort was the "Chicago College of the Air" which televised credit courses over WTTW, the educational television channel in Chicago. Closed circuit television is now used at all levels of education.[53] Today more than ten million students have received part of their formal education via television.[54]

The educational revolution of the 1960's also drew attention to the so-called "teaching machines" with programmed instruction. This system was a means of bringing the student to concept formation through a series of carefully graduated steps which provided him at the same time with a means of self-evaluation. Since the student was able to realize his successes and errors as rapidly as he made them, he could proceed at his own rate of speed. Programmed instruction, in the form of books or boxes, was particularly adaptable to the study of subjects which could be easily reduced to elemental steps. Programs in grammar, foreign languages, logic, and mathematics were developed.[55]

In addition to team teaching, educational television, and programmed instruction, numerous new ideas such as the nongraded school and individualized instruction were tried out. The growing problems of the inner city schools and culturally disadvantaged youth focused attention on the preparation of methods and materials designed to reach the children of the poor. The advances in educational technology made more sophisticated programs of teacher education necessary.

[52] Woodring, New Directions, p. 75.

[53] Theodore R. Conant, "Teaching by Television," in Gross and Murphy, Revolution in the Schools, pp. 32–35.

[54] Keppel, Revolution in American Education, pp. 129–30.

[55] Ibid., pp. 127–28.

If teacher education programs are to avoid the discrepancy between theory and practice, teacher preparation must provide experience with instructional technology. Although the new techniques and instruments are significant, it is important to keep them in proper perspective. They are merely instruments to be used by the teacher. They can serve many purposes, both good and ill. The essential element in education is a teacher with a broad philosophical perspective, who can use these technological innovations to advance man's rationality.

The effects of the new instructional technology on education should be cautiously interpreted. In the past, the educational establishment has strongly resisted change. Although originally introduced with vitality, many educational innovations later became formalized. New labels were used but instruction remained tied to traditional ways.

Although the experimental programs have made progress, it has usually required a lengthy period of time for reform to reach the schools. Concerted nationwide efforts by private foundations and the federal government may reduce this time lag. Despite the growing tendency to view education on a national level, the actual execution of the reforms remains with local administrators, teachers, and school districts.

## CONCLUSION:
## TRENDS IN TEACHER EDUCATION

The historical record clearly indicates the profound changes that have occurred in American teacher education. The unskilled school-keeper of colonial days has been replaced by the competent teacher who brings professional expertise to education. The one-room country schoolhouse of the frontier has been replaced by the massive complexes which are today's elementary and secondary schools. In the context of a complicated technological, industrialized, urban society, teaching can no longer remain the simple transmission of the basic skills of reading, writing, and arithmetic. Modern teachers find themselves participating in a complex process which has intellectual, social, ethical, political, economic, and aesthetic consequences for all those whom they seek to educate. Since education is so significant a process, it is not surprising that teachers find themselves scrutinized by a public which ranges from the concerned parent to the nation's President. Since American schools are a public concern, the professional preparation of American teachers will always be closely studied and by the same token subject to controversy. Although teacher education has undergone significant transformation since the 1950's, it is possible to survey briefly some of the major trends which seem likely to shape the patterns of the future:

1. Many teacher education programs are experiencing a great increase in the areas of general education and subject matter specialization. Since the 1950's, the trend has been toward higher "intellectual" or "academic" standards. While this has been especially true in the case of the secondary-school programs, elementary education has in some cases responded by also requiring subject matter specialization. 2. Variations in the professional education sequence still exist from state to state. However, every state requires a minimum of eighteen semester hours of professional course work for elementary teachers, and at the secondary level a minimum of twelve hours.[56] Significant experiments have been made in the structuring of the professional sequences as the teaching experience and related courses are concentrated within a single year or semester. The student is exposed to a concentrated sequence of professional courses within a relatively short period so that he may clearly see and understand the relationship between theory and practice. 3. The use of internships has attracted considerable attention. The teacher candidate is placed in a classroom situation where he learns the practice of teaching under the guidance of both the supervisors of the training institution and the faculty in the school. He is given the opportunity to synthesize his experiences in a series of seminars with his supervisors. He and his fellow apprentices discuss together the problems, methods, and materials related to the teaching experience. 4. Most states require a bachelor's degree following four years of successful collegiate preparation. Some states have added a fifth year requirement and others are moving in that direction. 5. State certification arrangements are being subjected to intensive study and reform. Some changes have been made in the direction of facilitating reciprocity, which makes it easier for teachers to be certified in a number of states. Other states have adopted "approved programs" approaches by which colleges and universities submit their teacher education course to the state for approval. Graduates of such approved programs are then automatically certified as teachers.

Teaching has come a long way from the lowly status it held during the colonial period to the present-day stress on teachers who are well trained to provide quality education for American youth. In recent times, some observers have related the quality of American education to national survival itself. In the United States, the educational program has expanded with an unparalleled rapidity. The American school is a major social institution which has assumed its share of responsibilities in shaping the nation. In the light of these responsibilities, teaching is a kind of leadership

[56] James B. Conant, *Education of American Teachers*, pp. 43–46.

resembling that exercised by statesmen who plot the course of the national experience. Prospective teachers need to be aware of the relationship which the school bears to the "great society" and to the future course of the American experience.

## References

ANDERSON, ROBERT H. *Teaching in a World of Change.* New York: Harcourt, Brace & World, Inc. 1966.

BARNARD, HENRY. *Normal Schools, and Other Institutions, Agencies, and Means Designed for the Professional Education of Teachers.* Hartford: Case, Tiffany, and Company, 1851.

BEGGS, WALTER K. *The Education of Teachers.* New York: The Center for Applied Research in Education, Inc., 1965.

CONANT, JAMES G. *The Education of American Teachers.* New York: McGraw-Hill Book Company, 1963.

COUNTS, GEORGE S. *The Social Foundations of Education.* New York: Charles Scribner's Sons, 1934.

DRAPER, ANDREW S. *A Teaching Profession: An Address Before the Massachusetts State Teachers' Association, at Worcester, Massachusetts, November 28, 1890.* Albany: Weed, Parsons, and Co., 1890.

*Elementary and Secondary Education Act of 1965,* Public Law 89–10, 89th Cong., H.R. 2362, April 11, 1965.

ELSBREE, W. S. *The American Teacher.* New York: American Book Company, 1939.

GROSS, RONALD, and MURPHY, JUDITH, eds. *The Revolution in the Schools.* New York: Harcourt, Brace & World, Inc., 1964.

HALL, SAMUEL. *Lectures to School-Masters on Teaching.* Boston: Carter, Hendee and Co., 1833.

HARPER, CHARLES. *A Century of Public Teacher Education.* Washington: National Education Association, 1939.

HELLER, MELVIN P. "Team Teaching: Professionalism for Professionals." *Catholic High School Quarterly Bulletin,* XXIII, No. 4 (January, 1966).

KENNEDY, JOHN F. *Message from the President of the United States Relative to an Educational Program.* H.R. Document No. 330, Feb. 6, 1962.

KEPPEL, FRANCIS. *The Necessary Revolution in American Education.* New York: Harper & Row, Publishers, 1966.

National Commission on Teacher Education and Professional Standards. *Changes in Teacher Education: An Appraisal.* Washington: National Education Association of the United States, 1964.

PAGE, DAVID P. *Theory and Practice of Teaching or the Motives and Methods of Good School-Keeping.* New York: A. S. Barnes and Co., 1885.

RAFFERTY, MAX. *What They Are Doing to Your Children.* New York: New American Library, 1963.

RICKOVER, H. G. *Education and Freedom.* New York: E. P. Dutton and Company, 1959.

SMITH, ELMER R., ed. *Teacher Education: A Reappraisal: Report of a Conference Sponsored by the Fund for the Advancement of Education.* New York: Harper & Row, Publishers, 1962.

STONE, JAMES C. *The Breakthrough in Teacher Education: A Study of the Impact of Venture Capital in Forty-two Colleges and Universities.* San Francisco: Jossey-Bass, Inc., 1968.

————, and HEMPSTEAD, ROSS. *California Education Today.* New York: Thomas Y. Crowell Company, 1968.

————, and ROBINSON, CLARK N. *The Graduate Internship Program in Teacher Education.* Berkeley and Los Angeles: University of California Press, 1965.

WOODRING, PAUL. "A Century of Teacher Education." In *A Century of Higher Education,* William Brickman and Stanley Lehrer, eds. New York: Society for the Advancement of Education, 1962.

————. *New Directions in Teacher Education.* New York: The Fund for the Advancement of Education, 1957.

# SELECTIONS

*The selection below is from Samuel R. Hall's Lectures to School-Masters on Teaching, 1833. Hall's Lectures was one of the first books written in the United States about teaching. As a lecturer and essayist on teacher education, Hall drew attention to the problem of preparing enough adequately trained teachers to staff the common district schools.*

## Lectures to School-Masters on Teaching

Having adverted in the preceding Lecture, to certain existing evils, unfriendly to the character and usefulness of common schools, I shall, in this, call your attention to *the requisite qualifications of an instructer*. This subject is of high importance. All who possess the requisite *literary* attainments, are not qualified to assume the direction of a school. Many entirely fail of usefulness, though possessed of highly cultivated minds. Other things are required in the character of a good school-master. Among these, *common sense* is the first. This is a qualification exceedingly important, as in teaching school one has constant occasion for its exercise. Many, by no means deficient in intellect, are not persons of *common* sense. I mean by the term, that faculty by which things are seen as they are. It implies judgment and discrimination, and a proper sense of propriety in regard to the common affairs of life. It leads us to form judicious plans of action, and to be governed by our circumstances, in the way which men in general will approve. It is the exercise of reason, uninfluenced by passion or prejudice. It is in man nearly what instinct is in brutes. Very different from genius or talent, as they are commonly defined, it is better than either. Never blazing forth with the splendor of noon, but it shines with a constant and useful light.

2. *Uniformity of temper* is another important trait in the character of an instructer. Where this is wanting, it is hardly possible to govern or to teach with success. He, whose temper is constantly varying, can never be uniform in his estimation of things around him. Objects change in their appearance as his passions change. What appears right in any given hour may seem wrong in the next. What appears desirable to-day, may be beheld with aversion tomorrow. An uneven temper, in any situation of life, subjects one to many inconveniences. But when

SOURCE: Samuel R. Hall, *Lectures to School-Masters on Teaching* (Boston: Carter, Hendee and Co., 1833), pp. 31–42.

placed in a situation where his every action is observed and where his authority, must be in constant exercise, the man who labors under this malady is especially unfortunate. It is impossible for him to gain and preserve respect among his pupils. No one who comes under the rule of a person of uneven temper, can know what to expect or how to act.

3. A capacity to *understand and discriminate character*, is highly important to him who engages in teaching. The dispositions of children are so various, the treatment and government of parents so dissimilar, that the most diversified modes of governing and teaching need to be employed. The instructer who is not able to discriminate, but considers all alike, and treats all alike, does injury to many. The least expression of disapprobation to one, is often more than the severest reproof to another; a word of encouragement will be sufficient to excite attention in some, while others will require to be urged, by every motive that can be placed before them. All the varying shades of disposition and capacity should be quickly learned by the instructer, that he may benefit all and do injustice to none. Without this, well meant efforts may prove hurtful, because ill-directed, and the desired object may be defeated, by the very means used to obtain it.

4. Teachers should possess much *decision of character*. In every situation of life this trait is important, but in none more so, than in that of which I am treating. The little world, by which he is surrounded, is a miniature of the older community. Children have their aversions and partialities, their hopes and fears, their plans, schemes, propensities and desires. These are often in collision with each other and not unfrequently in collision with the laws of the school, and in opposition to the best interest of themselves. Amidst all these, the instructer should be able to pursue a uniform course. He ought not to be easily swayed from what he considers right. If easily led from his purpose, or induced to vary from established rules, his school must become a scene of disorder. Without decision, the teacher loses the confidence and respect of his pupils. I would not say, that, if, convinced of having committed an error, or of having given a wrong judgment, you should persist in the wrong. But I would say, it should be known as one of your first principles in school-keeping, that what is required must be complied with in every case, unless cause can be shown why the rule ought, in a given instance, to be dispensed with. There should *then* be a frank and easy compliance with the reasonable wish of the scholar. In a word, without decision of purpose in a teacher, his scholars can never be brought under that kind of discipline, which is requisite for his own ease and convenience, or for the improvement in knowledge, of those placed under him.

5. A schoolmaster ought to be *affectionate*. The human heart is so constituted, that it cannot resist the influence of kindness. When affectionate intercourse is the offspring of those kind feelings which arise from true benevolence, it will have an influence on all around. It leads to ease in behavior, and genuine politeness of manners. It is especially desirable in those who are surrounded by the young. Affectionate parents usually see their children exhibit similar feelings. Instructers who cultivate affection, will generally excite the same in their scholars. No object is more important than to gain the love and good will of those we

are to teach. In no way is this more easily accomplished than by a kind interest manifested in their welfare; an interest which is exhibited by actions as well as words. This cannnot fail of being attended with desirable results.

6. A just *moral discernment,* is of pre-eminent importance in the character of an instructer. Unless governed by a consideration of his moral obligation, he is but poorly qualified to discharge the duties which devolve upon him. He is himself a moral agent, and accountable to himself, to his employers, to his country and to his God, for the faithful discharge of duty. If he have no moral sensibility, no fear of disobeying the laws of God, no regard for the institutions of our holy religion, how can he be expected to lead his pupils in the way that they should go? The cultivation of virtuous propensities is more important to children than even their intellectual culture. The *virtuous* man, though illiterate, will be happy, while the learned, if *vicious,* must be miserable in proportion to his attainments. The remark of the ancient philosopher, that 'boys ought to be taught that which they will most need to practise when they come to be men,' is most true. To cultivate virtuous habits, and awaken virtuous principles;—to excite a sense of duty to God and of dependence on Him, should be the first objects of the teacher. If he permits his scholars to indulge in vicious habits—if he regard nothing as sin, but that which is a transgression of the laws of the school, if he suffer lying, profaneness, or other crimes, to pass unnoticed and unpunished, he is doing an injury for which he can in no way make amends. An instructer without moral feeling, not only brings ruin to the children placed under his care, but does injury to their parents, to the neighborhood, to the town and, doubtless, to other generations. The moral character of instructers should be considered a subject of very high importance; and let every one, who knows himself to be immoral, renounce at once the thought of such an employment, while he continues to disregard the laws of God, and the happiness of his fellow men. Genuine piety is highly desirable in every one entrusted with the care and instruction of the young; but morality, at least should be *required,* in every candidate for that important trust.

7. Passing over many topics connected with those already mentioned, I shall now remark on the necessary literary qualifications of a schoolmaster. It will at once be apparent that no one is qualified for this business, who has not a thorough knowledge of the branches required to be taught in common schools. These are Reading, Spelling, Writing, Grammar, Arithmetic, Geography, and in some states the History of the United States. All these branches are necessary, to enable individuals to perform the common business and common duties of life. The four first are requisite in writing a letter on business or to a friend. The fifth is required in the business transactions of every day. The two last are necessary to enable every one to understand what he reads in the common newspapers, or in almost every book which comes within his reach. Of each of these branches, the instructer should certainly have a thorough knowledge; for he ought to have a full knowledge of what he is to teach. As he is to lay the *foundation* of an education, he should be well acquainted with the first principles of science. Of the letters of the alphabet such disposition is made, as to produce an immense num-

ber of words, to each of which a distinct meaning is given. 'The nature and power of letters, and just method of spelling words,' should be very distinctly understood. If there be defect in *knowledge* here, there must be a defect in teaching. A man cannot be expected to teach that which he does not know himself. Among all the defects I have witnessed in the literary qualification of instructers, the most common, by far the most common, have been here. Among a great number, both of males and females, I have found *very few* who possessed the requisite knowledge of the nature and power of letters, and rules of spelling. The defect originates in the fact, that these subjects are neglected after childhood, and much that is learned then is subsequently forgotten. Teachers, afterwards, especially of academies, presume that these subjects are familiar, and seldom make the inquiry of scholars, whether they have sufficient knowledge on these points. As a considerable part of every school is composed of those who are learning to spell and read, much importance is attached to the requisite qualifications of the teacher, to lay a proper foundation for subsequent attainments.

---

*Henry Barnard, Superintendent of Common Schools of Connecticut, devoted effort to advancing the cause of popular education. He recognized that the success of the common school movement depended upon well-ordered teacher educational institutions. To advance the cause of the normal school, Barnard collected a number of documents designed to promote the professional education of teachers. The "First Annual Circular of the State Normal School at New Britain," Connecticut was included in Barnard's work on normal schools.*

# First Annual Circular of the State Normal School at New Britain

The State Normal School or "Seminary for the training of teachers in the art of teaching and governing the Common Schools" of Connecticut was established by act of the legislature, May session, 1849, and the sum of eleven thousand dollars was appropriated for its support for a period of at least four years.

The sum appropriated for the support of the school is derived not from the income of the School Fund, or any of the ordinary resources of the Treasury, but from a bonus of ten thousand dollars paid by the State Bank, at Hartford, and of

SOURCE: Henry Barnard, *Normal Schools, and Other Institutions, Agencies, and Means Designed for the Professional Education of Teachers* (Hartford: Case, Tiffany and Co., 1851), pp. 47–50.

$1,000 paid by the Deep River Bank, for their respective charters. No part of this sum can be expended in any building or fixtures for the school, or for the compensation of the trustees.

The entire management of the Institution as to the application of the funds, the location of the school, the regulation of the studies and exercises, and the granting of diplomas, is committed to a Board of Trustees, consisting of the Superintendent of Common Schools, ex officio, and one member for each of the eight counties of the state, appointed by the Legislature, two in each year, and to hold their office for the term of four years, and serve without compensation. The Board must submit an annual report as to their own doings, and the progress and condition of the seminary.

The Normal School was located permanently in New Britain, on the 1st of February, 1850, after full consideration of the claims and offers of other towns, on account of the central position of the town in the state, and its accessibility from every section by railroad; and also in consideration of the liberal offer on the part of its citizens to provide a suitable building, apparatus, and library, to the value of $16,000 for the use of the Normal School, and to place all the schools of the village under the management of the Principal of the Normal School, as Schools of Practice.

The Building provided for the accommodation of the Normal School, and the Schools of Practice, when completed will contain three large study-halls, with nine class-rooms attached, a hall for lectures and exhibitions, a laboratory for chemical and philosophical experiments, an office for the Principal and trustees, a room for the library, and suitable accommodations for apparatus, clothes, furnaces, fuel &c. The entire building will be fitted up and furnished in the most substantial manner, and with special reference to the health, comfort and successful labor of pupils and teachers. In addition to the Normal School building, there are three houses located in different parts of the village for the accommodation of the primary schools belonging to the Schools of Practice.

The immediate charge of the Normal School and Schools of Practice, is committed to Rev. T. D. P. Stone, Associate Principal, to whom all communications relating to the schools can be addressed.

The school was opened for the reception of pupils on Wednesday, the 15th of May, 1850, and the first term closed on Tuesday, October 1st. The number of pupils in attendance during the term was sixty-seven; thirty males, and thirty-seven females.

The second term will commence on Wednesday, the 4th of December, 1850, and continue till the third Wednesday in April, 1851, divided into two sessions as given below.

*Terms and vacations.* The year is divided into two terms, Summer and Winter, each term consisting of two sessions.

The first session of the winter term commences on the first Wednesday of December, and continues fourteen weeks. The second session of the winter term commences on the third Wednesday of March, and continues six weeks.

The first session of the summer term commences on the third Wednesday of May, and continues twelve weeks. The second session of the summer term commences on the third Wednesday of August, and continues six weeks.

To accommodate pupils already engaged in teaching, the short session of each term will, as far as shall be found practicable, be devoted to a review of the studies pursued in the district schools in the season of the year immediately following, and to a course of familiar lectures on the classification, instruction and discipline of such schools.

*Admission of pupils.* The highest number of pupils which can be received in any one term, is two hundred and twenty.

Each school society is entitled to have one pupil in the school; and no society can have more than one in any term, so long as there are applicants from any society, at the time unrepresented. Until the whole number of pupils in actual attendance shall reach the highest number fixed by law, the Principal is authorized to receive all applicants who may present themselves, duly recommended by the visitors of any school society.

Any person, either male or female, may apply to the school visitors of any school society for admission to the school, who will make a written declaration, that their object in so applying is to qualify himself (or herself) for the employment of a common school teacher, and that it is his (or her) intention to engage in that employment, in this state.

The school visitors are authorized to forward to the Superintendent of Common Schools, in any year, the names of four persons, two of each sex, who shall have applied as above, for admission to the school, and who shall have been found on examination by them, "possessed of the qualifications required of teachers of common schools in this state," and whom they "shall recommend to the trustees as suitable persons, by their age, character, talents, and attainments, to be received as pupils in the Normal School."

Applicants duly recommended by the school visitors, can forward their certificate directly to the Associate Principal of the Normal School at New Britain, who will inform them of the time when they must report themselves to be admitted to any vacant places in the school.

Persons duly recommended, and informed of their admission, must report themselves within the first week of the term for which they are admitted, or their places will be considered as vacated.

Any persons, once regularly admitted to the Normal School, can remain connected with the same for three years, and will not lose their places, by temporary absence in teaching common schools in the state—such experience, in connection with the instruction of the Institution, being considered a desirable part of a teacher's training.

*Studies.* The course of instruction will embrace: 1. A thorough review of the studies pursued in the lowest grade of common schools. 2. An acquaintance with such studies as are embraced in the highest grade of common schools, authorized by law, and which will render the teaching of the elementary branch more thorough and interesting. 3. The art of teaching and its methods, including the history and progress of education, the philosophy of teaching and discipline, as drawn from the nature of the juvenile mind, and the application of those principles under the ordinary conditions of our common schools.

The members of the school will be arranged in three classes—Junior, Middle and Senior. All pupils on being admitted to the school, will be ranked in the *Junior Class*, until their familiarity with the studies of the lowest grade of common schools have been satisfactorily tested. The *Middle Class* will embrace those who are pursuing the branches usually taught in Public High Schools. The *Senior Class* will comprise those who are familiar with the studies of the Junior and Middle Classes, or who are possessed of an amount of experience in active and successful teaching, which can be regarded as a practical equivalent. All the studies of the school will be conducted in reference to their being taught again in common schools.

*Practice in the art of teaching and governing schools.* The several schools of the first school district, comprising the village of New Britain, are placed by a vote of the District, under the instruction and discipline of the Associate Principal, as Model Schools and Schools of Practice, for the Normal School. These schools embrace about four hundred children, and are classified into three Primary, one Intermediate and one High School. The course of instruction embraces all the studies pursued in any grade of common schools in Connecticut. The instruction of these schools will be given by pupils of the Normal School, under the constant oversight of the Associate Principal and Professors.

*Text books.* A Library of the best text books, in the various studies pursued in the schools, is commenced, and already numbers upward of four thousand volumes. Pupils are supplied with text books in such studies as they may be engaged, at a charge, barely sufficient to keep the books in good condition, and supply such as may be injured or lost. Arrangements have also been made to furnish teachers who wish to own a set of text books at the publishers' lowest wholesale price.

*Apparatus.* The sum of one thousand dollars is appropriated for the purchase of apparatus, which will be procured from time to time, as the wants of the school may require. As far as practicable, such articles of apparatus will be used in the class-rooms of the Normal School, as can be readily made by teachers themselves, or conveniently procured at low prices, and be made useful in the instruction of District Schools.

*Library.* The school is already furnished with the best works on the Theory and Practice of Education, which the Normal pupils are expected to read, and on several of which they are examined. The library will be supplied with Encyclopedias, Dictionaries, and other books of reference, to which free access will be given to members of the school.

*Board.* Normal pupils must board and lodge in such families, and under such regulations, as are approved by the Associate Principal.

The price of board, including room, fuel, lights and washing, in private families, ranges from $2.00 to $2.50 per week. Persons, expecting to join the school, should signify their intention to the Associate Principal, as early as practicable, before the commencement of a term, that there may be no disappointment in the place and price of board.

*Discipline.* The discipline of the institution is committed to the Associate Principal, who is authorized to secure the highest point of order and behavior by all suitable means, even to a temporary suspension of a pupil from the schools. The age of the pupils, the objects which bring them to a Normal School, and the spirit of the institution itself, will, it is believed, dispense with the necessity of a code of rules. The members are expected to exemplify in their own conduct, the order, punctuality, and neatness of good scholars, and exhibit in all their relations, Christian courtesy, kindness and fidelity.

*Examination and inspection.* The school will be visited each term by a committee of the trustees, who will report on the results of their examination to the Board.

There will be an examination at the close of each term, before the whole Board, and at the close of the summer term, the examination will be public, and will be followed by an exhibition.

The school is at all times open to inspection, and school visitors, teachers, and the friends of education generally in the state are cordially invited to visit it at their convenience.

*Diploma.* The time required to complete the course of instruction and practice, which shall be deemed by the trustees a suitable preparation for the business of teaching, and entitle any applicant to a Diploma of the Normal School, will depend on the age, attainments, mental discipline, moral character, and evidence of practical tact in instruction and government of each applicant.

No diploma will be given to any person who does not rank in the Senior Class, and has not given evidence of possessing some practical talent as a teacher in the Schools of Practice, or in the District Schools of the state.

## TEACHERS' INSTITUTES
A portion of the vacation in the spring and autumn, will be devoted by the Officers of the Normal School, to Teachers' Institutes or Conventions, in different parts of the state.

At least two of these Institutes will be held in the spring, for the special benefit of teachers who may be engaged, or expect to teach district schools in the summer following.

## COUNTY TEACHERS' ASSOCIATION
The Principal, or one of the Professors of the Normal School, will attend, on invitation and due notice, at every regular meeting of any County Teachers' Association, which shall continue in session through two evenings and one day, and assist in the lectures, discussions and other exercises of the occasion.

## STATE TEACHERS' ASSOCIATION

The State Teachers' Association has voted to hold an annual meeting at New Britain during the examination at the close of the summer term of the Normal School, and a special meeting at the dedicatory exercises at the completion of the Normal School in the spring. Arrangements will be made to entertain all members of the Association, during the meeting.

*Adopted at a meeting of the Board of Trustees, held at New Britain.* Oct. 1, 1850.

FRANCIS GILLETTE, *President.*

# 8

## Liberalizing
## Educational Methodology:
## The European Reformers

### INTRODUCTION

During the nineteenth century, the inertia of the inherited structure of education was being challenged by educational reformers on both sides of the Atlantic. In the United States, as common school education became more extensive across the land, the demand for teachers accelerated. As the government became involved and the church relinquished some of its control, new criteria were developed for the certification of teachers. With doctrinal conformity no longer the major requirement for engaging in teaching, more attention was devoted to educational methodology. Horace Mann and Henry Barnard, as well as other educational reformers such as Calvin Stowe of Ohio and James Carter of Massachusetts, were deeply impressed with the developments taking place in Europe in this area. Indeed, many American educational leaders toured Europe and returned with glowing accounts of the work of the European educational methodologists.

### ROUSSEAU'S *EMILE*

Foremost among the European theorists was the French social philosopher, Jean Jacques Rousseau (1712–1778). Like other thinkers of the eighteenth-century Enlightenment, Rousseau sought to discover the laws of nature and to establish a society based on their application. In such a natural society, artificial social conventions would be eliminated and human progress would ensue. Rousseau felt that traditional schools were based on an excessive verbalism which construed education as the mastery of abstract bodies of literature. In his educational novel, *Emile*, Rousseau condemned artificial education and developed a naturalistic theory which rested on three premises: first, that nature was the great educator, instructing man through his senses; second, that instruction should be adapted to the gradually unfolding capacities of the child; third,that instruction should be active and based on the child's experiences.

Rousseau structured his educational method around five clearly defined periods of human growth: infancy, childhood, boyhood, adolescence, and youth. For each stage of development, there was an appropriate set of educational activities. In relating education to these stages, Rousseau was arguing that the whole of childhood be recognized as a legitimate and necessary sequence in human growth: "Childhood has its place in the scheme of human life. We must view the man as a man, and the child as a child." [1] In recognizing the dignity of childhood, Rousseau rejected the Calvinist conception that man was depraved and that children were conceived in sin and born in corruption. This latter concept held that the child should be treated like a miniature adult and that his propensity to evil might be exorcised through harsh discipline and external coercion. Rousseau, considering the child naturally good, held that his interests were also good and should form the basis for his education. In emphasizing the learner's interests and needs, Rousseau was anticipating the child-centered progressive educators of the twentieth century.

During infancy, from birth until age five, Rousseau described Emile as completely helpless and dependent upon others for his needs. Nature had given superabundant energy to the infant in order that he might develop physically through self-activity. Rousseau advised parents to allow the child the greatest possible freedom of movement.

Childhood, from ages five to twelve, constituted Rousseau's second stage of human development. Becoming conscious of his own personal life, the child experienced feelings of happiness and unhappiness. He was a natural egotist motivated by self-love and self-preservation. During this stage, the boy was incapable of reasoning or forming judgments. Such words as obedience, obligation, and duty were meaningless and should have no bearing on the child's education.

In the third state, boyhood, twelve to fifteen, the child's strength increased more rapidly than his needs. This stage of rapid physical develop-

---

[1] William Boyd, *The Emile of Jean Jacques Rousseau: Selections* (New York: Teachers College Press, Teachers College, Columbia University, 1966), p. 34.

ment indicated that the time of mental development was approaching. Following his natural curiosity, the child learned by experimenting and by making and doing. As a part of this experimentation, Rousseau urged that Emile be taught a manual skill in order that he have a proper combination of physical and manual labor.

During the fourth stage, from fifteen to eighteen, adolescence, Emile was to come to know and to live in the social order. To live in the world, the adolescent had to know how to live with others; he must be aware of the forces which motivate people. At this stage Emile was now capable of developing moral values. History, biographical exemplars, and religion were introduced as sources of moral values.

During the final stage of education, from eighteen to twenty, Emile broadened his awareness of the world by extensive travels during which he learned foreign languages, studied natural history, diverse peoples, laws and governments. Upon completion of his travels he took a wife, Sophy.

Rousseau's concept of natural education motivated other educational theorists to investigate child growth and development. These theorists, studying under the influence of the eighteenth century Enlightenment, sought to discover in nature a pattern of revealing but inflexible natural patterns of development. Among the many innovators of the period the names of three stand out especially: Johann Heinrich Pestalozzi, Friedrich Froebel, and Johann Friedrich Herbart. These men influenced the educational institutions of Europe tremendously and indirectly helped to shape the emergent American common school.

## JOHANN HEINRICH PESTALOZZI

The famous Swiss educator was born in 1746, the second of the three surviving children of Johann Baptist Pestalozzi. After his father's early death, he was raised by his mother, Susanna, and a devoted servant, Babeli, Barbara Schmid. During his growing years, young Pestalozzi was carefully sheltered from the outside world. As a result, he was socially inept and as an adult tended to be disorganized when dealing with the practicalities of life. As a youth, he attended the Collegium Humanitatis and the Collegium Carolinum, both classical Swiss schools. Though he enjoyed his studies, he felt that they had not prepared him for the real world.

Upon reaching manhood, Pestalozzi developed a number of interests, each of which absorbed him for short periods of time. His activities ranged from membership in the Helvetic Society, a Swiss patriotic organization, to farming. He was the author of numerous tracts on politics, morals, sociology, and philosophy. As politician, agriculturalist, and industrialist, he was unsuccessful. After a long process of trial and error, he finally found his life's work in education. Familiar with the writings of Rousseau, Pestalozzi attempted to apply *Emile* to the rearing of his own child. As a result of this experience, he was able to see many of the weaknesses and strengths of Rousseau's ideas. He dedicated himself to the education of the poor and founded schools at Neuhof, Stans, Burgdorf, and Yverdon. At the last one he developed his theory of education, which was based on natural principles of sense experience.

From 1774–1779, Pestalozzi conducted an industrial school for poor children at his estate at Neuhof. He believed that the poverty-ridden Swiss peasants might be educated out of their economic and social deprivation by means of a system of instruction which combined both literacy and useful occupations. His students were engaged in learning farming, spinning, and weaving, as well as reading and arithmetic. Unrealistically, Pestalozzi believed that his primitive school could be economically self-sufficient, but this first educational venture failed. Nevertheless, he remained committed to improving the condition of the poor by developing a methodology of natural education that would regenerate society itself.

Taking a cue from Rousseau, in 1781 he too published a novel as a vehicle for his educational theory, *Leonard and Gertrude*.[2] The book depicted the social reformation which took place in the Swiss village of Bonal because of the insight and educational methods of a simple peasant woman, Gertrude. Pestalozzi hoped that what occurred in his mythical village would actually occur in the larger real society.

In 1798 he took charge of an orphanage at Stans, where he tried to combine moral, physical, and intellectual education. Unfortunately, Stans soon became a battleground between the French and the Austrians and the school was abruptly closed. The following year Pestalozzi was assigned to the village of Burgdorf where a private school, partially endowed by the Helvetian government, had been established. From 1799 until 1804, Pestalozzi labored at Burgdorf to develop a natural theory of education. As a result of his pedagogical experiments he published *How Gertrude Teaches Her Children* in 1801.[3]

When support was withdrawn from the school at Burgdorf, Pestalozzi went to Yverdon, where he conducted his most famous experimental school from 1804 until 1825. Here he established a gentle environment

---

[2] Johann H. Pestalozzi, *Leonard and Gertrude*, trans. Eva Channing (Boston: D. C. Heath and Co., 1907).

[3] Johann H. Pestalozzi, *How Gertrude Teaches Her Children*, trans. Lucy E. Holland and Francis Turner (London: Swan Sonnenschein and Co., 1907).

very different from the harsh modes of traditional schooling. Pestalozzi's school resembled a home where discipline was mild, children were treated as equals, and no one was coerced through fear. Pestalozzi believed that genuine learning could take place only within an institution where children were emotionally secure.

Since Pestalozzi's writing is obscure, systematic treatment of his educational methodology is difficult. However, certain salient features of his work appear. Holding that man was composed of moral, physical, and intellectual powers, Pestalozzi believed that natural education should develop all three of these powers simultaneously and harmoniously.

Like Rousseau, Pestalozzi believed that all knowledge comes to the human mind through sensation. He believed that conceptualization involved the following stages: one, determining the form and outline of the object; two, determining the number of objects present; three, naming the object. Pestalozzi's famous object lesson was based on the teaching of form, number, and language and was directed to the development of the skills of measuring, numbering, and speaking rather than to the traditional literary skills of reading and writing. Only after a firm foundation had been established in form, number, and language was the learner permitted to go on to these literary skills.[4]

Basically, Pestalozzi urged that all instruction begin with the simplest elements in the learner's immediate environment and then proceed gradually to those more distant and complex, gradually culminating in abstract ideas. Pestalozzi's educational method was a forerunner of the progressive experience curriculum of the twentieth century. Following Dewey, progressive educators emphasized that all education should be based upon the learner's experience. Both Pestalozzi and Dewey opposed an education which was so abstract that it bore no relevance to the child's own experience.

Using his principle of natural education based on sense perception, Pestalozzi inaugurated changes in his instructional methodology. In arithmetic, students began learning with concrete objects such as marbles or peas and then moved to an understanding of mathematical symbols and computations. In geography, the lesson began with the child's immediate environment. The child made clay models of the local rivers, land forms, and topographical features and gradually began to draw maps. Treating drawing as a prelude to writing, Pestalozzi began with simple lines and then moved to more complex letters. In summary, these are the general principles of Pestalozzian methodology:

[4] Gerald L. Gutek, *Pestalozzi and Education* (New York: Random House, Inc., 1968), p. 95.

1. Sensation is the basis of all instruction.
2. Language should always be related to observation.
3. Instruction should begin with the simplest elements and gradually proceed to the abstract and complex.
4. Teachers should always respect the individuality of the learner.
5. Natural education should harmoniously develop the moral, intellectual, and physical powers of the student.

While Pestalozzi's principles may seem commonplace to the modern teacher, these were revolutionary educational concepts at the beginning of the nineteenth century. Educators flocked to Switzerland to observe the schools at Burgdorf and Yverdon. Pestalozzi's teaching assistants carried his methods to France, England, Germany, and the United States.

The Pestalozzian method of education was first introduced to the United States under the auspices of the American philanthropist William Maclure. During his European travels Maclure had visited Pestalozzi's schools and was impressed with the educational practices he saw. He decided to introduce the Pestalozzian method to the United States and contracted to subsidize Joseph Neef, one of Pestalozzi's assistants, in a school near Philadelphia. In 1808 Neef published his *Sketch of a Plan and Method of Education,* which was the first book to be written in English in the United States on teaching methodology. Neef conducted a number of schools on the Pestalozzian plan in Pennsylvania. In 1826 he joined Maclure and the English utopian socialist Robert Owen in the communitarian experiment at New Harmony, Indiana. The schools of New Harmony attracted a number of Pestalozzian teachers but they failed to have a significant influence on American education because Owen's social experiment was short-lived.

During the second half of the nineteenth century, Pestalozzianism was again popularized through the efforts of Edward A. Sheldon, 1823–1897. As president of the Oswego Normal School of New York, Sheldon made the Pestalozzian method a part of the teacher preparation of many American teachers. Concentrating on the object lesson, Sheldon said:

> To lead children to observe with attention the objects which surround them and then to describe with accuracy the impressions they convey, appears to be the first step in the business of education.[5]

Under Sheldon's influence the object lesson became the dominant educational method used in American schools, as modified Pestalozzian

[5] Edward A. Sheldon, *Lessons on Objects* (New York: Charles Scribner's Sons, 1863), p. 22.

principles were diffused throughout the United States. Henry Barnard was also well disposed toward Pestalozzian theories and practices and helped to popularize them in his educational writings in the *American Journal of Education*. Thus Pestalozzi, though often unsuccessful in his other ventures, earned a place in the history of education by developing a methodology that liberalized instruction by rejecting sterile, rote memorization and dogmatic indoctrination, and by placing in its stead an organized, albeit simplified, approach to teaching and learning problems.

## FRIEDRICH FROEBEL

Friedrich Froebel, 1782–1852, was another of the many visitors drawn to the Pestalozzian school at Yverdon. A native of southern Germany, Froebel, like his Swiss mentor Pestalozzi, had experienced many "black nights of the soul" as he sought the vocation which would provide him with direction and purpose. As a youth, he studied religion, and was always somewhat drawn to mysticism. Later, as a university student at Gottingen, he studied physics, chemistry, minerology, and natural history. His investigations of natural science produced in him a deep love of nature, which he interpreted within the context of philosophic Idealism. Although he worked variously as a forester, an accountant, a surveyor, and a museum assistant, none of these vocations satisfied him.

At the age of twenty-three, Froebel decided to become a schoolteacher and obtained a position in the Pestalozzian Institute at Frankfurt. Here he met Anton Gruner, a disciple of Pestalozzi's, and became convinced that an educational career would give meaning to his life. After several years of study with Gruner, Froebel went to Yverdon, where he observed Pestalozzi's educational experiments.

Although impressed with his innovations, Froebel believed the Pestalozzian method needed refinement. In 1816, he founded a school at Keilhau where he hoped to work out his own system. In 1831, he went back to Switzerland to become an instructor in teacher education. In 1837 he returned to Germany, where he established his famous kindergarten in the village of Blankenburg. As a result of these experiments he wrote his most famous pedagogical work, *The Education of Man*, in which he defined education as ". . . leading man, as a thinking, intelligent being, growing into self-consciousness, to a pure and unsullied, conscious and free representation of the inner law of Divine Unity, and in teaching him ways and means thereto." [6]

[6] Friedrich Froebel, *The Education of Man*, trans. W. N. Hailmann (New York: Appleton and Co., 1896), p. 1.

For Froebel, a mystical idealist, there was a spark of the Divine present in all men. The process of child growth and development was the unfolding and the externalization of this essence. Growth was the process of unfolding according to a built-in design in much the same way as the flower bud unfolds as the blossom or the oak unfolds from the acorn. The educator was not to interfere with the natural unfolding of the child's latent abilities but was rather to guide the process by encouraging the child's self-activity in the environment of the kindergarten—the child's garden.

Froebel regarded the child's play as an important form of self-activity. For the child, play was simply his natural way of living. Further, play furnished an important form of socialization of the child with his peer group. Hence, the kindergarten was an institution based upon play.

## Froebel's Gifts and Occupations

Froebel arranged a series of gifts and occupations to provide the core of the kindergarten program. Paramount among the series of gifts to encourage the child's development was the ball. According to Froebel's mystical conception of child growth, the ball was the first plaything of the child's development. The ball represented the spherical nature of the world and epitomized the concept of the unity of mankind with the Absolute Reality. The ball was an undifferentiated unity; the other symbols were derived from the ball but still retained a unity of origin in it. Other symbolic gifts were the cube, the brick, the surface, and the point.[7] The Froebelian occupation was designed to involve the child in working with construction materials such as paper, clay, or thread. Occupations such as needlework, sewing, or weaving furnished opportunities for the child to engage in purposeful activity.

## The Kindergarten

While the gifts and occupations and their attendant symbolism have been discarded by modern educators as mysticism, major elements of Froebel's ideas have remained to become a definite contribution to education.[8] First, he stressed the spiritual nature of the child as a precious human being. Along with Pestalozzi's work, Froebel's concept of the child as a child helped to render obsolete the doctrine of child depravity. Second, Froebel's emphasis on play, games, and songs liberated school practices. Today, nursery play is designed to awaken in the child his first

---

[7] Kate D. Wiggin and Nora A. Smith, *Froebel's Gifts* (Boston: Houghton Mifflin Company, 1896), pp. 6–30.

[8] William Heard Kilpatrick, *Froebel's Kindergarten Principles: Critically Examined* (New York: The Macmillan Company, 1916), pp. 195–200.

awareness of human relationships and social interaction. ⌊Third, Froe-belian pedagogy stimulated the examination of child growth and development.⌉

The kindergarten was first transported to the United States by the German refugees from the unsuccessful Revolution of 1848. William Torrey Harris, superintendent of schools in Saint Louis, introduced the kindergarten as part of the public school system. By 1888 there were 15,145 children enrolled in the public kindergartens of the United States. By 1954, the number had increased to 1,479,000. The rapid growth of support and stress on preschool education have made the kindergarten an enduring educational institution.

## JOHANN FRIEDRICH HERBART

The third major educator of this period was Johann Friedrich Herbart, 1776–1841, a German philosopher and psychologist. He too visited Pestalozzi, staying at the Swiss educator's school at Burgdorf in 1799. Herbart was much more emotionally stable than Pestalozzi or Froebel, and not as romantic as they or Rousseau in his educational theory. Herbart devoted himself to the systematic study of philosophy, and applied his keen sense of logic to a critical analysis of the process of education. During his life he was professor of philosophy at the Universities of Gottingen and Konigsburg. As a part of his teaching duties he developed a series of lectures on pedagogy, from which he derived his theory and practice of education. As a university professor he was most concerned with their usefulness and application to education on the secondary and higher levels. He wrote two books that were major contributions to pedagogy: *The Science of Education*, 1806, and *Outlines of Educational Doctrine*, 1835. Both these sources offer some indications of the elements of his theory.

Like most educational theorists, Herbart regarded the ultimate goal of education as that of moral development. His idea of the end product of education, the "cultured man," comprised five basic elements of morality: freedom, perfection, good will, righteousness, and retribution. To develop as a moral man, the student was provided with the broadest possible range of experience.

Herbart conceived of interest as an internal tendency that facilitated the retention of an idea in consciousness or contributed to its return to consciousness. The power of interests increased with the frequency with which an idea was presented to consciousness and with the association of ideas in what Herbart called the "apperceptive mass." Basing his reasoning upon the doctrine of "many-sidedness of interests" and "apperceptive mass," Herbart arrived at two pedagogical laws: frequency and association. The more times an idea is presented to consciousness, the greater the tendency of the idea to find a locus in the apperceptive mass of the learner. Also, ideas tend to cluster, similar ideas attracting each other. The teacher was to stress by repeated presentation those ideas which he wanted to dominate the student's life, and then point out the similarities between clusters of ideas.

Since he considered morality the final aim of education, Herbart emphasized the humanistic studies of history and literature. If history were taught as the study of the lives of great men, it could provide students with illustrative examples of how to behave. Students could study the historical models and seek to imitate the virtues exemplified by each one. In addition to providing models of value, history and literature also formed a cultural base around which other subject matter was to be correlated. For example, religious events and scientific discoveries could be placed in a historical context. Herbart's concern with literature and history encouraged the adoption of these studies into the curriculum at a time when secondary education was still dominated by Greek, Latin, and mathematics.

From his logical-psychological researches Herbart concluded that the mind assimilated all ideas in the same way. It was therefore possible to arrive at one methodology of instruction which would be suitable for any subject. Although Herbart's original system was divided into four steps— clarity, association, system, and method—his interpreters established five clearly defined phases of teaching method: [9]

1. *Preparation.* During this first stage, the student's mind was prepared for the assimilation of the new idea into his apperceptive mass. Past ideas, experiences, and other memories were recalled and related to the new idea being introduced in the lesson. This was designed to bring the student into a state of readiness for the lesson.

2. *Presentation.* During the second stage the new idea was actually presented to the student. The teacher's instruction was to be so clear and definite that the student completely understood the new idea.

3. *Association.* The new idea was compared and contrasted with ideas which the student already knew. This step was to facilitate his assimilation of the new idea by associating it with familiar and related ideas.

4. *Generalization.* A general definition or principle was formed upon the basis of the combined new and old learning.

[9] Johann Friedrich Herbart, *Outlines of Educational Doctrine,* trans. Alexis F. Lange, annot. Charles de Garmo (New York: The Macmillan Company, 1901). (De Garmo was one of the leading American figures in the popularization of the Herbartian method.)

5. *Application.* The last step tested the principle with appropriate problems and exercises.

Herbart's educational theory won wide popularity among American educators during the late nineteenth century. As a theoretical rationale for the study of education, it contributed to the acceptance of pedagogy as a university discipline. As a practical teaching method, Herbart's five steps were used by many teachers as a systematic guide to the organization of classroom instruction. The positive Herbartian contribution to American education was three-fold: his emphasis on history and literature as a cultural core helped to enrich the curriculum; his logically structured methodology encouraged precise lesson planning; he influenced the organization of subject matter content in relation to educational methodology.

On the negative side, Herbartian influence imposed a precise, rigid approach on the process of instruction. Because it emphasized the role of the teacher as planner, presenter of material, and source of knowledge, the student's function became the passive one of receiving information. Herbartianism overemphasized the past to the neglect of the present and its problems. Finally, its exaggeration of formal methodology stifled creativity.

## CONCLUSION

Evaluation of the work of the European methodologists Pestalozzi, Froebel, and Herbart shows that their contributions to education were most significant in that they channeled educational effort into new directions. Pestalozzi and Froebel, in particular, were instrumental in directing more attention to the nature of the child. They felt that the actual practices of schooling had neglected to consider the child's interests and needs. Although their views may be primitive by our standards, they both contributed to the genesis of an enlightened concept of childhood. After their work, children could no longer be considered miniature adults. They also focused greater attention on the educational environment. Froebel's kindergarten, especially, stressed the necessity of a prepared environment, a child's garden, where through play and directed instruction the child would develop freely according to nature's laws. Foremost in the methods of Pestalozzi and Froebel was the building of emotional security in the young student. They felt he could best grow to healthy adulthood with love, sympathy, and understanding. Perhaps, more than their specific methodology, the idea of understanding the child as a child was their greatest contribution.

In terms of specific contributions to educational methodology, Pestalozzi's emphasis on direct experience and sense observation and Froebel's stress on stories, songs, and play liberated educational practices from excessive verbalism, rote memorization, and harsh corporal punishment. Unfortunately, both the Pestalozzian attempts to reduce all learning to the simplest elements and the Froebelian obsession with highly structured "gifts and occupations" tended to minimize the general concept of child understanding and love. Some of the followers of both educators neglected the general features of their theories and concentrated on particular aspects of the methodologies. Hence, Pestalozzianism was reduced to "object teaching" in England and the United States. Froebelianism was more fortunate in that its emphasis on child love and sympathy has been passed down through the generations of kindergarten practitioners.

Herbart's attempts to reduce teaching and learning to a number of highly structured steps found rapid acceptance among many educators. The attempt to apply logical methods to teaching was a step in the direction of the construction of a science of education. Indeed, Herbartianism seemed a ready-made rationale for the growing field of professional education that was struggling for academic acceptance in many American colleges and universities. Yet at the time Herbartianism reached its peak it was already doomed to virtual extinction by the rising tides of experimentalism which characterized twentieth-century American education.

# References

BOYD, WILLIAM. *The Emile of Jean Jacques Rousseau: Selections.* New York: Teachers College Press, Teachers College, Columbia University, 1966.

FROEBEL, FREDERICK. *The Education of Man.* Translated by W. N. Hailmann, New York: Appleton and Company, 1896.

GUTEK, GERALD L. *Pestalozzi and Education.* New York: Random House, Inc., 1968.

HERBART, JOHANN FREDERICK. *Outlines of Educational Doctrine.* Translated by Alexis F. Lange, annotated by Charles de Garmo. New York: The Macmillan Company, 1901.

KILPATRICK, WILLIAM H. *Froebel's Kindergarten Principles: Critically Examined.* New York: The Macmillan Company, 1916.

PESTALOZZI, JOHANN H. *How Gertrude Teaches Her Children.* Translated by Lucy E. Holland and Francis Turner. London: Swan Sonnenschein and Co., 1907.

——. *Leonard and Gertrude.* Translated by Eva Channing. Boston: D. C. Heath and Co., 1907.

SHELDON, EDWARD A. *Lessons on Objects.* New York: Charles Scribner's Sons, 1863.

WIGGIN, KATE D., and SMITH, NORA A. *Froebel's Gifts.* Boston: Houghton Mifflin Company, 1896.

# SELECTIONS

*Johann Heinrich Pestalozzi, one of the leading educational reformers of the nineteenth century, had a profound influence upon both European and American education. His educational methodology, which emphasized sense realism, directly contributed to the re-organization of the Prussian schools. The ideas of many American educators such as Henry Barnard, Edward A. Sheldon, and others were also greatly affected by Pestalozzi's methodology. Trying to explain his new approach to education, Pestalozzi wrote the following report to the "Friends of Education," a Swiss society organized to support his reformed pedagogy.*

## The Method: A Report by Pestalozzi

I am trying to psychologize the instruction of mankind; I am trying to bring it into harmony with the nature of my mind, with that of my circumstances and my relations to others. I start from no positive form of teaching, as such, but simply ask myself:—

"What would you do, if you wished to give a single child all the knowledge and practical skill he needs, so that by wise care of his best opportunities, he might reach inner content?"

I think, to gain this end, the human race needs exactly the same thing as the single child.

I think, further, the poor man's child needs a greater refinement in the methods of instruction than the rich man's child.

Nature, indeed, does much for the human race, but we have strayed away from her path. The poor man is thrust away from her bosom, and the rich destroy themselves both by rioting and by lounging on her overflowing breast.

. . . . .

The most essential point from which I start is this:—

Sense impression of Nature is the only true foundation of human instruction, because it is the only true foundation of human knowledge.

SOURCE: Johann H. Pestalozzi, *How Gertrude Teaches Her Children*, trans. Lucy E. Holland and Francis C. Turner (London: Swan Sonnenschein and Co., 1907), pp. 199–211. The report has been abridged by the author.

All that follows is the result of this sense impression, and the process of abstraction from it. Hence in every case where this is imperfect, the results also will be neither certain, safe nor positive; and in any case, where the sense impression is inaccurate, deception and error follow.

I start from this point and ask:—"What does Nature herself do in order to present the world truly to me, so far as it affects me? That is,—By what means does she bring the sense impressions of the most important things around me, to a perfection that contents me?" And I find,—She does this through my surroundings, my wants, and my relations to others.

Thus all the Art (of teaching) men is essentially a result of physico-mechanical laws, the most important of which are the following:—

1. Bring all things essentially related to each other to that connection in your mind which they really have in Nature.

2. Subordinate all unessential things to essential, and especially subordinate the impression given by the Art to that given by Nature and reality.

3. Give to nothing a greater weight in your idea than it has in relation to your race in Nature.

4. Arrange all objects in the world according to their likeness.

5. Strengthen the impressions of important objects by allowing them to affect you through different senses.

6. In every subject try to arrange graduated steps of knowledge, in which every new idea shall be only a small, almost imperceptible addition to that earlier knowledge which has been deeply impressed and made unforgettable.

7. Learn to make the simple perfect before going on to the complex.

8. Recognize that as every physical ripening must be the result of the whole perfect fruit in all its parts, so every just judgment must be the result of a sense impression, perfect in all its parts, of the object to be judged. Distrust the appearance of precocious ripeness as the apparent ripeness of a worm-eaten apple.

9. All physical effects are absolutely necessary; and this necessity is the result of the art of Nature, with which she unites the apparently heterogeneous elements of her material into one whole for the achievement of her end. The Art, which imitates her, must try in the same way to raise the results at which it aims to a physical necessity, while it unites its elements into one whole for the achievement of its end.

10. The richness of its charm and the variety of its free play cause the results of physical necessity to bear the impress of freedom and independence. Here, too, the Art must imitate the course of Nature, and by the richness of its charm and the variety of its free play, try to make its results bear the impress of freedom and independence.

11. Above all, learn the first law of the physical mechanism, the powerful, universal connection between its results and the proportion of nearness or distance between the object and our senses. Never forget this physical nearness or distance of all objects around you has an immense effect in determining your positive sense impressions, practical ability and even virtue. But even this law of your nature converges as a whole towards another. It converges towards the

centre of our whole being, and we ourselves are this centre. Man! never forget it! All that you are, all you wish, all you might be, comes out of yourself. All must have a centre in your physical sense impression, and this again is yourself. In all it does, the Art really only adds this to the simple course of Nature.—That which Nature puts before us, scattered and over a wide area, the Art puts together in narrower bounds and brings nearer to our five senses, by associations, which facilitate the power of memory, and strengthen the susceptibility of our senses, and make it easier for them, by daily practice, to present to us the objects around us in greater numbers, for a longer time and in a more precise way.

Pestalozzi.

*Burgdorf, June 27th, 1800.*

---

*Friedrich Froebel, who developed the Kindergarten, presented his most systematic work on educational theory in* The Education of Man. *Although the style of this work is complicated by the mystical overtones of Froebel's philosophic idealism, the book provides valuable insight into his concepts of man, the child, and education.*

# Froebel: The Education of Man

In all things there lives and reigns an eternal law. To him whose mind, through disposition and faith, is filled, penetrated, and quickened with the necessity that this can not possibly be otherwise, as well as to him whose clear, calm mental vision beholds the inner in the outer and through the outer, and sees the outer proceeding with logical necessity from the essence of the inner, this law has been and is enounced with equal clearness and distinctness in nature (the external), in the spirit (the internal), and in life which unites the two. This all-controlling law is necessarily based on an all-pervading, energetic, living, self-conscious, and hence eternal Unity. This fact, as well as the Unity itself, is again vividly recognized, either through faith or through insight, with equal clearness and comprehensiveness; therefore, a quietly observant human mind, a thoughtful, clear human intellect, has never failed, and will never fail, to recognize this Unity.

This Unity is God. All things have come from Divine Unity, from God, and

Source: Friedrich W. Froebel, *The Education of Man*, trans. W. N. Hailmann (New York: D. Appleton and Company, 1887). Hailmann was a well-known lecturer on education in the United States and at the time he translated Froebel's work was Superintendent of Public Schools at LaPorte, Indiana. *The Education of Man* was a volume in the series edited by W. T. Harris, U.S. Commissioner of Education. The author has selected representative selections from the text.

have their origin in the Divine Unity, in God alone. God is the sole source of all things. In all things there lives and reigns the Divine Unity, God. All things live and have their being in and through the Divine Unity, in and through God. All things are only through the divine effluence that lives in them. The divine effluence that lives in each thing is the essence of each thing.

It is the destiny and life-work of all things to unfold their essence, hence their divine being, and, therefore, the Divine Unity itself—to reveal God in their external and transient being. It is the special destiny and life-work of man, as an intelligent and rational being, to become fully, vividly, and clearly conscious of his essence, of the divine effluence in him, and, therefore, of God; to become fully, vividly, and clearly conscious of his destiny and life-work; and to accomplish this, to render it (His essence) active, to reveal it in his own life with self-determination and freedom.

*Education consists in leading man, as a thinking, intelligent being, growing into self-consciousness, to a pure and unsullied, conscious and free representation of the inner law of Divine Unity, and in teaching him ways and means thereto.*

The knowledge of that eternal law, the insight into its origin, into its essence, into the totality, the connection, and intensity of its effects, and knowledge of life in its totality, constitute *science, the science of life;* and, referred by the self-conscious, thinking, intelligent being to representation and practice through and in himself, this becomes *science of education.*

The system of directions, derived from the knowledge and study of that law, to guide thinking, intelligent beings in the apprehension of their life-work and in the accomplishment of their destiny, is *the theory of education.*

The self-active application of this knowledge in the direct development and cultivation of rational beings toward the attainment of their destiny, is *the practice of education.*

The object of education is the realization of a faithful, pure, inviolate, and hence holy life.

Knowledge and application, consciousness and realization in life, united in the service of a faithful, pure, holy life, constitute the wisdom of life, pure wisdom.

*To be wise is the highest aim of man,* is the most exalted achievement of human self-determination.

To educate one's self and others, with consciousness, freedom, and self-determination, is a twofold achievement of wisdom: it *began* with the first appearance of man upon the earth; it *was manifest* with the first appearance of full self-consciousness in man; it *begins now* to proclaim itself as a necessary, universal requirement of humanity, and to be heard and heeded as such. With this achievement man enters upon the path which alone leads to life; which surely tends to the fulfillment of the inner, and thereby also to the fulfillment of the outer requirement of humanity; which, through a faithful, pure, holy life, attains beatitude.

By education, then the divine essence of man should be unfolded, brought out, lifted into consciousness, and man himself raised into free, conscious obedience to the divine principle that lives in him, and to a free representation of this principle in his life.

Education, in instruction, should lead man to see and know the divine, spiritual, and eternal principle which animates surrounding nature, constitutes the essence of nature, and is permanently manifested in nature; and, in living reciprocity and united with training, it should express and demonstrate the fact that the same law rules both (the divine principle and nature), as it does nature and man.

Education as a whole, by means of instruction and training, should bring to man's consciousness, and render efficient in his life, the fact that man and nature proceed from God and are conditioned by him—that both have their being in God.

*Education should lead and guide man to clearness concerning himself and in himself, to peace with nature, and to unity with God;* hence it should lift him to a knowledge of himself and of mankind, to a knowledge of God and of nature, and to the pure and holy life to which such knowledge leads.

### FROEBEL'S KINDERGARTEN

Would you, O parents and educators, see in miniature, in a picture, as it were, what I have here indicated, look into this education-room—of eight boys, seven to eight years old.

This unifying and, at the same time, self-reliant spirit unites all things that come near and seem adapted to its nature, its wants, and inner status—unites stones and human beings in a common purpose, a common endeavor. And thus each one soon forms for himself his own world; for the feeling of his *own power* implies and soon demands also the possession of his *own space* and his *own material* belongings exclusively to him.

Be his realm, his province, his land, as it were, a corner of the court-yard, of the house, or of the room; be it the space of a box, of a chest, or of a closet; be it a grotto, a hut, or a garden—the human being, the boy at this age, needs an external point, if possible, chosen and prepared by himself, to which he refers all his activity.

When the room to be filled is extensive, when the realm to be controlled is large, when the whole to be represented or produced is complex, then brotherly union of similar-minded persons is in place. And when similar-minded persons meet in similar endeavor, and their hearts find each other, then either the work already begun is extended, or the work begun by one becomes a common work.

On the large table of the much-used room there stands a chest of building-blocks, in the form of bricks, each side about one sixth of the size of actual bricks, the finest and most variable material that can be offered a boy for purposes of representation. Sand or sawdust, too, have found their way into the room, and fine, green moss has been brought in abundantly from the last walk in the beautiful pine-forest.

It is intermission, and each one has begun his own work. There in a corner stands a chapel quite concealed, a cross and an altar indicate the meaning of the structure: it is the creation of a small, quiet boy. There on a chair two boys have united to undertake a considerably greater piece of work: it is a building of several stories, and probably represents a castle, which looks down from the chair as from a mountain into a valley. But what has quietly grown under the hands of that boy at the table? It is a green hill crowned by an old, ruined castle. The others, in the meanwhile, have erected a village in the plain below.

Now, each one has finished his work; each one examines it and that of the others. In each one rises the thought and the wish to unite all in a connected whole; and scarcely has this wish been recognized as a common one, when they establish common roads from the village to the ruin, from this to the castle, and from the castle to the chapel, and between them lie brooks and meadows.

At another time some had fashioned a landscape from clay, another had constructed from pasteboard a house with doors and windows, and a third had made miniature ships from nut-shells. Each one examines his work: it is good, but it stands alone. He sees his neighbor's work: it would gain so much by being united. And immediately the house, as a castle, crowns the hills, and the tiny ship floats on the small artificial lake, and, to the delight of all, the youngest brings his shepherd and sheep to graze between the mountain and the lake. Now they all stand and behold with pleasure and satisfaction the work of their own hands.

Again, what busy tumult among those older boys at the brook down yonder! They have built canals and sluices, bridges and sea-ports, dams and mills, each one intent only on his own work. Now the water is to be used to carry vessels from the higher to the lower level: but at each step of progress one trespasses on the limits of another realm, and each one equally claims his right as lord and maker, while he recognizes the claims of the other. What can serve here to mediate? Only *treaties*, and like states, they bind themselves by strict treaties. Who can point out the varied significance, the varied results of these plays of boys? Two things, indeed, are clearly established. They proceed from one and the same spirit of boyhood and the playing boys made good pupils, intelligent, and quick to learn, quick to see and to do, diligent and full of zeal, reliable in thought and feeling, efficient and vigorous. Those who played thus are efficient men, or will become so.

Particularly helpful at this period of life is the cultivation of gardens owned by the boys, and their cultivation for the sake of the produce. For here man for the first time sees his work bearing fruit in an organic way, determined by logical necessity and law—fruit which, although subject to the inner laws of natural development, depends in many ways upon his work and upon the character of his work!

This work fully completes, in many ways, the boy's life with nature, and satisfies his curiosity concerning her workings, his desire to know her—a desire that urges him again and again to give thoughtful and continuous attention and observation to plants and flowers. Nature, too, seems to favor these promptings and occupations, and to reward them with abundant success; for a glance upon these gardens of children reveals at once the fact that, if a boy has given his plants only moderate care and attention, they thrive remarkably well; and that the plants and flowers of the boys who attend to them with special care live in sympathy with these boys, as it were, and are particularly healthy and luxuriant.

If the boy can not have the care of a little garden of his own, he should have at least a few plants in boxes or pots, filled not with rare and delicate or double plants, but with common plants that have an abundance of leaves and blossoms, and thrive easily.

The child, or boy, who has guarded and cared for another living thing, although it be of a lower order, will be led more easily to guard and foster his own life. At the same time the care of plants will gratify his desire to observe other living things, such as beetles, butterflies, and birds, for these seek the vicinity of plants.

# 9

# John Dewey's Influence on American Education

## INTRODUCTION

John Dewey was a keen observer, critic, and theorist of American society and education who exercised tremendous influence on the development of twentieth-century American education. Born in Burlington, Vermont, in 1859, he devoted his efforts to educational theory and practice, although he was trained in formal philosophy. A prolific author, Dewey wrote such works as *The School and Society*, 1898, in which he described his educational practices at the laboratory school he founded at the University of Chicago in 1896. In 1910 he wrote *How We Think*, in which he stressed problem-solving as the mode of complete thought. In 1913, *Interest and Effort in ·Education* further demonstrated his keen interest in educational theory and practice. *Individualism Old and New*, 1929, was a penetrating study of social change in relation to American civilization. *Art as Experience*, 1934, contained his views on aesthetic experience. While all of Dewey's works have influenced American intellectual life, *Democracy and Education*, written in 1916, remains his classic statement of educational theory. In addition to these books, Dewey produced an extensive number of other works and articles.

## EDUCATIONAL THEORY

To appreciate Dewey's impact on American education, it is necessary to examine some of the various elements of his theories. Dewey's philosophy of instrumentalism or experimentalism was affected by his exposure to Hegelian idealism and the Darwinian revolution.

As a graduate student at Johns Hopkins University, young Dewey studied under the Hegelian idealists who dominated philosophy at American universities during the closing years of the nineteenth century. The Hegelians believed that the increasingly complex patterns of social life were in reality a more complete unfolding of the Absolute in the course of human history. Although Dewey later rejected Hegelianism, he interpreted man's progress to mean that human intelligence was capable of devising more comprehensive modes of shared experiences or interrelationships.

Even more important than his exposure to Hegelianism was the impact of the Darwinian revolution upon Dewey. Darwin's theory of evolution postulated an environment in which the organism lives, adjusts, and adapts itself to survive. The terms "organism" and "environment" were adopted by Dewey and became crucial to his educational philosophy. He viewed the organism as a living creature, composed physiologically of living tissue and possessing a set of impulses or drives designed to maintain the life of that tissue. Every organism lives within an environment which both threatens and nourishes its life.

During the life of the organism it encounters problems or situations which threaten its continuing existence. The successful organism is able to solve these problems, or blocks to activity, and regain its balance. The interaction of the organism with its environment constitutes experience. Each successive solution of a problem helps build a network of experience between the organism and its environment.

The human organism lives in a social as well as a physical environment. In his struggle to sustain life man forms groups promoting life. This associative experience, Dewey felt, enriches and adds to experience by complicating it and providing opportunities for increased human interaction.

Even in this brief description of Dewey's ideas, it can be seen that experience was a key element in his experimentalist or instrumentalist philosophy of education. While the collective experience of man was individually built in associative life, the individual man experienced a more complex set of interactions and hence had the greatest opportunities for growth. Mind was built socially as a result of this total experience.

Dewey found every form of human association to be educational. As a means of social continuity, education transmitted the society's experience from its mature to its immature members. It also preserved the culture by imposing, at any particular time and place, its customs, mores, folkways, and languages upon the children of the cultural group. Without this transmission each generation would be forced to begin life in savagery. Formal education was, then, the deliberate, organized process of introducing the immature to their culture by providing them with the tools appropriate for participation and communication in the associative life of the group sustaining the particular culture. The cultural tools, language, number, and symbolic systems were the survival patterns perfected by man to enhance survival and master the environment.

Education, for Dewey, was a selective process. The cultural environment was vast and complex, containing the total experience of the society. Some of this total experience was of value, but other parts were detrimental to human growth.

The school, the specialized environment of society for the enculturation of the young, had a threefold function: to simplify, purify, and balance the cultural heritage which it transmitted to the immature members of society. The school simplified the complex environment by selecting parts of it and reducing its complexity to units which the immature would be able to comprehend according to their level of maturation and readiness for learning. The school purified the environment by choosing those parts of greatest social value and eliminating the elements detrimental to society. It then balanced the selected and purified experiences by integrating them into a harmonious totality, in an effort to produce integrated individuals in an integrated environment. The school thus represented a simplified, purified, and balanced environment in which the immature human organism encountered problems to be faced and solved. As the child learned to accomplish this he added to his experience or his growth.

For Dewey, the scientific method, broadly conceived, constituted man's most accurate and efficient means of controlling the process of change. By means of the scientific method, man could use change to manage his environment to effect his own purposes. Dewey framed the "complete act of thought" as a methodology of problem-solving, as a means of controlling environment. He structured the problem-solving method in a sequential process embracing five steps or phases:

1. The problematic situation: the individual experienced perplexity, confusion, and doubt since he was involved in an incomplete situation whose full character was still undetermined. In this phase, the individual's activity was impeded by an obstacle which was something new in terms of his prior experience.
2. Definition of the problem: in the second stage, the individual tried to locate and identify the difficulty.
3. Analysis: the individual made a careful survey, examination, exploration, and analysis of all aspects of the problem. This phase required the use of skills and knowledge to resolve the problem.
4. Hypothetical resolution: the individual conjectured possible alter-

native courses of action which might be used to resolve the problematic difficulty.

5. Solution: the individual selected that alternative which he believed would satisfactorily solve the problem and tested it by acting upon it. If the problem was resolved, the individual resumed activity until he encountered another problem.[1]

Dewey's "complete act of thought" was a rendition of an educational methodology which was used by some educators as the activity method or the problem-solving approach to learning. Students were to be involved in problems, rather than inert subject matter courses. The problems were to be based on the interests and needs of the learner. The child was to attempt to solve the problem by scientific procedure. The school did not offer preparation for solving future problems. It was anticipated that as a result of applying the method of science, the child would learn to use the process, which he would then transfer to situations in and out of school.

As the student applied the scientific approach to problem-solving, he was disciplining himself. Discipline was thus internal rather than a matter of external coercion as had often been the case in the more traditional school. Traditional educators had stressed that discipline should first be externally administered by the teacher. After a period of this deliberate coercion, the child would internalize the once imposed discipline. Dewey, however, disagreed with the traditionalists. Discipline came, he said, from the problem itself. It was intrinsic to the task, and the requirements of the task were what guided the learning process. The teacher was not to apply external coercion but was to supply guidance to aid the learner in solving his problems.

As the student learned to discipline himself in the use of the scientific method, his intelligence was socially built. The cooperative experience of working with others in mutual and associative problem-solving enriched the experience of the individual. As part of a group, he learned to cooperate with others, to discuss, to deliberate, and finally to act. The cooperative act, based on open, mutual communication, was at heart the democratic method. Because of this, the title of Dewey's major work, *Democracy and Education,* was made an article of pedagogical faith in the experimentalist-oriented progressive school.

The end of education, for Dewey, was simply growth leading to still further growth. In other words, education was to produce experience for the sake of experience. The experiencing, growing organism was the living

---

[1] John Dewey, *Democracy and Education* (New York: The Macmillan Company, 1964), p. 150. (Originally published in 1916.)

organism. When the processes of growth ceased, the organism was no longer alive. Growth involved the ability to relate one experience to other experiences, to relate one thing learned to other things learned. Knowledge gained through experience in solving problems meant that education, like life, was a process of continuous reconstruction of experience.

## THE DEWEY LABORATORY SCHOOL

Perhaps the most effective manner of discussing Dewey's experimental progressivism is to examine the work of his Laboratory School at the University of Chicago from 1896 to 1903. The most significant literature on the school is his own book, *The School and Society*, 1899, and *The Dewey School* by K. C. Mayhew and A. C. Edwards, published in 1936. According to Mayhew and Edwards, who were associates of Dewey's at the Laboratory School:

> As regards the spirit of the school, the chief object is to secure a free and informal community life in which each child will feel that he has a share and his own work to do. This is made the chief motive towards what are ordinarily termed order and discipline. It is believed that the only genuine order and discipline are those which proceed from the child's own respect for the work which he has to do and his consciousness of the rights of others who are, with himself, taking part in this work. As already suggested, the emphasis in the school upon various forms of practical and constructive activity gives ample opportunity for appealing to the child's social sense and to his regard for thorough and honest work.[2]

The same authors relate one of the experimental activities conducted by the students at the school:

> . . . One year there was a discussion of all the metals known to the children, together with their uses. Iron, lead, tin, copper, and zinc were compared as to their hardness, weight, and the amount of heat required to bring them to the melting point. Tin, zinc, and lead were melted over a bunsen burner and poured into water to cool. Since all the children had handled shot, they were interested in the spherical form assumed in cooling when the metal was poured from a height. In heating the metals, they noted the time necessary to melt lead and tin and learned that copper and iron wire did not melt, but became red hot and could be flattened easily by hammering. They were shown metals in the natural state and given

[2] Katherine Camp Mayhew and Anna Camp Edwards, *The Dewey School* (New York: D. Appleton-Century Co., 1936), p. 32. Copyright 1936 by D. Appleton-Century Company. Reprinted by permission of Appleton-Century-Crofts, division of Meredith Publishing Company.

the word ore as a general term. They discussed how metals were probably discovered. It was suggested that people may have found melted copper in the charcoal on the hearth, and they were given the various stories about the discovery of iron.

The next step was the construction of a smelting place of clay or stones. The chief problems for the children to solve in this undertaking were the position of the chimney and the arrangement for proper draught. They found by experience the advantage of a steady draught, how to protect the fire from sudden changes of wind, and that hard wood makes a hotter fire than soft. Further experimentation was necessary before they could understand the principle of draught. With the help of a taper, they investigated the currents of air in the room and found the current of cold air from the windows sinking to the floor and a current of warm air leaving the room at the top of the door. They then appreciated that the hot air in their furnace would rise and understood the necessity of a chimney for an intake of a continuous supply of cold air. Tin and zinc were melted successfully in a few of the best constructed smelters, and the group, now quite intelligent as to the principle, pooled their experience and labor to construct a larger one in which ore was to be melted for the tribe's arrow heads. . . .[3]

In the foregoing paragraphs, several key features of Dewey's experimental progressivism are evident. First of all, the emphasis on shared discussion was important. At several stages in the process, the children engaged in discussion. The discussion led to a sharing or pooling of experience. Secondly, at certain crucial stages, the ideas brought up in the discussion were actually tested in the children's experiments. In the case of their study of the principle of draught, they transformed the theory into actual constructive materials and tested it.

After Dewey concluded his educational experimentation at the Chicago Laboratory School, he returned to his work in formal philosophy and the philosophy of education. As professor of philosophy at Columbia University he completed his works on experimentalism. The philosophy of education that Dewey developed exerted a profound influence on American education in general and the "new education" of the twentieth century in particular.

## THE PROGRESSIVE MOVEMENT IN AMERICAN EDUCATION

While Dewey's experimental philosophy contributed substantially to the progressive movement in American education, it is inaccurate to consider

[3] *Ibid.*, pp. 109–10.

them synonymous. Experimental philosophy of education was based on a systematic theory according to the tenets of science. Progressive education, although it embraced experimentalism, enjoyed a much broader base of support among educators, and was less specific in character.

To study the origins of progressive education, one must begin by examining the ideas of the naturalistic educators of the late eighteenth and nineteenth centuries. Rousseau, Pestalozzi, and Froebel had developed theoretical positions that challenged traditional school practices. The eighteenth-century Enlightenment and nineteenth-century social reform had produced the new notion of "progress." Man could shape his environment, the reformers claimed, by using the instruments of reason and science. They thought that an educational methodology based on the laws of natural development could free man and move him along the path toward a better world.

In the United States, the early decades of the twentieth century have been referred to by historians as the era of the progressive movement in politics. Robert LaFollette, Theodore Roosevelt, and Woodrow Wilson led a national crusade against graft, corruption, decay, and monopoly. LaFollette's Wisconsin Idea was based on an intimate relationship between education and political reform. Although Wilson's New Freedom and Roosevelt's New Nationalism varied on some specifics, both Presidents believed that an enlightened citizenry could use the democratic process to achieve political, social, and economic reformation. The social work of Jane Addams, the journalism of Lincoln Steffens, and the legal opinions of Oliver W. Holmes, Jr., were expressions of the spirit of progressivism applied to society, letters, and law. Progressivism in education and in politics were parallel movements which challenged traditionalism and sought to offer creative responses to the problems of the twentieth century. Both movements optimistically placed their faith in the ability of the common man to use the democratic process as a means of achieving social progress.

The progressive educators, continuing to be infected by the spirit of Mann's optimism, believed that education could exercise a reforming influence. However, formal education itself first had to be reformed and rendered a progressive instrument. A number of teachers and administrators joined together in the Progressive Education Association, which was founded in 1919 under the early leadership of Stanwood Cobb. Although educational progressives, like political and social progressives, embraced a variety of programs, certain features emerged as basic to the reform pedagogy. Among them were the freedom of the child to develop naturally; stress on the interests and needs of the learner; recommendations for the scientific study of pupil growth; emphasis on the teacher's role as guide rather than taskmaster; and greater cooperation between the school and the society.[4]

## William Heard Kilpatrick

One of the great popularizers of Dewey's experimentalist philosophy of education was William Heard Kilpatrick. Born in rural Georgia in 1871, the son of a Baptist minister, Kilpatrick for a time taught in country schools in his native state and at Mercer College. As a teacher, Kilpatrick reacted strongly against the traditional approach to education, which he felt was characterized by a devitalized, bookish approach to knowledge. Focused entirely in the past, book learning tended to be a mechanical affair which an external authority imposed on the child. When Kilpatrick encountered the work of John Dewey, he found a theoretical structure to support his conviction that education needed to be involved in the interests and needs of the learner.

As professor of education at Teachers College of Columbia University Kilpatrick developed the project approach, which he patterned after Dewey's conception of the scientific method. He recommended that schoolwork be organized into activities that would demand the learner's effort. Kilpatrick distinguished four classes of projects:

One:    The constructive or creative project, whose purpose was for the students to formulate a plan or design which could be concretized.

Two:    The appreciation project, whose purpose was the enjoyment of an aesthetic experience such as reading, art appreciation, or hearing a musical composition.

Three:  The problem project, whose purpose was the solving of an intellectual difficulty.

Four:   The drill project, or specific learning project, whose purpose was the learning of a skill such as swimming, typing, writing.[5]

Kilpatrick attracted large numbers of students of education to his lectures at Teachers College. Many of these students themselves became educational leaders who advocated the project method. During the 1920's and 1930's this method of learning became immensely popular and characterized the new progressive education. One of the major attitudes which

[4] Adolph E. Meyer, *The Development of Education in the Twentieth Century* (Englewood Cliffs, N. J.: Prentice-Hall, Inc., 1949), p. 71.

[5] William H. Kilpatrick, "The Project Method," *Teachers College Record*, XIX, 4 (September, 1918), 319–35.

Kilpatrick sought to develop in his students, as did Dewey, was that of participation or democratic sharing. The group of students working on a given project was regarded as a kind of embryonic democratic society. If students learned to employ the methodology of science in solving the problems related to the group project, educators anticipated employing the method in a broader context to solve social, political, and economic problems as well.

## Conflicts and Criticism of Progressivism

Although Kilpatrick was concerned with both the individual child and the social context, many progressive educators were more narrowly concerned with the child. During the depression period of the 1930's, the excessively child-centered orientation of progressive education was challenged by George S. Counts who, in *Dare the School Build a New Social Order?*, urged progressive educators to direct their efforts toward effecting social reform through the schools.[6] The conflicts and counter-arguments between the child-centered and the socially oriented wings of the movement weakened progressivism. However, what was more important was that much of the progressive program was included in the program of the schools. Gradually the pedagogical reforms of progressivism became regular practices in the schools. Shortly after World War II, the Progressive Education Association disbanded as a formal organization.

Like any reform movement, progressive education was attacked by numerous critics. Among them was a group of prominent educators, such as William Chandler Bagley and Isaac Kandel, who were termed "essentialists." These people felt that the task of education was the cultivation of intellectual skills and knowledge. To them, the most efficient means of cultivating an intelligent citizenry was by systematically training its children in the basic subjects of reading, writing, arithmetic, history, English, and foreign languages. The essentialists felt that education should be a matter of hard work and discipline. They also believed that education was mainly the transmission of the social heritage. They did not believe that the school should be concerned with seeking to influence social, economic, or political change directly.

In the post-Sputnik era of the 1950's, a number of critics of public school education appeared. In *Educational Wastelands* and *The Restoration of Learning*, Arthur Bestor attacked what he saw as the "educationist establishment." Bestor urged a return to basic education grounded on

---

[6] George S. Counts, *Dare the School Build a New Social Order?* (New York: The John Day Company, 1932).

subject matter. Max Rafferty, former superintendent of California schools, in his book *Suffer Little Children*, charged the influence of the progressive reformers with contributing to the weakening of educational standards.

## CONCLUSION

It is an extremely difficult task to assess the progressive contribution to American education. As in any reform movement, there could be found extremists whose excesses did not represent its true spirit, as well as adherents who did not really understand its meaning and program. The confusion was compounded by many progressives engaging in internecine warfare and thereby further weakening the movement.

As a movement, progressive education never really succeeded in dominating the American public schools. Many of the outstanding progressive experiments were conducted in private schools. While certain public schools included problem-solving, projects, and activities in their programs, their over-all educational pattern remained geared to the subject-matter curriculum.

Despite these limitations, the movement did make certain contributions. The work of John Dewey, William H. Kilpatrick, and George S. Counts helped to build a philosophy of education based upon the scientific method, and the school was the testing ground of that philosophy. Within the experimentalist framework, theory and practice were closely connected.

The progressive advocates of experimentalism and the "new education" also recognized the intimate relation of the school to society. Education came to be considered a social enterprise which involved the highest moral leadership. In the 1930's, socially oriented progressives urged that the schools actively encourage social, economic, and political reform to aid the nation in overcoming economic depression. In the 1960's, educational leaders have viewed the school as an instrument for bringing about social and racial integration.

Progressive educators brought about a more enlightened view of the child. The principles of psychology were used in the reconstruction of method in the classroom. The new stress on activities and problem-solving encouraged a concept of knowledge as a working tool of man. The instrumental concepts of knowledge and education posited a future for man in which he could control the course of change and reshape his environment according to his own plans.

# References

BESTOR, ARTHUR E. *Educational Wastelands.* Urbana: University of Illinois Press, 1953.

COUNTS, GEORGE S. *Dare the School Build a New Social Order?* New York: The John Day Co., 1932.

CREMIN, LAWRENCE A. *The Transformation of the School.* New York: Alfred A. Knopf, 1962.

DEWEY, JOHN. *Democracy and Education.* New York: The Macmillan Company, 1916.

——. *Experience and Education.* New York: The Macmillan Company, 1938.

KILPATRICK, WILLIAM H. *Education and the Social Crisis.* New York: Liveright Corporation, 1932.

——. "The Project Method." *Teachers College Record,* XIX, 4 (September, 1918), 319–35.

MAYHEW, K. C., and EDWARDS, A. C. *The Dewey School.* New York: D. Appleton-Century Co., 1936.

MEYER, ADOLPH E. *The Development of Education in the Twentieth Century.* Englewood Cliffs, N.J.: Prentice-Hall, Inc., 1949.

# SELECTION

*In John Dewey's short book entitled* Experience and Education, *written in 1938, he took to task the defenders of educational traditionalism and extremist advocates of educational progressivism as well. Both schools of thought, he observed, were laboring under the difficulties of an "either-or" attitude. He urged progressives to develop a positive plan of action, a genuine philosophy of education, rather than being content with maintaining a purely negative attitude to traditional schooling. In the selection which follows, Dewey discusses the nature of freedom.*

## Experience and Education

. . . The only freedom that is of enduring importance is freedom of intelligence, that is to say, freedom of observation and of judgment exercised in behalf of purposes that are intrinsically worth while. The commonest mistake made about freedom is, I think, to identify it with freedom of movement, or with the external or physical side of activity. Now, this external or physical side of activity cannot be separated from the internal side of activity; from freedom of thought, desire, and purpose. The limitation that was put upon outward action by the fixed arrangements of the typical traditional schoolroom, with its fixed rows of desks and its military regimen of pupils who were permitted to move only at certain fixed signals, put a great restriction upon intellectual and moral freedom. Strait-jacket and chain-gang procedures had to be done away with if there was to be a chance for growth of individuals in the intellectual springs of freedom without which there is no assurance of genuine and continued normal growth.

But the fact still remains that an increased measure of freedom of outer movement is a *means*, not an end. The educational problem is not solved when this aspect of freedom is obtained. Everything then depends, so far as education is concerned, upon what is done with this added liberty. What end does it serve? What consequences flow from it? Let me speak first of the advantages which reside potentially in increase of outward freedom. In the first place, without its existence it is practically impossible for a teacher to gain knowledge of the indi-

SOURCE: John Dewey, *Experience and Education* (New York: The Macmillan Company, 1938), pp. 69–76. Used by permission of Kappa Delta Pi, An Honor Society in Education, owners of the copyright.

viduals with whom he is concerned. Enforced quiet and acquiescence prevent pupils from disclosing their real natures. They enforce artificial uniformity. They put seeming before being. They place a premium upon preserving the outward appearance of attention, decorum, and obedience. And everyone who is acquainted with schools in which this system prevailed well knows that thoughts, imaginations, desires, and sly activities ran their own unchecked course behind this façade. They were disclosed to the teacher only when some untoward act led to their detection. One has only to contrast this highly artificial situation with normal human relations outside the schoolroom, say in a well-conducted home, to appreciate how fatal it is to the teacher's acquaintance with and understanding of the individuals who are, supposedly, being educated. Yet without this insight there is only an accidental chance that the material of study and the methods used in instruction will so come home to an individual that his development of mind and character is actually directed. There is a vicious circle. Mechanical uniformity of studies and methods creates a kind of uniform immobility and this reacts to perpetuate uniformity of studies and of recitations, while behind this enforced uniformity individual tendencies operate in irregular and more or less forbidden ways.

The other important advantage of increased outward freedom is found in the very nature of the learning process. That the older methods set a premium upon passivity and receptivity has been pointed out. Physical quiescence puts a tremendous premium upon these traits. The only escape from them in the standardized school is an activity which is irregular and perhaps disobedient. There cannot be complete quietude in a laboratory or workshop. The non-social character of the traditional school is seen in the fact that it erected silence into one of its prime virtues. There is, of course, such a thing as intense intellectual activity without overt bodily activity. But capacity for such intellectual activity marks a comparatively late achievement when it is continued for a long period. There should be brief intervals of time for quiet reflection provided for even the young. But they are periods of genuine reflection only when they follow after times of more overt action and are used to organize what has been gained in periods of activity in which the hands and other parts of the body beside the brain are used. Freedom of movement is also important as a means of maintaining normal physical and mental health. We have still to learn from the example of the Greeks who saw clearly the relation between a sound body and a sound mind. But in all the respects mentioned freedom of outward action is a means to freedom of judgment and of power to carry deliberately chosen ends into execution. The amount of external freedom which is needed varies from individual to individual. It naturally tends to decrease with increasing maturity, though its complete absence prevents even a mature individual from having the contacts which will provide him with new materials upon which his intelligence may exercise itself. The amount and the quality of this kind of free activity as a means of growth is a problem that must engage the thought of the educator at every stage of development.

There can be no greater mistake, however, than to treat such freedom as an end in itself. It then tends to be destructive of the shared cooperative activities which are the normal source of order. But, on the other hand, it turns freedom which should be positive into something negative. For freedom from restriction, the negative side, is to be prized only as a means to a freedom which is power: power to frame purposes, to judge wisely, to evaluate desires by the consequences which will result from acting upon them; power to select and order means to carry chosen ends into operation.

Natural impulses and desires constitute in any case the starting point. But there is no intellectual growth without some reconstruction, some remaking, of impulses and desires in the form in which they first show themselves. This remaking involves inhibition of impulse in its first estate. The alternative to externally imposed inhibition is inhibition through an individual's own reflection and judgment. The old phrase "stop and think" is sound psychology. For thinking is stoppage of the immediate manifestation of impulse until that impulse has been brought into connection with other possible tendencies to action so that a more comprehensive and coherent plan of activity is formed. Some of the other tendencies to action lead to use of eye, ear, and hand to observe objective conditions; others result in recall of what has happened in the past. Thinking is thus a postponement of immediate action, while it effects internal control of impulse through a union of observation and memory, this union being the heart of reflection. What has been said explains the meaning of the well-worn phrase "self-control." The ideal aim of education is creation of power of self-control. But the mere removal of external control is no guarantee for the production of self-control. It is easy to jump out of the frying-pan into the fire. It is easy, in other words, to escape one form of external control only to find oneself in another and more dangerous form of external control. Impulses and desires that are not ordered by intelligence are under the control of accidental circumstance. It may be a loss rather than a gain to escape from the control of another person only to find one's conduct dictated by immediate whim and caprice; that is, at the mercy of impulses into whose formation intelligent judgment has not entered. A person whose conduct is controlled in this way has at most only the illusion of freedom. Actually he is directed by forces over which he has no command.

# 10

# Education and Integration

## INTRODUCTION

Horace Mann and Henry Barnard both believed that the common school was designed to promote the integration of Americans into a national community. Children of varied social, racial, ethnic, economic, and religious backgrounds would share in one democratic system of education which would unite these several separate peoples into one, indivisible union. Throughout the nineteenth century the common school served to assimilate more than thirty-five million immigrants into American life. Yet despite its success in Americanizing immigrants, the common school failed to realize completely the goal of social integration. Large numbers of Americans were still excluded from full economic, political, and social participation in their nation's life. Although American educators theorized about equality of educational opportunity, many American children were still educationally disenfranchised because of race and poverty.

The military victory of the northern armies in the Civil War liberated almost four million Negro slaves. In 1865, ratification of the Thirteenth Amendment to the Constitution abolished slavery in the United States; in 1866, the Fourteenth Amendment specified that no state should "deprive any person of life, liberty, or property, without due process of law." While these Constitutional amendments formally ended Negro servitude, many of the effects of over two hundred years of slavery remained to plague both black and white in the years after the Civil War.

Although they were legally free, many American Negroes were excluded from the national democratization by the doctrine of "separate but equal" which legalized practices of racial segregation. After 1875, southern states enacted laws which segregated public transportation, accommodations, and other facilities. In 1896, the Supreme Court in the *Plessy v.*

*Ferguson* decision upheld these practices. The "separate but equal" doctrine had a particularly pernicious effect upon the theory of equal educational opportunity. Although the states claimed that white and black schools received equal support, some spent much more money to educate the white than the Negro children. The following pages outline the struggle of the American Negro to begin to take part in the common dream of the promise of American life by describing some of the major events that have helped to overturn the "separate but equal" doctrine.

## BROWN V. BOARD OF EDUCATION OF TOPEKA

In the 1950's and 1960's, the attention of the American public was focused on the problem of racial integration as Negro citizens actively sought the social, racial, political, and educational equality so long promised them by law. In terms of education, the most significant event in securing equal opportunity was the 1954 decision by the United States Supreme Court in the case of *Brown v. the Board of Education of Topeka*. It was also one of the major events in recent years which gave substantial impetus to the movement—and all its ramifications—of the Negro Americans to achieve recognition of their civil rights in every area. In this case the Court overthrew the 1896 *Plessy v. Ferguson* decision which had upheld the state's maintenance of separate schools for white and Negro children as a valid exercise of its legislative rights. In the light of sociological and psychological evidence, Chief Justice Warren, speaking for the Court, stated:

> Segregation of white and colored children in public schools has a detrimental effect upon the colored children. The impact is greater when it has the sanction of the law; for the policy of separating the races is usually interpreted as denoting the inferiority of the Negro group. A sense of inferiority affects the motivation of a child to learn. Segregation with the sanction of law, therefore, has a tendency to retard the education and mental development of Negro children and to deprive them of some of the benefits they would receive in a racially integrated school system.[1]

The civil rights movement had two major lines of development in relation to the schools. At first civil rights advocates concentrated on the schools of the old South and the border states, where segregation had the force of long-standing law as well as custom. Although the decision of 1954 reversed the "separate but equal" doctrine, much actual legal spadework had to be done to make enforcement of the decision a reality. The second area concerned the schools of the northern states, especially in the large

[1] *Brown v. Board of Education*, 347 U.S. 483 (1954).

cities, where there had been an influx of Negro migration from the South. In these northern metropolitan areas the patterns of racial segregation took a more subtle form. Here segregation came to be referred to as *de facto*, having its basis usually in the residential patterns that developed rather than in actual legislation.

## The Southern White Reaction

The southern white reaction to the events of 1954 was at first one of disbelief and defiance of the Supreme Court's decision, and then of token acceptance. Almost immediately, some southern white politicians resurrected the "states' rights" argument against the anti-segregation decision. The legislature of South Carolina passed a Resolution on February 16, 1954, "condemning and protesting the usurpation and encroachment on the Reserved Powers of the States by the Supreme Court." On March 12, 1956, seventeen United States Senators and seventy-seven Representatives to Congress presented this statement:

> Without regard to the consent of the governed, outside agitators are threatening immediate and revolutionary changes in our public school systems. If done, this is certain to destroy the system of public education in some of the States.

Grudgingly, politicians in some of the southern states complied with the Court's decision, but not without testing the federal government's willingness to implement it. In 1957, Governor Faubus of Arkansas attempted to block the integration of the Little Rock schools. President Eisenhower met the Governor's tactics with an executive order which authorized the use of federal troops. In 1962, Governor Barnett of Mississippi attempted to halt the enrollment of James Meredith, a Negro, in the University of Mississippi. Governor Barnett claimed to base his action of interposition on the Tenth Amendment of the United States Constitution. He alleged that the interests of order and safety required him to "interpose and invoke the police powers of the state." The use of the word "interpose" harked back to John C. Calhoun's long buried but equally futile doctrine of "interposition." President Kennedy ordered federal troops into the state of Mississippi to end violence in Oxford, and to secure Meredith's admission to the University.

## THE ORIGINS OF THE SOUTH'S PROBLEMS

An examination of the effects of the events of the 1950's and 1960's on southern racial relations that is based solely on the question of states' rights versus federal power is insufficient for an adequate interpretation of the situation. To understand the racial crisis in the South we must at least briefly review the history of the South and the history of the Negro.

Historically, the existence of Negro slavery as a part of the plantation economy had made southern social developments different from those in the northern states. Slavery came to be regarded as the South's peculiar institution. Some southern leaders during the revolutionary and early national periods had regarded slavery as a necessary evil. A few, like Jefferson, favored the gradual emancipation of the slaves and their resettlement in Africa. In 1793, Eli Whitney invented a cotton gin that made it possible to easily separate the cotton fibers from the seeds. This made it economically efficient to cultivate cotton on a large scale in the South, and a vast area of land extending from Georgia and South Carolina westward to Texas was opened to "King Cotton" and the plantation system. The growth of the textile industry in England and in the North gave the cotton planters a market for their produce which stimulated the southern economy and led to a rapid increase in the number of Negro slaves.

Until the 1840's, southern leaders had apologized for slavery as a necessary evil. When northern abolitionists such as William Lloyd Garrison and Horace Greeley attacked slavery in the decade before the Civil War, southerners went further and began to try to justify it. Articles in *De Bow's Review*, a leading southern publication, contained a positive defense of slavery. Edmund Ruffin, a noted agriculturalist, argued that Negro slavery had produced a well-ordered society based on the model in Plato's *Republic*. Other writers, such as Governor Hammond of South Carolina, found it justified in the Old Testament. Although the Civil War, fought from 1861 to 1865, destroyed slavery by armed force, some southerners continued to accept the doctrine of Negro inferiority that had been part of the rationale used to justify the South's "peculiar institution."

The southern Negro faced hostility from whites who had been raised from birth on the theory of white supremacy. In addition to this racial hostility, he was victimized by the debilitating effects of the slave system in other ways. Since slave marriages had no legal status, there was no reliable family structure. Many southern states had made it a legal offense to teach Negroes to read during the slave period and as a result most of them were illiterate. Further, the system was such that most of them were forced into a condition of childish dependence upon white masters.

At the close of the Civil War the Negro population, nearly four and a half million, was located almost entirely in the South. Only about 300,000 Negroes lived in northern states. It has been estimated that only three per cent of the Negro population were literate. Since Negroes had been denied education during slavery, the task of teaching them was enormous.

As the Union Army entered the South, northern charitable and religious groups sent funds and teachers to educate the newly freed former slaves. Schools were established and staffed by the "New England school marms" who were much maligned by some white southerners. Although these voluntary and charitable efforts made some inroads, they were inadequate to deal with the magnitude of the problem of Negro education. In 1865, the federal government established the Freedmen's Bureau under the direction of General Oliver O. Howard. From its founding until 1870, the Bureau maintained a school system which enrolled almost a quarter of a million black students.

During the Reconstruction period, which began with the Confederate defeat in 1865 and lasted in some southern states until 1877, Negroes had their first encounters with democratic government. During these years, southern state governments were controlled by black representatives in coalition with radical Republicans. Although some historians have interpreted Reconstruction as an era of political corruption and graft on the part of blacks, "scalawags," and "carpetbaggers," there has been in recent years a revision and reinterpretation of the times. Critics of the Reconstruction legislatures neglected to mention their constructive contributions such as abolition of property requirements for suffrage, reform of penal institutions, construction of roads and highways, and most significantly the establishment of free public schools. Prior to the Civil War, most southern states had not established common schools. It was not until Reconstruction that these states inaugurated systems of public education.

After the post-Civil War period of Reconstruction ended in 1877, the Negro's position as a freed man was determined by the economic and political conflicts among the divided white southerners. Three major socioeconomic classes had emerged in the post-war era: the land-owning and industry-owning white leadership, the socio-economically disadvantaged "poor whites," and the Negro. The only thing separating the Negro and the "poor white" was the color line. The "poor white" had been antagonistic toward the Negro before the Civil War, and emancipation only served to harden his hatred of the latter as an economic competitor.

Toward the end of the nineteenth century, racial rivalries intensified as political fuel was added to the burning embers of antagonism. Until the 1880's, the Democratic Party was the sole political force in the South. In the late 1880's and 1890's, the Populist Party was organized. Thus the Negroes became the balance of power between the two hostile white groups who were seeking political power among the voters. Gradually the "poor white" agriculturalists gained control, and determined that Negroes should never again exercise the role of political balance in the South.

Leaders of the "poor white" element such as Pitchfork Ben Tillman of South Carolina and Cole Blease of Mississippi stirred up racial antagonism and maintained their factions in power. At first, by restricting the primaries to white voters only, Negro voters were excluded but not actually disenfranchised. By the late 1890's and early 1900's, however, rigid segregation laws had been enacted, and the Negro was actively disenfranchised by property qualification, literacy tests, poll taxes, and the white primary. Every area of southern life became segregated, to the point of maintaining separate drinking fountains and transportation requirements. The disenfranchisement took place with little protest from the northern white community. Many northern progressives failed to include a place for Negro citizens in their programs of social reform, as well. The prevailing mood of social Darwinism, with its emphasis on white Anglo-Saxon superiority, produced a climate of opinion that tolerated and tacitly approved the segregation legislation. The growth of these attitudes reinforced the already existing pattern of separate schools for the races. It is interesting to note that much of what compulsory common-school legislation was enacted in the South owed its existence to the much maligned Reconstruction period and the so-called "carpetbag" legislatures.

## BOOKER T. WASHINGTON

After the Reconstruction period, the task of Negro leadership fell to an Alabama educator, Booker T. Washington, president of Tuskegee Institute. Concerning himself with educating Negroes in vocations and trades, Washington urged them to avoid the political arena. Thus, at the very time when Negroes were being disenfranchised and excluded from sharing the growing opportunities of American life, their own leading spokesman urged caution and patience. Washington felt that Negroes had tried to move too quickly into professional and political life and first needed to establish themselves by building a solid economic base as skilled workers and craftsmen.

As an educational statesman, Washington worked hard to cultivate amicable relations between members of both races. His autobiography, *Up From Slavery*, recounts his own career and the difficult early history of Tuskegee.[2] Some idea of Washington's social theory can be gained from his famous Atlanta Exposition Address, which he delivered at the opening of the Cotton States Exposition in Atlanta in 1895. In this address, which

[2] Booker T. Washington, *Up From Slavery* (New York: Doubleday & Company, 1938).

has been referred to as the Atlanta Compromise, Washington urged Negroes to cultivate friendly relations with southern whites. He expressed regret that some Negroes believed participation in politics more important than property ownership or the acquisition of skills. He urged Negroes to improve themselves by seeking occupations in agriculture, mechanics, commerce, domestic service, and the professions.[3] Washington also believed that they should remain in the South, where they should work out their destiny with the co-operation of the white community:

> As we have proved our loyalty to you in the past, in nursing your children, watching by the sick bed of your mothers and fathers, and often following them with tear-dimmed eyes to their graves, as in the future, in our humble way, we shall stand by you with a devotion that no foreigner can approach, ready to lay down our lives, if need be, in defense of yours, interlacing our industrial, commercial, civil, and religious lives with yours in a way that shall make the interests of both races one. In all things that are purely social we can be as separate as the fingers, yet one as the hand in all things essential to mutual progress.[4]

As a practical educator, Washington sought to make Tuskegee Institute into a national example of successful educational effort. He recognized a close relationship between theory and practice, building a curriculum that combined industrial work and academic training as complementary subjects, and teaching that "working with the hands" was a source of uplifting moral power. Washington designed Tuskegee's educational program to teach the dignity of labor, to thoroughly and effectively teach the trades, to supply the demand for trained leaders, and to help students meet their educational expenses.[5]

In assessing Washington's social and political influence on the course of Negro-white racial relations, it must be remembered that he contributed to a climate of opinion that prevailed until the time when the Negro began to re-assert himself in the struggle for equality. Washington labored at a time when he could have counted on few white or northern voices to aid him had he attempted to lead a struggle for racial equality. Washington's speech and attitude was at best an uneasy compromise with the racial *status quo*.

[3] E. Davidson Washington, ed., *Selected Speeches of Booker T. Washington* (New York: Doubleday, Doran, and Co., 1932), pp. 31–36.

[4] *Ibid.*, p. 34.

[5] Booker T. Washington, *Working with the Hands* (New York: Doubleday, Page, and Co., 1904), pp. 80–81.

## NEGRO SELF-ASSERTION

The days of Washington's Atlanta Compromise may have represented temporary acceptance of the *status quo* by some Negroes, but not for all. The noted Negro historian W.E.B. Du Bois became a strong critic of Washington's rationale for Negro social progress. According to Du Bois, Washington's position involved a triple paradox:

. . . . Is it possible, and probable, that nine millions of men can make effective progress in economic lines if they are deprived of political rights, made a servile caste, and allowed only the most meagre chance for developing their exceptional men? If history and reason give any distinct answer to these questions, it is an emphatic No. And Mr. Washington thus faces the triple paradox of his career:

1. He is striving nobly to make Negro artisans business men and property owners; but it is utterly impossible, under modern competitive methods, for workingmen and property owners to defend their rights and exist without the right of suffrage.

2. He insists on thrift and self-respect, but at the same time counsels a silent submission to civic inferiority such as is bound to sap the manhood of any race in the long run.

3. He advocates common-school and industrial training, and depreciates institutions of higher learning; but neither the Negro common schools, nor Tuskegee itself, could remain open a day were it not for teachers trained in Negro colleges or trained by their graduates.[6]

As a result of criticism from Du Bois and others, interested individuals, both Negro and white, who were concerned with the advancement of the cause of racial equality organized the Niagara Movement in 1905. Among the principles of the new movement were freedom of speech and criticism, abolition of distinctions based on color and race, recognition of human brotherhood, and the right of all to education.

The first decade of the twentieth century witnessed a number of violent race riots. In August of 1908, a bloody race riot occurred in Springfield, Illinois, within view of Lincoln's home. Between 1880 and 1920 more than 3,000 lynchings occurred in the United States, 70 per cent of whom were Negro victims. In the light of these events the Atlanta Compromise was not a working agreement.

In 1910, under the leadership of the constitutional lawyer Moorfield Storey and Du Bois, the National Association for the Advancement of Col-

[6] W. E. Burghardt Du Bois, *The Souls of Black Folk: Essays and Sketches* (Chicago: A. C. McClurg and Co., 1903), pp. 51–52.

ored People was founded. The NAACP rejected the submissiveness of Washington's Atlanta Compromise and advocated:

1. The strict enforcement of the civil rights guaranteed by the Fourteenth Amendment;
2. Equal educational opportunities for all and in all the states, and the same public school expenditure for the Negro and the white child;
3. In accord with the Fifteenth Amendment, that the right of the Negro to vote on the same terms as other citizens be recognized in all parts of the country.

The work of the NAACP consisted of advancing the arguments for racial equality through the courts under the leadership of first Storey and in later years Thurgood Marshall. The NAACP's efforts culminated in the famous Supreme Court decision of 1954, which struck at the heart of legal segregation. At first, observers believed that the jurisdiction of the decision was limited to *de jure* [7] segregation in the South. However, the second phase in the movement toward racial equality was the attack launched against *de facto* segregation in the large northern cities.

## THE CIVIL RIGHTS MOVEMENT

A number of cities such as Chicago, New York, Philadelphia, Los Angeles, and others each had a growing Negro community that was fed by the continuing in-migration from the South. These population centers required a complicated readjustment of racial relations. The integration of the Negro into urban life was not only a racial problem though; it was complicated by socio-economic factors which had definite educational consequences. One of the consequences of racial prejudice for the Negro has been his economic suffering. His lower economic class status has usually resulted in lack of educational opportunity and little social mobility. Much of the burden of readjustment or reconstruction has fallen upon the American public school. Several factors have contributed to the complexity of racial relations in terms of education:

[7] The terms *de jure* and *de facto* are Latin phrases which are descriptively applied to certain legal situations. *De jure* means by right, or by lawful title. *De jure* segregation has come to refer to a separation of the races which is enforced by law. For example, southern school segregation prior to 1954 had the force of law. In contrast, *de facto* means actually, in fact, or in reality. *De facto* segregation has come to refer to racial separation, accidental or deliberate, which exists but without the sanction of law. For example, the residential patterns of many large northern cities are racially segregated but without force of law.

1. The typical northern metropolitan area did not have legal or *de jure* segregation laws: schools were not segregated on the basis of law.

2. The large northern city was made up of residential areas or extensive neighborhoods. Many of these residential areas were populated by people of similar economic and often ethnic backgrounds. Partly because of long-standing residential patterns and partly because of increased racial tensions, some neighborhoods evolved into strictly Negro and strictly white sections. The genuinely integrated residential area was rare. The Negro population tended to be confined in the center of the city where residential buildings were deteriorating. The white population was located on the periphery of the city or in adjacent suburban areas. As the Negro gradually moved outward from the central city, the white moved farther away to the fringes of the city or to the suburban areas. Examples of this racial movement can be found in the south side of Chicago, the Harlem area of New York, and the Watts area of Los Angeles.

3. The schools had been the scene of racial segregation in the South. As a result of the Court's decision, they now became the focal point of the struggle for racial equality. Civil rights leaders viewed the school as a means of bringing about social, political and economic mobility. The common school had been intended as a great welder of an integrated community. The northern public school also became the center for a movement toward racial integration.

4. The public school in the United States has usually been located in the residential area of the children who were to attend it. In fact, an attitude developed which considered the public school a "neighborhood school." As had been pointed out, there were very few genuinely integrated neighborhoods in the large northern communities. Since residential patterns were for the most part either white or Negro, neighborhood schools based upon the population of a specific residential area tended to be attended by either white or Negro children. Civil rights leaders attacked the *status quo* in northern education as *de facto* segregation and urged that something be done to improve the situation.

The 1960's have witnessed large-scale protests against what has been termed northern *de facto* segregation. While still using the courts and other legal means, some civil rights groups have turned to more directly activist methods of achieving their goals such as non-violent demonstrations or school boycotts. School administrators have found themselves the targets of these and other pressures. In such cities as Chicago and Milwaukee, school boycotts were held in which Negro parents kept their children out of the public school for short periods of time in order to protest school policies. In order to examine the racial balance in the schools, some boards of education have conducted racial head-counts and other surveys. Chicago's Hauser Report is one example of such surveys.[8]

Since they have been different from place to place, it is difficult to generalize about the educational programs of the various civil rights organizations. Yet they do have certain features in common. All of the major civil rights organizations remain committed to the American ideal of providing equality of educational opportunity to all children. All of them believe that equality can best be achieved through programs of genuinely integrated education. Both the National Urban League and the NAACP recommend that: 1) inner city children be taught by qualified teachers; 2) remedial reading programs and other forms of compensatory education be instituted where needed; 3) integrated education be regarded as a national opportunity for all American children regardless of color. In addition to sharing these goals, the Southern Christian Leadership Conference has expressed a special commitment to securing improved educational opportunities for the poor and has recommended more adult education programs and preferential programs to overcome cultural deprivation. Most of the civil rights organizations have also favored the inclusion of Afro-American history in the curriculum.

Although they have generally agreed on certain educational recommendations, there have been differences over specific programs designed to achieve integrated education. Some have suggested the bussing of students from one racial area to another within the large cities in order to achieve racial balance in classrooms. Others have recommended overlapping school districts to embrace both black and white areas. Civil rights leaders have also charged that the quality of education in the inner city schools is usually inferior to that of the fringes of the city and the suburban areas. To upgrade educational programs in the inner city schools, compensatory and remedial programs, recruitment of qualified teachers, increased expenditures, extended school years, reduction of class enrollments, and expanded vocational programs have been urged.

The problem of achieving real racial integration and equal educational

[8] The Advisory Panel of Integration of the Public Schools, *Report to the Board of Education City of Chicago*, March 31, 1964, p. 15. This *Report*, prepared by a panel headed by Professor Philip M. Hauser, indicated that the great majority of Chicago public school students attended schools which were segregated on a *de facto* basis. For example, among all students from grades one through twelve, exclusive of special education students, 84% of the 207,000 Negro students were in Negro schools and 86% of the 225,000 white students were in white schools. The *Report* concluded that *de facto* school segregation results mainly from residential segregation, which is reinforced by a policy of geographically determined school attendance areas based on a system of neighborhood schools.

opportunity for all Americans will not be easily solved. Irrational and emotional elements have also urged non-democratic methods of solving the problem. The Ku Klux Klan, the White Citizens' Council, and the Black Nationalists have advocated various means of resolving the racial situation that would call for a segregated pattern of life. Other groups, like the Southern Christian Leadership Conference, the National Association for the Advancement of Colored People, and the Urban League, have recognized that school integration is only one part of a much larger problem that involves economic, social, and political integration. The fact that the school is a focal point in the struggle shows how much the majority of Americans continue to rely on education as a democratic means of building a community that can solve such pressing problems.

## THE CULTURALLY DISADVANTAGED

Educators working in the 1950's, and 1960's have coined a new term, the "culturally disadvantaged." In 1964, the Johnson administration launched a "war on poverty" designed to alleviate conditions of economic desperation that have plagued certain segments of our population. "Cultural disadvantage" usually results from poverty; it is not necessarily a racial problem. Pockets of unemployment in rural areas have infected the white Appalachian region as well as the "Big City" slums populated by Negroes, Puerto Ricans, and other minority groups. Although the problems of educating the culturally disadvantaged have long been neglected, a concerted effort has been made by both the federal government and local communities to improve educational possibilities for this large group of Americans. Retraining programs have been initiated to provide adults with employable skills. More emphasis has been placed on encouraging adolescents to complete high school. With a growing awareness of the psychological and educational effects produced by cultural deprivation, educators have begun to prepare new instructional materials and methods for use in deprived areas. New programs of teacher education have been introduced to prepare teachers for the special problems of the inner city school.

The problem of educating the culturally disadvantaged has been aggravated by what sociologists and philosophers of education have called the value-clash in the schools between the middle and lower socioeconomic classes.[9] By definition, education is involved with the selection,

---

[9] Carlton E. Beck, Normand R. Bernier, James B. Macdonald, Thomas W. Walton, and Jack C. Willers, *Education for Relevance: The Schools and Social Change* (Boston: Houghton Mifflin Company, 1968), pp. 57–129, deals extensively with the question of alienation and the school.

preservation, and transmission of societal values. Not only are school programs concerned with information, understanding, and skills; they also have to do with preferences about how one should live and what one should prize or value. By and large, the American public school subscribes to and reflects the life patterns of the majority of the population, which tends to fall into the category that is commonly referred to as the "American middle class." The school is an institution established by this majority, and it has reflected the middle-class educational values of literacy, utilitarianism, preparation for employability, respect for property and for gradual and peaceful processes of social change. American schoolteachers have been largely drawn from the middle class, and their lives as well as their teaching have reflected the values of their socio-economic group.

People in the lower socio-economic classes, especially the culturally disadvantaged, have experienced long periods of frustration in which the avenues of social mobility have been closed to them due to their lack of competence in the cultural skills and tools considered so important by the middle class. Because of racial discrimination and economic deprivation, the culturally disadvantaged often feel that the program of the middle-class school is irrelevant to their needs. These groups frequently feel alienated from the values which the school seeks to cultivate. As a result of this frustration, the disadvantaged group does not share the middle class's broad value preferences and has evolved its own set. When its members are confronted with the seemingly alien values of the school, the result is often disinterest or rebellion against the teacher and the school on the part of the students.

An important phase of the "war on poverty" has been to foster the predisposition toward schooling that is needed for educational success. In particular, the federally financed "Project Head Start" has attempted to provide pre-school experiences for the culturally deprived youngster so that he may develop a favorable attitude to the school program. The success of this and other projects depends upon the amount of time, money, and skill that the majority is willing to spend on the disadvantaged minority.

## EDUCATION AND THE URBAN CRISIS

A major thesis of this book has been that formal education is a social process and that the school is a social institution. Educational issues have been presented as closely interwoven with economic, social, political, and religious issues. In this context, formal education cannot be considered as isolated within four walls of a building, but rather as it projects its consequences throughout society. In turn, the currents of social change also affect the educational situation in terms of the school's goals, curriculum, program, and processes. This chapter has dealt with racial and social integration which is one of the most crucial issues facing both the American school and American society.

Although racial and social integration affect schools nationally, the problem is most acute in the large urban areas. It is in these population centers that the black ghettos have developed and that conditions of dire poverty exist. During the summer of 1967, especially violent race riots erupted in the cities of Newark and Detroit. Again, following the assassination of Martin Luther King in the spring of 1968, there were further disorders in several cities, including Chicago and the nation's capital, Washington, D. C.

On July 28, 1967, President Lyndon Johnson established a National Advisory Commission on Civil Disorders, headed by Governor Otto Kerner of Illinois as chairman and Mayor John Lindsay of New York City as vice-chairman. The report of this Commission will probably be one of the most revealing documentary sources for the future historian who attempts to unravel the threads of racial conflict in the United States. The Kerner Commission considered various aspects of the racial disorders in terms of their historical, sociological, economic, legal, and educational causes. The members of the President's Commission on Civil Disorders were very much aware of the interrelationship of the urban school with its society.[10]

The Commission found that the quality of education in the inner-city school of the black ghetto was inadequate and unequal to that provided for most white children. According to the report:

> . . . for many minorities, and particularly for the children of the racial ghetto, the schools have failed to provide the educational experiences which could help overcome the effects of discrimination and deprivation.
>
> This failure is one of the persistent sources of grievance and resentment within the Negro community. The hostility of Negro parents and students toward the school system is generating increasing conflict and causing disruption within many city school districts.[11]

The Commission identified many sources of the inadequacy of the inner city schools. Most of these schools were still rigidly segregated, with

---

[10] The National Advisory Commission on Civil Disorders, *Report of the National Advisory Commission on Civil Disorders* (New York: Bantam Books, Inc., 1968), pp. 424–56, deals specifically with education.

[11] *Ibid.*, pp. 424–25.

the result that 90 per cent of Negro students were attending classes in schools where the majority of the enrollment was Negro. Rather than decreasing in the period since 1954, segregation was actually growing.

Schools attended by disadvantaged Negro children, it was discovered, had teaching staffs with less experience and lower qualifications than schools attended by white middle-class children. Severe overcrowding in inner-city schools resulted in large class sizes and shortages of necessary textbooks and supplies. Located in the oldest areas of the city, these schools were housed in obsolete and poorly equipped buildings. These conditions, along with the complex problem of cultural deprivation, contributed to low verbal and reading achievements among the Negro children attending such schools.

Inner-city schools were also caught up in the financial crisis that plagues most cities. Because of the declining taxation base, education budgets were too limited to begin to solve the massive problem of financing quality education. On the other hand, state contributions and federal assistance were inadequate to provide the funds needed for compensatory educational programs to equalize educational opportunities.

Along with the burden of financial and physical difficulties of the schools, students and parents in the ghetto often felt alienated from formal educational processes and institutions. In many instances the Commission found that ghetto schools were apparently unresponsive to the community, and that communications had broken down between school administrators and the communities they served. The ghetto youth found formal education irrelevant to both their needs and their culture. Parents were often distrustful of school officials who were responsible for formulating and implementing educational policies.

The Kerner Commission recommended several broad strategies to improve education within the inner city. The most pressing problem was that of eliminating *de facto* racial segregation. Not only was integration a priority in education, it was a national necessity to the future of American society. Compensatory education was needed to improve the quality of instruction in the ghetto schools and to facilitate maximum achievement in integrated schools as well. Along with programs designed to affect instruction directly, the Commission urged improvement of school-community relations by expanding opportunities for community and parental participation in the school system. It also recommended expanded opportunities for higher and vocational education.

In terms of suggesting specific programs, the Kerner Commission urged that increased financial assistance be given by local, state, and federal authorities for innovative experiments to eliminate *de facto* racial segregation. For example, exemplary or magnate schools might be established on an integrated basis, offering special programs to attract students of varying racial and socio-economic backgrounds. Year-round education might be provided for disadvantaged students. These extended programs would include a wide range of educational experiences directed toward improving verbal skills, providing job training, and embracing cultural, aesthetic, and recreational activities. Emphasis should be on early childhood education and preschool programs, such as Head Start, to overcome early deprivation of language skills and conceptual disabilities. Textbooks and curricula should be revised to include recognition of the culture, history, and contributions of minority groups to American civilization. Underlying all of the Commission's recommendations was a strong plea for intensive concentration on the improvement of basic verbal skills in reading and writing, since these are the necessary foundations for later educational achievements.

In many respects, the Kerner Commission's recommendations re-echoed the arguments made by Horace Mann and Henry Barnard in the early nineteenth century when they advocated public support for the common school. Mann and Barnard had pointed to public education as the great equalizer of American society and as the most effective means of building an integrated national community with mutual interests and aspirations. When John Dewey wrote about the "great society," he too regarded education as a social process working toward the same ends. When George S. Counts wrote about the American public school, he called it *The American Road to Culture*. If the school is to help fulfill the promise of American life, then its energies must be directed to the unsolved problems of racial and social integration which beset this generation of Americans.

## References

ANDERSON, ARCHIBALD; CLIFT, VIRGIL A.; and HULLFISH, H. GORDON, eds. *Negro Education in America*. New York: Harper & Row, Publishers, 1962.

BECK, CARLTON E.; BERNIER, NORMAND R.; MACDONALD, JAMES B.; WALTON, THOMAS W.; and WILLERS, JACK C. *Education for Relevance: The Schools and Social Change*. Boston: Houghton Mifflin Company, 1968.

BOND, HORACE MANN. *The Education of the Negro in the American Social Order*. Englewood Cliffs, N.J.: Prentice-Hall, Inc., 1934.

DU BOIS, W.E. BURGHARDT. *Black Reconstruction*. New York: Harcourt, Brace & Co., 1935.

———. *The Souls of Black Folk*. Chicago: A. C. McClurg and Co., 1903.

FRAZIER, E. FRANKLIN. *The Negro in the United States*. New York: The Macmillan Company, 1949.

National Advisory Commission on Civil Disorders. *Report of the National Advisory Commission on Civil Disorders.* New York: Bantam Books, Inc., 1968.

WASHINGTON, BOOKER T. *The Future of the American Negro.* Boston: Small, Maynard and Co., 1900.

———. *Working With the Hands.* New York: Doubleday, Page, and Co., 1904.

WASHINGTON, E. DAVIDSON, ed. *Selected Speeches of Booker T. Washington.* New York: Doubleday, Doran, and Co., 1932.

# SELECTIONS

Booker T. Washington, the Negro educator who first attempted to lead Negro Americans up from slavery, believed that social improvement for Negroes would follow if they had a solid economic base. He urged Negroes to seek economic betterment through the trades and crafts rather than through political means. By nature Washington seems to have been a gradualist, a conservative, and a practical man. Although his attitude is not widely accepted today, it does represent an important historical attitude on the gradualistic method of bringing about social and economic change through education. In the selection below, taken from The Future of the American Negro, Washington discusses the role of education in that future.

# The Future of the American Negro

One of the main problems as regards the education of the Negro is how to have him use his education to the best advantage after he has secured it. In saying this, I do not want to be understood as implying that the problem of simple ignorance among the masses has been settled in the South; for this is far from true. The amount of ignorance still prevailing among the Negroes, especially in the rural districts, is very large and serious. But I repeat, we must go farther if we would secure the best results and most gratifying returns in public good for the money spent than merely to put academic education in the Negro's head with the idea that this will settle everything.

In his present condition it is important, in seeking after what he terms the ideal, that the Negro should not neglect to prepare himself to take advantage of the opportunities that are right about his door. If he lets these opportunities slip, I fear they will never be his again. In saying this, I mean always that the Negro should have the most thorough mental and religious training; for without it no race can succeed. Because of his past history and environment and present condition it is important that he be carefully guided for years to come in the proper use of his education. Much valuable time has been lost and money spent in vain, because too many have not been educated with the idea of fitting them to do well

Source: Booker T. Washington, The Future of the American Negro (Boston: Small, Maynard, and Co., 1900), pp. 67–69, 78–82.

the things which they could get to do. Because of the lack of proper direction of the Negro's education, some good friends of his, North and South, have not taken that interest in it that they otherwise would have taken. In too many cases where merely literary education alone has been given the Negro youth, it has resulted in an exaggerated estimate of his importance in the world, and an increase of wants which his education has not fitted him to supply.

But, in discussing this subject, one is often met with the question, Should not the Negro be encouraged to prepare himself for any station in life that any other race fills? I would say, Yes; but the surest way for the Negro to reach the highest positions is to prepare himself to fill well at the present time the basic occupations. This will give him a foundation upon which to stand while securing what is called the more exalted positions. The Negro has the right to study law; but success will come to the race sooner if it produces intelligent, thrifty farmers, mechanics, and housekeepers to support the lawyers. The want of proper direction of the use of the Negro's education results in tempting too many to live mainly by their wits, without producing anything that is of real value to the world. Let me quote examples of this.

. . . . .

. . . . the skilled labour has been taken out of the Negro's hands; but I do mean to say that in no part of the South is he so strong in the matter of skilled labour as he was twenty years ago, except possibly in the country districts and the smaller towns. In the more northern of the Southern cities, such as Richmond and Baltimore, the change is most apparent; and it is being felt in every Southern city. Wherever the Negro has lost ground industrially in the South, it is not because there is prejudice against him as a skilled labourer on the part of the native Southern white man; the Southern white man generally prefers to do business with the Negro mechanic rather than with a white one, because he is accustomed to do business with the Negro in this respect. There is almost no prejudice against the Negro in the South in matters of business, so far as the native whites are concerned; and here is the entering wedge for the solution of the race problem. But too often, where the white mechanic or factory operative from the North gets a hold, the trades-union soon follows, and the Negro is crowded to the wall.

But what is the remedy for this condition? First, it is most important that the Negro and his white friends honestly face the facts as they are; otherwise the time will not be very far distant when the Negro of the South will be crowded to the ragged edge of industrial life as he is in the North. There is still time to repair the damage and to reclaim what we have lost.

I stated in the beginning, that industrial education for the Negro has been misunderstood. This has been chiefly because some have gotten the idea that industrial development was opposed to the Negro's higher mental development. This has little or nothing to do with the subject under discussion; we should no longer permit such an idea to aid in depriving the Negro of the legacy in the form of skilled labour that was purchased by his forefathers at the price of two hundred and fifty years of slavery. I would say to the black boy what I would say to the white boy, Get all the mental development that your time and pocket-book will allow of,—the more, the better; but the time has come when a larger proportion —not all, for we need professional men and women—of the educated coloured men and women should give themselves to industrial or business life. The professional class will be helped in so far as the rank and file have an industrial foundation, so that they can pay for professional service. Whether they receive the training of the hand while pursuing their academic training or after their academic training is finished, or whether they will get their literary training in an industrial school or college, are questions which each individual must decide for himself. No matter how or where educated, the educated men and women must come to the rescue of the race in the effort to get and hold its industrial footing. I would not have the standard of mental development lowered one whit; for, with the Negro, as with all races, mental strength is the basis of all progress. But I would have a large measure of this mental strength reach the Negroes' actual needs through the medium of the hand. Just now the need is not so much for the common carpenters, brick masons, farmers, and laundry women as for industrial leaders who, in addition to their practical knowledge, can draw plans, make estimates, take contracts; those who understand the latest methods of truck-gardening and the science underlying practical agriculture; those who understand machinery to the extent that they can operate steam and electric laundries, so that our women can hold on to the laundry work in the South, that is so fast drifting into the hands of others in the large cities and towns.

---

*One of the most significant decisions of the United States Supreme Court affecting public education was that of the 1954 decision in* Brown v. the Board of Education of Topeka. *Prior to this decision, state laws requiring or permitting racial segregation in public schools were presumed constitutional, according to the "separate but equal" provisions of the* Plessy v. Ferguson *case in 1896. In 1954 the Court heard cases from Delaware, Kansas, South Carolina, and Virginia which questioned the constitutionality of the "separate but equal" provision. The decision of 1954, quoted below, declared that racially segregated public schools had no place in American life. This decision was one of far-reaching social, political, legal, and educational significance.*

# Brown v. Board of Education of Topeka

These cases come to us from the States of Kansas, South Carolina, Virginia, and Deleware. They are premised on different facts and different local condi-

SOURCE: *Brown v. Board of Education of Topeka,* 347 U.S. 483 (1954).

tions, but a common legal question justifies their consideration together in this consolidated opinion.

In each of the cases minors of the Negro race, through their legal representatives, seek the aid of the courts in obtaining admission to the public schools of their community on a nonsegregated basis. In each instance, they have been denied admission to schools attended by white children under laws requiring or permitting segregation according to race. This segregation was alleged to deprive the plaintiffs of the equal protection of the laws under the Fourteenth Amendment. In each of the cases other than the Delaware case, a three-judge federal district court denied relief to the plaintiffs on the so-called "separate but equal" doctrine announced by this Court in *Plessy* v. *Ferguson*, 163 U.S. 537. Under that doctrine, equality of treatment is accorded when the races are provided substantially equal facilities, even though these facilities be separate. In the Delaware case, the Supreme Court of Delaware adhered to that doctrine, but ordered that the plaintiffs be admitted to the white schools because of their superiority to the Negro schools.

The plaintiffs contend that segregated public schools are not "equal" and cannot be made "equal," and that hence they are deprived of the equal protection of the laws. Because of the obvious importance of the question presented, the Court took jurisdiction. Argument was heard in the 1952 Term, and reargument was heard this Term on certain questions propounded by the Court.

Reargument was largely devoted to the circumstances surrounding the adoption of the Fourteenth Amendment in 1868. It covered exhaustively consideration of the Amendment in Congress, ratification by the states, then existing practices in racial segregation, and the views of proponents and opponents of the Amendment. This discussion and our own investigation convince us that, although these sources cast some light, it is not enough to resolve the problem with which we are faced. At best, they are inconclusive. The most avid proponents of the post-War Amendments undoubtedly intended them to remove all legal distinctions among "all persons born or naturalized in the United States." Their opponents, just as certainly, were antagonistic to both the letter and the spirit of the Amendments and wished them to have the most limited effect. What others in Congress and the state legislatures had in mind cannot be determined with any degree of certainty.

An additional reason for the inconclusive nature of the Amendment's history, with respect to segregated schools, is the status of public education at that time. In the South, the movement toward free common schools, supported by general taxation, had not yet taken hold. Education of white children was largely in the hands of private groups. Education of Negroes was almost nonexistent, and practically all of the race were illiterate. In fact, any education of Negroes was forbidden by law in some states. Today, in contrast, many Negroes have achieved outstanding success in the arts and sciences as well as in the business and professional world. It is true that public education had already advanced further in the North, but the effect of the Amendment on Northern States was generally ignored in the congressional debates. Even in the North, the conditions of public education did not approximate those existing today. The curriculum was usually rudimentary; ungraded schools were common in rural areas; the school term was but three months a year in many states; and compulsory school attendance was virtually unknown. As a consequence, it is not surprising that there should be so little in the history of the Fourteenth Amendment relating to its intended effect on public education.

In the first cases in this Court construing the Fourteenth Amendment, decided shortly after its adoption, the Court interpreted it as proscribing all state-imposed discriminations against the Negro race. The doctrine of "separate but equal" did not make its appearance in this Court until 1896 in the case of *Plessy* v. *Ferguson, supra,* involving not education but transportation. American courts have since labored with the doctrine for over half a century. In this Court, there have been six cases involving the "separate but equal" doctrine in the field of public education. In *Cumming* v. *Board of Education of Richmond County,* 175 U.S. 528, and *Gong Lum* v. *Rice,* 275 U.S. 78, the validity of the doctrine itself was not challenged. In more recent cases, all on the graduate school level, inequality was found in that specific benefits enjoyed by white students were denied to Negro students of the same educational qualifications. *State of Missouri ex rel. Gaines* v. *Canada,* 305 U.S. 337; *Sipuel* v. *Board of Regents of University of Oklahoma,* 332 U.S. 631; *Sweatt* v. *Painter,* 339 U.S. 629; *McLaurin* v. *Oklahoma State Regents,* 339 U.S. 637. In none of these cases was it necessary to reexamine the doctrine to grant relief to the Negro plaintiff. And in *Sweatt* v. *Painter, supra,* the Court expressly reserved decision on the question whether *Plessy* v. *Ferguson* should be held inapplicable to public education.

In the instant cases, that question is directly presented. Here, unlike *Sweatt* v. *Painter,* there are findings below that the Negro and white schools involved have been equalized, or are being equalized, with respect to buildings, curricula, qualifications and salaries of teachers, and other "tangible" factors. Our decision, therefore, cannot turn on merely a comparison of these tangible factors in the Negro and white schools involved in each of the cases. We must look instead to the effect of segregation itself on public education.

In approaching this problem, we cannot turn the clock back to 1868 when the Amendment was adopted, or even to 1896 when *Plessy* v. *Ferguson* was written. We must consider public education in the light of its full development and its present place in American life throughout the Nation. Only in this way can it be determined if segregation in public schools deprives these plaintiffs of the equal protection of the laws.

Today, education is perhaps the most important function of state and local governments. Compulsory school attendance laws and the great expenditures for education both demonstrate our recognition of the importance of education to our democratic society. It is required in the performance of our most basic public responsibilities, even service in the armed forces. It is the very foundation of good citizenship. Today it is a principal instrument in awakening the child to cultural values, in preparing him for later professional training, and in helping him to adjust normally to his environment. In these days, it is doubtful that any child may reasonably be expected to succeed in life if he is denied the opportunity of an education. Such an opportunity where the state has undertaken to provide it, is a right which must be made available to all on equal terms.

We come then to the question presented: Does segregation of children in public schools solely on the basis of race, even though the physical facilities and other "tangible" factors may be equal, deprive the children of the minority group of equal educational opportunities? We believe that it does.

In *Sweatt* v. *Painter, supra* (339 U.S. 629, 70 S.Ct. 850), in finding that a segregated law school for Negroes could not provide them equal educational opportunities, this Court relied in large part on "those qualities which are incapable of objective measurement but which make for greatness in a law school." In *McLaurin* v. *Oklahoma State Regents, supra* (339 U.S. 637, 70 S.Ct. 853), the Court, in requiring that a Negro admitted to a white graduate school be treated like all other students, again resorted to intangible considerations: ". . . his ability to study, to engage in discussions and exchange views with other students, and, in general, to learn his profession." Such considerations apply with added force to children in grade and high schools. To separate them from others of similar age and qualifications solely because of their race generates a feeling of inferiority as to their status in the community that may affect their hearts and minds in a way unlikely ever to be undone. The effect of this separation on their educational opportunities was well stated by a finding in the Kansas case by a court which nevertheless felt compelled to rule against the Negro plaintiffs:

"Segregation of white and colored children in public schools has a detrimental effect upon the colored children. The impact is greater when it has the sanction of the law; for the policy of separating the races is usually interpreted as denoting the inferiority of the Negro group. A sense of inferiority affects the motivation of a child to learn. Segregation with the sanction of law, therefore, has a tendency to retard the educational and mental development of Negro children and to deprive them of some of the benefits they would receive in a racially integrated school system."

Whatever may have been the extent of psychological knowledge at the time of *Plessy* v. *Ferguson*, this finding is amply supported by modern authority. Any language in *Plessy* v. *Ferguson* contrary to this finding is rejected.

We conclude that in the field of public education the doctrine of "separate but equal" has no place. Separate educational facilities are inherently unequal. Therefore, we hold that the plaintiffs and others similarly situated for whom the actions have been brought are, by reason of the segregation complained of, deprived of the equal protection of the laws guaranteed by the Fourteenth Amendment. This disposition make unnecessary any discussion whether such segregation also violates the Due Process Clause of the Fourteenth Amendment.

Because these are class actions, because of the wide applicability of this decision, and because of the great variety of local conditions, the formulation of decrees in these cases presents problems of considerable complexity. On reargument, the consideration of appropriate relief was necessarily subordinated to the primary question—the constitutionality of segregation in public education. We have now announced that such segregation is a denial of the equal protection of the laws. In order that we may have the full assistance of the parties in formulating decrees, the cases will be restored to the docket, and the parties are requested to present further argument. . . . The Attorney General of the United States is again invited to participate. The Attorneys General of the states requiring or permitting segregation in public education will also be permitted to appear as *amici curiae* upon request to do so by September 15, 1954, and submission of briefs by October 1, 1954.

It is so ordered.

# 11

# Conclusion

## SUMMING UP

The record of the trials, achievements, and contributions of American education remains an unfinished account. As a growing, continuing, and wholly public experience, American education has incorporated the contributions of many individuals. Some of them are well-known figures who have won recognition in the annals of American educational history, such as Horace Mann, Henry Barnard, James Carter, John Dewey, and William H. Kilpatrick. The quiet service of others, including millions of classroom teachers, has frequently gone unacknowledged. Since such an account does not have a conventional conclusion, it is more appropriate for this last chapter to review those major aspects of our educational history that have made it such a uniquely American experience.

The outstanding institution in American education is the common school, whose evolution has been closely related to the concepts of equal educational opportunity and of cultural integration. From Mann and Barnard through Dewey to the present, educational leaders have regarded the common school as a publicly controlled and publicly responsible institution accessible to children of all races, religions, and socio-economic backgrounds. As an agency of assimilation, the common school was one of the most effective instruments of fashioning millions of immigrants into one people.

The single-track system of American education is also derived from the democratic concept of education. In contrast to the European dual-track or class-oriented form of education, our "educational ladder" is now publicly supported and controlled, extending from elementary school all the way through the high school, college, and university. Thus, an American child can receive a free and complete formal education in this graduated, articulated system.

The American educational experience developed from the interaction between the American people and their unique environment. American education, developing in the equalitarian spirit of its pioneers, has reflected in the programs of the schools a broadly based commitment to the democratic ethic. Since education is responsible at each point to the public and its demands, control has been vested at the local level, in boards of education composed of laymen, and the schools' particular programs and practices vary accordingly.

The question of local control still requires serious study and reappraisal by both laymen and professional educators. As discussed in an earlier chapter, the concept originated in New England and spread during the nineteenth century with the common-school district system. Because of their fear of centralized governmental power, the framers of the United States Constitution had made no specific reference to education. As a result, in the early national period state governments assumed the role of educational authorities, and then in turn delegated substantial powers to local boards. It was not until the mid-twentieth century that the federal government became involved, with the enactment of programs of general aid to education.

Although a nominal allegiance to the concept of local control has persisted to the present, actual administrative, organizational, and financial practices have rendered much of it merely theoretical. Individual state governments have gained control in many places by distributing funds to schools which meet various state-imposed criteria. The large school aid programs enacted by the federal government have brought with them a set of requirements to be met by schools receiving those funds. State and federal courts have handed down a number of decisions directly concerning education; the United States Supreme Court's anti-segregation decision was only one among many. Since both state and federal programs of financial aid have included minimum conditions of their recipients, some tendencies toward uniformity in educational policies and programs have resulted. However, American schools, their facilities, and their programs still vary tremendously in both quantitative and qualitative aspects.[1]

The current educational system has evolved as the nation has grown from a rural, frontier environment to a complex, industrialized, technological society. Reflecting this transition, education, too, has become a large-scale enterprise, and the teaching profession has grown with it. The American teacher is better trained in both subject matter content and pedagog-

---

[1] For a succinct and direct discussion of the question of educational control, see Truman M. Pierce, *Federal, State, and Local Government in Education* (Washington: The Center for Applied Research in Education, 1964).

ical methodology than the pioneer teacher of the "little red schoolhouse" ever dreamed of being.

A summary of the unique features of American education indicates those achievements and developments which have made public education an integral part of the national heritage. However, it should also mention the challenges that must be solved if American education is to show continuing progress.

## QUALITY AND QUANTITY IN EDUCATION

The continuing role of American education can best be interpreted in the context of the quantitative and qualitative challenges it faces.[2] Through the history of this country there has been a never-ending demand for more schools, more teachers, and more facilities. Today, massive expenditures, large-scale construction programs, and greater experimentation with educational technology are being expedited to an ever higher degree. Yet while these quantitative aspects are constantly being expanded, they still lag behind the needs of a growing and mobile population. Because of the population growth, a most important task in education will be finding means to make it more available to more people. Those concerned with the American school must find new sources of school support and devise more efficient methods of educating.

But the problem is not only one of providing increased opportunities for more students; it is also a matter of providing worthwhile and enriching educational experiences. Efforts to do so must incorporate the answers to such questions as: What values and attitudes should the school help to shape? What are personal and social excellence? What should be the aims or goals of the American school? The qualitative aspects of education are mainly theoretical, which makes them difficult to define and much harder to solve. Educational leaders need the perspective and insight of both theory and practice.

## SOME SPECIFIC CHALLENGES

This book is primarily intended to present and analyze the development of American education in historical perspective. Some of the major challenges facing public education today have been examined in that context, and their definition, analysis, and resolution in the years to come will form

[2] The recent book by Francis Keppel, *The Necessary Revolution in American Education* (New York: Harper & Row, Publishers, 1966), contains an excellent discussion of the quantitative and qualitative revolutions which have affected the American school.

the next chapters in its story. Current problems will require solutions to the following important needs:

1. Definition of aims and goals in such a way that the broad purpose of education can most effectively realize the democratic ideal of American life.

2. The need for continued efforts to come to grips with the problems of racial, social, and economic integration so that educational opportunities are made available to all.

3. Identification and investigation of the problems raised by life in a mass society so that education can be carried on as a quest for the cultivation of personal excellence.

4. Acceleration of programs that will tap the potential of the gifted student.

5. Large-scale programs specially designed to cope with the problems of racial discrimination, social isolation, and cultural deprivation. Such massive programs will necessitate a basic restructuring of urban patterns of education.

6. More intensive efforts to help the growing child become more independent, more creative, and freer to develop his own intelligence and capabilities to the fullest possible extent.

7. Reappraisal of the traditional concept of local school control in the light of increasing social, political, and economic interdependence.


## THE AMERICAN EDUCATIONAL COMMITMENT

The seven major challenges which have been raised here are only a few of the myriad issues, problems, and conflicts facing contemporary American education. The successful response of both the American people and their schools in meeting these challenges rests in the last analysis on their continued commitment to public education, its potential excellence, and the ideal of equal educational opportunity. Perhaps the greatest contribution that the study of the history of American education can make is a greater understanding of the origins and development of this commitment.

Arriving in the New World wilderness, the transplanted European colonists established schools to preserve their civilization. During the early years of the American Republic, common education throughout the country built loyalties to the new nation. Throughout the nineteenth century, the public school did a great deal to assimilate the streams of immigrants who came to the United States, and forge their loyalty likewise. As industry and technology transformed rural America into an urban society, the public high school extended educational opportunity to the secondary level. In the last few decades the opportunities for college attendance were extended to larger numbers of American youth. More than halfway through the twentieth century, the greatest goal of education is still to make equal educational opportunity a reality for the disadvantaged youth in both urban and rural areas. As educational opportunities are extended to more and more individuals, the teaching profession, as well as the public, remains firmly committed to the highest standards in education. Thus, equal opportunity and excellence continue to be the twin goals which sustain the American educational commitment.

# Index

abolitionists, 208
academy, 71, 73-76
  curriculum and administration of, 74-75
  decline of, 75-76
  functions of, 74
  origin of, 73-74
accreditation of high schools, 80-81
Addams, Jane, 197
agricultural and mechanical colleges, rise of, 105, 107
Allen, Hollis P., 104n
American Association of Junior Colleges, 117
American (The) High School Today (Conant), 84-85
American Higher Education (Brown & Mayhew), 107-8, 109
American Lyceum movement, 52
American Philosophical Society, 32
American Revolution, see Revolutionary period education
American (The) Road to Culture (Counts), 220
anarchism, rise of, 57
Andrews, Benjamin F., 106n
Annapolis Naval Academy, 104
apprenticeship system in colonial South, 18
Art as Experience (Dewey), 191
association, educational value of, 192-93
automation, education and, 118, 146
Axt, Richard G., 104n

Babbidge, Homer D., 104n
Bagley, William Chandler, 199
Barnard, Henry, 3, 52, 71, 105, 131, 172n, 184

Barnard, Henry (cont.)
  biographical sketch of, 58-59
  common school movement and, 58-60, 166, 205, 220
  educational philosophy of, 59-60
  Pestalozzian principles and, 177-78, 184
  on teacher education, 133-34, 135, 166-71
Barnett, Ross, 207
Beck, Carlton, E., 216n
Beck, Hugo E., 152n
Beggs, Walter K., 140n
Bell, Andrew, 29, 50
Bernier, Normand R., 216n
Bestor, Arthur, 199-200
"Bill (A) for the More General Diffusion of Knowledge" (Jefferson), 34-36, 42-48
Black Nationalists, 216
Blease, Cole, 210
boards of education, power of, 230
Boyd, William, 173n
Breakthrough (Stone), 153-54
Brown, Elmer, 138
Brown, Hugh S., 107-8, 109n
Brown, J. Stanley, 116
Brown University, 100
Brown v. Board of Education of Topeka (1954), 146, 206-7, 213, 224-26
Brubacher, John S., 101n
Bruner, Jerome S., 157
Buchanan, James, 106
Burton, Warren: District (The) School As It Was, 67-70

Calhoun, John C., 207
California

235